The
Navy Wife

☆

*Anne Briscoe Pye
and Nancy Shea*

THE
NAVY
WIFE

New York | H♦B | London

HARPER & BROTHERS
PUBLISHERS

This book is complete and unabridged
in contents, and is manufactured in strict
conformity with Government regulations
for saving paper.

Contents

FOREWORD

BETWEEN the day when, immensely flattered, I promised to write a foreword to *The Navy Wife*, and today when, through the grace of God and the almost incredible bravery of our boys in blue and khaki, I am able to fulfill that promise, there has intervened a day that we Service wives in Hawaii have written into our lives with a Capital D—D, you understand, as in Double Duty. And we know, through radio broadcasts and the messages of love and encouragement coming to us, that you on the mainland, civilian and military, have written it, with a Capital D, into your lives as well—D, God bless you, as in Dedication.

If I "Remember Pearl Harbor," it is to point up the fact that December 7th, 1941, makes this book twice timely. *The Navy Wife* is now more than a perfect companion piece to Nancy Shea's first book, *The Army Wife*; it is practically a Siamese twin. For whatever impression you may have formed of the rivalry between our Services, whether from attending an Army-Navy football game or from shuddering at the vocal vehemence with which we "Sink the Army, sink the Army Gray," we are one now in a solid, unbroken front.

It has been my privilege to read *The Navy Wife* in manuscript form and to claim friendship with its authors. As a Navy wife and a writer, myself, I can appreciate the splendid piece of work they have turned out in this guidebook for young Navy wives. As for their qualifications, since this is WAR and not an Army-Navy football game, and remembering the above-mentioned United Front, I can take down my back hair and admit that Nancy Shea, though an Army wife (there I go . . .), is the most indefatigable digger-upper I know and one of the best co-ordinators. Merely watching her set out on the trail of an elusive fact has been known to lay me low, and I hope she writes her next book in the Grand Canyon, or somewhere. As for Anne Briscoe Pye, wife of Vice-Admiral William Satterlee Pye, U.S.N., she has Navy Blue for blood. Love of our Navy is evident in her every action, while understanding of its traditions and procedure practically oozes out of her pores.

The Navy Wife, like its twin, *The Army Wife*, is a common-sense guidebook, not as opposed to etiquette but as superimposed upon it for the benefit of wives new to the Service. It is addressed equally to the new brides of officers in the Regular Navy and to those wives of officers in the Naval Reserve who are so gallantly breaking their home ties to come and stand shoulder to shoulder with us old-timers in the defense of our country. For each Navy wife has a definite part in this war. This book tells you how and why.

While it is true that our customs and social usage are more or less in abeyance for the duration, the traditions upon which they are founded will endure forever. (Note to myself: Get off that platform, lug, and leave it to your betters.) What I am trying to say, and saying it badly because the evacuators not only have packed my Thesaurus but are threatening to take the very chair out from under my slacks, is that this book is something I would have given my eyeteeth for during the last war when my husband came into the Navy as a reserve officer in the Civil Engineer Corps. I had already suffered the pangs of a Post-ish education, though Emily was then unknown to fame, so which fork didn't worry me. But which officers' families we were supposed to call on at once, and which were supposed to call on us, worried me a lot. I learned by the monkey-see-monkey-do method, which really shouldn't be allowed outside a zoo, and which, thanks to Mrs. Shea and Mrs. Pye, will no longer be necessary. However, more than these superficialities, what interested me was the vast number of Regular Navy and Marine Corps wives I met upon presumably equal ground. Their spirit under trial made me at once humble and proud; it was not until I had learned a number of things the hard way that I understood what made them click. Then, at the close of the war, my husband transferred into the Regular Navy and lo! I was clicking, myself. Many Reserve officers will, at the end of this war, be following in my husband's steps, and many Reserve wives, turned Regular, will bless the day they bought *The Navy Wife*.

This book, it seems to me, should also have a special and timely appeal to all civilian women. For you will come across us in your home towns, strange evacuees from the far lands, each living her half-life in her own way. And, since our husbands are fighting side by side with your husbands and your sons, you will want to know about us, too; about our peacetime life and what it does to prepare us for—this.

MARGARET TAYLER YATES

Pearl Harbor, T.H.
December 15, 1941

ACKNOWLEDGMENTS

THE authors desire to acknowledge their very great debt to those Navy officers and Navy wives who have assisted so materially with their advice and suggestions in the preparation of the manuscript of this book.

Our thanks are especially due to Margaret Tayler Yates, wife of Commander Robert R. Yates, U.S.N., for her encouragement and help.

To Dr. Willard Wilson, of the Department of English of the University of Hawaii, we especially wish to express our appreciation for his untiring efforts in the revision and edition of parts of the original manuscript.

Acknowledgments are also extended to:

Vice-Admiral William S. Pye, U.S.N.
Rear Admiral Thomas Withers, U.S.N.
Rear Admiral P. N. L. Bellinger, U.S.N.
Rear Admiral John F. Shaforth, U.S.N.
General L. M. Little, U.S.M.C.
General Frank E. Evans, U.S.M.C.
Mrs. Stark, wife of Admiral Harold Stark, U.S.N.
Mrs. Kimmel, wife of Admiral Husband Kimmel, U.S.N.
Mrs. Spruance, wife of Rear Admiral R. A. Spruance, U.S.N.
Captain D. B. Beary, U.S.N.
Captain Harold Train, U.S.N.
Captain Worral Carter, U.S.N.
Captain E. A. M. Gendreau, U.S.N.
Captain Reynolds Hayden, U.S.N.
Captain John W. Gates, U.S.N.
Captain Leland P. Lovette, U.S.N.
Colonel Alton A. Gladden, U.S.M.C.
Mrs. Robinson, wife of Captain Stephan Robinson, U.S.N.
Mrs. Bernhard, wife of Captain Alva D. Bernhard, U.S.N.
Mrs. Cutts, wife of Captain Elwin F. Cutts, U.S.N.
Mrs. Benson, wife of Captain W. W. Benson, U.S.N.

Mrs. Hanson, wife of Captain E. W. Hanson, U.S.N.
Mrs. Patterson, wife of Captain D. F. Patterson, U.S.N.
Mrs. Selden, wife of Colonel John T. Selden, U.S.M.C.
Commander Charles B. Momsen, U.S.N.
Commander J. R. Tate, U.S.N.
Commander John Perry, U.S.N.
Commander T. H. Hederman, U.S.N., and Mrs. Hederman
Commander Howell C. Fish, U.S.N., and Mrs. Fish
Mrs. Kane, wife of Commander Joseph L. Kane, U.S.N.
Major William Lemly, U.S.M.C.
Chaplain Stanton Salisbury, U.S.N.
Chaplain John W. Moore, U.S.N.
Mrs. West, wife of Major Ralph E. West, U.S.M.C.
Mrs. Johnson, wife of Major Chandler Johnson, U.S.M.C.
Mrs. Pefley, wife of Major A. R. Pefley, U.S.M.C.
Lt. Commander John O. R. Coll and Mrs. Coll
Mrs. Forney M. Knox
Mrs. Fred Mullikin
Mrs. McKillip, wife of Lt. John C. McKillip, U.S.N.
Mrs. Byron Freeland
Lt. Commander G. B. Gelly, U.S.C.G.
Lt. Commander C. F. Greber, U.S.N.
Lt. Commander W. Sihler, U.S.N.
Lt. F. A. Erickson, U.S.C.G.
Lt. Commander Walton Hinds, U.S.N.
Mrs. Stuart, wife of Lt. Commander C. Stuart, U.S.N.
Mrs. Fitzgerald, wife of Lt. Commander Charles T. Fitzgerald,
    U.S.N.
Mrs. Quinby, wife of Lt. Commander C. F. M. Quinby
Lt. Charles Cushman, U.S.N., and Mrs. Cushman
Lt. John Briscoe Pye, U.S.N., and Mrs. Pye
Lt. S. Perkins, U.S.N., and Mrs. Perkins
Lt. G. S. Coleman, U.S.N.
Lt. Lawson Ramage
Lt. Owen Atkinson, U.S.N.R.
Mrs. McCloskey, wife of Lt. Robert McCloskey, U.S.N.
Lt. C. J. Ryan, U.S.N.
Mrs. Rice, wife of Lt. George F. Rice, U.S.N.
Ensign Richard E. Foster, U.S.N.
Ensign C. R. Burton, U.S.C.G.

Miss Arnest, U.S. Nurse Corps
Miss Lally, U.S. Nurse Corps
Mrs. Combe, U.S. Nurse Corps
James Humkey, U.S.M.C.
Miss Margaret Abigail Woods
Miss Opal Hadley

The
Navy Wife

Chapter I

THE NAVY DRAG AT ANNAPOLIS
ANCHOR'S AWEIGH!

Stand Navy down the field
Sails set to the sky
We'll never change our course
So Army you steer shy-y-y-y!

IN TIME of peace, the most thrilling phrase in the English language to a Navy wife is—*The Fleet's in.* Crowds line the water front to watch the officers and bluejackets on deck and liberty parties preparing to go ashore. Excited young Navy brides are always in the front line at the officers' landing, each one hoping to catch a glimpse of her Ensign or Lieutenant husband. The seasoned Navy wives are there too, but they remain in the background. It is an old story to them, but nevertheless they are there. The Fleet is in, their men are home, and life is filled with the electric excitement that only a Navy wife can understand.

There is a lure about the sea, a glamour about men who go down to the sea in ships; and the names of far-off ports like Hong Kong, Rio, Guantanamo, and Manila take on an added charm when "Bill's ship has been there." From the days of the old sailing vessels' return to New England harbors, until yesterday, when the sleek, streamlined cruisers and stolid battle-wagons proudly sailed into port, the scene was stirring. Today, naval orders are secret and the ships slide in silently, and in an even more sinister manner depart—destination unannounced and unknown except by those in key commands. *C'est la guerre!*

But when the ships are in port everyone is happy. There is something about a Navy blue uniform, starched whites, and

gleaming gold buttons that appeals to all members of the feminine sex, young or old. Everybody loves a sailor.

Meet Nancy Lee

Nancy Lee Patterson is what we might call a landlocked citizen or a landlubber; that is, she claims a little inland town in South Carolina by the name of Pinecrest as her home, and what she doesn't know about the Navy will fill this book and probably more. Nancy Lee is a smart girl, however, and she learned much in the short week that she knew Midshipman William Satterlee Tyler while he was on leave, visiting in her Southern home town.

Now, two months later, Nancy Lee is beginning her first year at a fashionable Washington preparatory college, and to date she has been terribly homesick. But the following invitation in the morning's mail alters all that.

(Here is the actual letter taken from the 1941 *Lucky Bag*.)

2002 Bancroft Hall
Saturday

Dear Nancy Lee:

Next week end is the end of an exam week for Uncle Sam's "Pampered Pets" and there is going to be a really good hop. I have been promising myself to ask you down for a week end since we met during my last week of leave. I'd like you to see my chummy little home, the U.S. Naval Academy.

You can help me drown my sorrows or celebrate my joys of exam week with "cokes" at the Greasy Spoon! Be sure to bring something to wear for sailing, as we're going out on the Bounding Main!

Anxiously,
Bill

To Bill, Nancy Lee wrote:

Dear Bill:

Thanks so much for the wonderful invitation. I'll be down on Saturday on the one o'clock bus with bells on! I'm looking forward to seeing the Academy, as I've never been down before. I'm interested to see if what the movies show about Annapolis is true.

I'll be sure to bring my water wings so I can get ashore if we run aground while sailing on the bounding blue waters of the Severn.

Till Saturday . . . be good.

Nancy Lee

(From now on, Nancy Lee, I shall talk directly to you.)
You are beset with several very important questions. What to take and what not to take? Where will you stay? How much will the week end cost? How does one reach this more or less inaccessible state capital of Maryland that shelters the Naval Academy?

So it is your first visit to Annapolis! For a successful visit plans are laid well in advance, and letters are exchanged. Then after a week of anxious anticipation Saturday finally arrives, and the week end of all week ends is under way.

There are various ways of reaching Annapolis. Believe it or not, none of these is by a bona fide railroad. The easiest approach from Washington, forty miles distant, is by bus or private motorcar. From Baltimore, thirty-three miles away, the favored conveyance is the Baltimore and Annapolis interurban, which resembles the Toonerville Trolley and is referred to as "The Galloping Goose." The other way is to motor, the only difficulty being that your private car may prove too great a temptation to your Midshipman. First classmen only are allowed to ride in automobiles, and even they have restricted privileges.

You are wise in planning to arrive on the one o'clock bus, because Midshipmen are not allowed to leave the Yard until after luncheon on Saturday. By that time Bill will be able to meet you at the bus stop at Carvel Hall. Upon your first visit you will appreciate this attention. No doubt he will have suggested that you put up at Carvel Hall, and probably he already will have made a reservation for you. If you want to make a hit with Bill, don't arrive hungry. Just before you take the bus in Washington fortify yourself with a good substantial lunch, enough food to keep you happy until you dine with him in the evening. There are two reasons for this tip. In the first place, Bill already will have lunched when he meets you. Secondly, Saturday minutes are precious at Annapolis. There may be a football game scheduled and you won't want to be late for the kick-off. He will begrudge even the amount of time that it takes you to register and settle in your room.

Very likely you will strike up an acquaintance on the bus, or you may know some of your fellow passengers. It will be a special bus marked Annapolis and will be filled with young, attractive, well-dressed girls who are going to the Naval Academy for the week end and a good time. There will be young careerists, college girls, débutantes, and a host of the youthful government employees with whom Washington is teeming now. The entire group will radiate happiness, good cheer, and the spirit of youth.

The first and most important one in every woman's life is *clothes*. They can make or mar the most exciting of week ends. Reduce your clothes and your luggage to a minimum. For the bus, motor, or trolley trip down, you will probably wear a tailored suit or a spectator sports dress and carry a topcoat or fur coat. Spotless gloves, a crisp blouse, and a nosegay in the lapel of your jacket are fresh little extra touches. Look your best and remember that first impressions are most important. By all means wear comfortable walking shoes, because if Bill meets you there will be the walk over the uneven brick sidewalks to the Academy grounds. Also, choose the lightest piece of luggage you possess, and confine your choice to one piece, unless you want to carry one of those little extra train-boxes or make-up kits. The airplane variety is best if you own it, because your host will have to carry it unless you succumb to the wide smile of the little Negro urchins who are always anxious and willing to "tote for Missy" for a small consideration.

Your wardrobe need not be extensive, as the week-end activities usually consist of the following: Saturday afternoon, a sail, a hike, or a football game; Saturday night, a formal hop, perhaps, or an informal hop at Smoke Hall. On Sunday afternoon you may be invited by an officer and his wife to

Sunday dinner, but such good fortune is not likely on your first visit.

You should take

For a sail: Slacks, of fairly warm material; the most becoming color and the best-tailored ones that you can afford. A cardigan or top coat, rubber-soled shoes.

For a football game and a hike: Tailored suit or spectator sports dress you wore down, with a warm topcoat or fur coat. Walking shoes.

For dinner and dance: Your very best evening dress, evening wrap or fur coat, carriage boots (not that you'll ever see a carriage but galoshes—lined—will protect those gold and silver slippers on a wettish night). A foldable pliofilm raincoat is an added protection.

For Sunday morning: A daytime dress, or suit.

This wardrobe should see you through your first week end, and after that you may wish to add to or subtract from your clothes budget. If you must go nautical, then take your own seafaring togs. Remember, the penalty for putting on a Midshipman's cap is a kiss—so forewarned is forearmed. Remember too that a Midshipman's buttons, belts, and insignia are expensive items, and parts of his uniform which he must replace immediately. Don't make off with them or ask to wear any part of your host's uniform. Many a budding romance has been blighted by a filched buckle, and girls have been wished into "the brig" for less.

Rates at Carvel Hall are $2.50 per day for single rooms without bath and $5.00 per day for private rooms with bath. Double rooms are from $3.50 to $6.00 per day. Meals cost $0.50 to $0.75 for breakfast, $1.00 for lunch, $1.00 for supper, and $1.25 for dinner. During June week the rates are advanced about 40 per cent.

Upon your second visit (if you are invited down again), you can find out about the private homes in Annapolis that take paying guests. A list of these is kept by the official hostess, and it is wise to make a reservation. The cost is nominal, as low as $1.00 per night, but these homes should be regarded as exactly what they are: the private homes of old Annapolis families. In most cases the hosts are F.F.Ms'. and are entitled to the respect of their guests. It is a nice touch to show them some courtesy, and at least express your appreciation.

The homes on the approved list measure up to the highest moral standards. At Carvel Hall or in any of the private houses your escort carries your luggage only to the parlor. And, my dear, I mean parlor; so does the hotel staff, so does the Commandant, and so does the whole Naval Academy faculty. Going upstairs or into a guest's bedroom is definitely not to be considered by a Midshipman, and the hostesses of private homes on the list to take paying guests are most particular on this point. A Mrs. Grundy seems to be tactfully in evidence at every turn. Of course, the case of a midshipman's mother, grandmother, father, or visiting Congressman is something else; but you are not interested in his family connections on this particular week end.

Upon your second or succeeding visits, you may choose to take an earlier bus to Annapolis in order to avoid the rush. In this case don't expect your escort to meet you, but take a taxi for thirty-five cents to the private home where you have a reservation. Then you will have time to freshen up, lunch at any one of the numerous attractive tearooms—Mignon's, Cruise Inn, or the Mirror Grill—even get your hair dressed or have a manicure before the time to meet Bill arrives.

Being an Annapolis Drag!

Since you received a special invitation from Bill, you are his "drag" for the week end. It may not sound particularly flattering at first, but "drag" is Academy lingo. If you spend frequent week ends at the Academy with Bill as your host, you will be known as his O.A.O. It means "One and Only," or as some cynic has said, "One Among Others"!

Remember, it sometimes requires even more effort to be an agreeable guest than it does to be the perfect host. Midshipmen are universally famous for their gallantry, their good manners, and for the wonderful hospitality they extend to their feminine guests. Your host will spend his all, if need be, to show you a good time, and he will strain his wallet as far as Uncle Sam will let him. In this regard, he has the edge on a West Point cadet. The latter is not allowed to carry any of the filthy lucre, nor is he permitted to sign anything except chits at the Boodler's Shop.

The drag always pays at West Point, and if she invites her host to dinner at the Thayer-West Point Inn, again she pays. Not so at Annapolis! Uncle Sam permits a Midshipman to take his drag to dinner (outside the Yard). If your host is very careful about movies and magazines during the month he may even save out enough for a modest corsage, but don't expect this extravagance. A *Plebe* draws two dollars spending money a month. It is referred to as the "monthly insult"; however, since a Plebe is not allowed to attend hops he hasn't much use for playboy money.

A *Youngster*, or second-year man, draws four dollars a month, which allows him possibly one riotous week end. But remember that out of this princely sum he must also buy magazines, postage stamps, and a holiday ice-cream soda or malted milk. A *Second Classman* draws seven dollars a month, while a *First Classman* advances to eleven dollars. You'll find it slightly different from going to week-end hops and proms at Yale or Princeton, so go easy on your host's bank roll. He has every penny budgeted and undoubtedly has or will have to deny himself many little comforts in order to show you a good time, so be appreciative of what he has to offer, and accept it graciously.

For some years there has been a very vicious custom in vogue among certain merchants in Annapolis, called the 4 Year Plan, whereby a Midshipman could secure credit and pay when he was commissioned. Unscrupulous drags or gold diggers have been known to hint for jewelry and, what is more, get it! Before the generous Midshipman realized his danger,

he was in serious debt. These practices are frowned on
heavily by the powers that be, and a girl who is thoughtful
and wise will not goad the enamored Midshipman toward
insolvency.

A drag is expected to pay her own transportation both ways,
her hotel bill, and all of her meal checks except those for
Saturday night dinner and Sunday luncheon. If there is a
football game, your host will have tickets. You will be his
guest at dinner and for the hop, also for any informal hops
and refreshments that may be sandwiched in on Saturday
afternoon and Sunday.

Midshipmen enjoy being invited out for a meal when visited
by their mothers, relatives, or Congressmen. It is also a
gracious gesture for a chaperon to invite the Midshipman who
is escorting her charge, or for the drag herself to invite him,
after she has accepted his hospitality more than once, to
Sunday dinner at Carvel Hall. This is not expected, but it
is a nice thing to do if a girl wishes to show her appreciation.
About the only way this courtesy can be handled tactfully
is for the drag who is a guest at Carvel Hall to arrange beforehand to have the dinner charge placed on her bill. Thus,
no money changes hands visibly, and the Midshipman is not
embarrassed.

After the football game in Thompson Stadium there may
be time for a coke at the Midshipmen's Canteen or one or
two dances, before he must fall in to muster. By this time
you must hurry away to dress for dinner and the evening hop.

You may dine amid the splendors of Carvel Hall, in gleaming candlelight, or within short walking distance of the Yard,
where there are many quaint little tearooms, such as the
Blue Lantern, the Port Lounge, the Little Campus, and the
Mirror Grill. The prices are modest to suit the wallets of the
Midshipmen. Happy couples linger over coffee and talk after
dinner until it is time to stroll back through the Academy
gates and to the Armory, officially known as Dahlgren Hall,
where the hops are usually held.

FORMAL HOPS

The regular Saturday evening hops are always formal and are presided over by a hostess who receives the guests. She is selected from among the wives of officers on duty at the Academy. The First Lady, the wife of the Superintendent, or the wife of the Commandant always receives at the opening ball in the fall and at the Graduation Hop. On these occasions, the chairman of the Hop Committee receives with the selected lady, stands first in line and presents the Midshipmen and their guests by name to her.

Be very gracious when you are being introduced. There is no need to say anything except "How do you do," but be natural and *smile*. Not one of those revealing toothpaste smiles, for remember, "the eyes of the Navy are upon you."

And how many pairs of eyes! The stag line is probably the longest in the world—something to make any girl's heart skip a beat. All three classes attend, and encircling the balcony above are the cherubic faces of the Plebes, who are allowed only to gaze enviously upon their betters from afar and dream of the time next year when they will take their places in line. Everything comes to him who waits, they hope, and Plebes are painfully chronic waiters.

The hops begin shortly after nine o'clock. By nine-thirty all the guests have passed through the receiving line and the dance is in full swing. Your very best evening dress is appropriate, but do not go in for exotic, extreme styles. The girl in the simple dress of good material and youthful, becoming design is often the belle of the ball.

And by this time you are beginning to wonder, to just what type of girl do these "pampered pets of Uncle Sam" give a rating of 4.0![1] Well, styles change in everything these days— from automobiles to girls and back again; but after a very

[1] The passing mark of 2.5 is equivalent to 62.5 per cent, on the scale of 4.0. Just why the scale of 4.0 was selected in preference to the conventional scale of 100 is not clear—perhaps 4 was decided to be as good as any other number. (Taken from Kendall Banning's *Annapolis Today*.)

thorough survey was made and Midshipmen had sized up all
types of girls who have been and are guests at the Naval
Academy, it was concluded that this is the preferred model:

The Natural Girl. To begin with she is easy on the eyes.
Her pretty soft brown hair has a semblance of a natural wave,
her features are good, she has pretty teeth and a ready smile.
She is slim and has a willowy figure. She dresses well, and
knows how to wear her clothes. She is adaptable, is understanding, and can make the best of regulations and conditions
as she finds them. She is a good cheery companion, an *excellent dancer*, never catty, has good manners, and appreciates
Midshipman Gish's hospitality.

Other types are divided by Midshipmen into eight cate-
gories—and when I say "divided" I mean divided! These boys
are connoisseurs of females, and they can dissect a woman's
whole inner soul with a merciless precision that any surgeon
might envy.

The Regal Girl, they claim, is too hard to live up to. She
has a terrible line and talks too much. *The Athletic Girl* may
prove an excellent companion, unless she is too mannish and
beats Midshipman Gish at his own sports. This he won't
like, especially if he discovers that intellectually she is a nit-
wit. If she is intelligent to boot, then he will find some other
deficiency—she is a bit too muscular, or not feminine enough.
The Clinging Vine acts as though she has had a footman to
open doors for her all her life. She is very, very feminine and
usually pretty in a delicate, fragile, flower-like sort of way.
This type goes over far better than the athletic girl, and often
gives the Natural Girl a bit of stiff competition. She goes over
fine with the Midshipmen from Dixie, who like their women
to appear helpless, weak, and willing.

The Childish Girl, who is naïve and kittenish, can be
charming at times, though usually her scatterbrained chatter
is boring after the first hour. The pose is hard to hold over
week ends. Then there is *The Motherly Type,* who is a good
companion, but too practical and with much too much com-

mon sense for one so young. She is on the serene, serious side—the very serious side. Midshipman Gish knows that if he is not wary she will soon be wearing his miniature.

The Beautiful but Dumb Girl we always have with us. She is usually disgustingly ignorant, especially about Naval Academy lingo and terms. She makes a grand appearance and is a good dancer, and as long as Midshipman Gish does all of the talking in public, he feels safe. In private he must tell her how beautiful she is at least every five minutes, and that gets pretty tiresome. *The Coquette* is usually the vest-pocket, or half-pint size, and her appeal, though general, is temporary. She is well mannered, makes a good impression, but is as fickle as a weather vane. *The Personality Girl* seems to have only one fault! "She always gets in your hair and won't let you forget her." She may or may not be good looking, but you can count on startling make-up, with nail polish to match. She may even have the American flag etched on the nail of her index finger, but if she is as intelligent as she appears, she will not be guilty of this unethical show of patriotism in the future. She is entertaining, good fun, and will be a hit with the stag line.

Moral, Miss America: psychoanalyze yourself, and choose the type you can best live up to. Recognize its weaknesses, but be consistent. If you start as a *Clinging Vine*, stay with it. Don't try to switch to the riding, golfing, hiking athlete, or Gish will know you're phony!

SPECIAL DANCES

Army mule—Army mule—You can kick and balk and bray,
But football you can not play—Army mule!

Whenever Navy defeats the Army in football, a Victory Ball is given in Dahlgren Hall, and it is always a very grand celebration. The Superintendent and his wife often give a supper for the football squad and their drags before the dance, and at the dance members of the team are presented with special souvenir awards or mementos.

"N" Dance

In the Maryland springtime, during June week, chairs and tables are set out on crew floats that are gaily decorated with Chinese lanterns, and a dance is held in Hubbard Hall, the boathouse. This is a very exclusive affair and is given in honor of the athletes who have won the coveted initial "N" during the current academic year. Special favors are planned for the drags, usually a gold "N" pin, and rides in gondolas over the moonlit waters add to the luxurious charm of the occasion. Blue coats and white trousers, called the "Yachting Uniform," are reserved for this occasion alone.

The Ring Dance

Perhaps the biggest evening of a Midshipman's life at the Naval Academy is the Ring Dance, when he receives his class ring. If humanly possible, he has his O.A.O. there to enjoy the momentous occasion with him. The June Ball or Graduation Hop may be more colorful, but it is the memory of the Ring Dance that lingers on. On occasion, the Secretary of the Navy and his wife have received, and always a famous orchestra is imported to furnish the music. "The crowning event of the evening arrives when each couple mounts the carpeted dais, and passes through the large gilded replica of the class ring." Each Midshipman usually invites his O.A.O., although sometimes sisters and even mothers pass through the enchanted circle. "As each couple approaches the archway, the lady takes her host's ring, suspended from a silken cord, and christens it by baptizing it successively in three bowls, one containing water from the Atlantic Ocean, one from the Pacific, and one from the Caribbean."[2] These bowls symbolize the oceans which are later to be called HOME. She then places the ring upon her host's finger, and in return he presents her with a favor bearing the class crest. Mirrors permit each couple to observe its own passage through the huge ring

[2] Quoted sentences from Kendall Banning, *Annapolis Today*. Funk & Wagnalls Company, New York, 1938.

replica, but gone is the honored kiss to accompany it.[3] If you are the real O.A.O., then a miniature of his class ring may be in the offing for you. This is really an engagement ring if worn by anyone except the Midshipman's mother or sister. While couples are merely engaged, the class seal is supposed to be worn on the inside of the finger; but after the marriage vows the Navy seal is worn on the outside. With dimmed lights, and a favorite orchestra playing "Navy Blue and Gold," this will be one of the evenings you will never forget.

Graduation Ball

The Graduation or Farewell Ball is always held the evening before graduation, and Dahlgren Hall is elaborately decorated in blue and gold bunting for the occasion. This ball, which is given for the graduating class and is attended by all four classes, marks the debut of the Plebes into the social life of the Academy. With the early graduation exercises which will undoubtedly be the rule for "the duration," the ball may have to be omitted altogether.

Other Hops

Hallowe'en, St. Valentine's Day, or St. Patrick's Day may raise a regular formal hop to a special occasion. There are also occasional informal hops. These are usually held in Smoke Hall on Saturday and Sunday afternoons between four and six o'clock. Any Midshipman of the three upper classes may bring one drag and no more. Even visiting parents are taboo.

June Week

June week at Annapolis is a glorious six days of happiness during peacetime! Every midshipman who has looked forward to June week with its attendant colorful festivities and traditions must feel a bit cheated when his class is graduated

[3] In 1941 Rear Admiral Russell Willson permitted the revival of the custom of the kiss during the Ring Ceremony, and also reinstated the Color Girl. As Lee Shores' note in *Shipmate* explained, "it may not be sanitary but it's damned satisfying."

early. However, that is life. June weeks will be held again and, let us hope, soon.

One of the high spots of June week is the Presentation of the Colors parade, when the colors are formally presented to the Color Company. The points in competition are awarded for aptitude, class standing, athletics, and drill. The commander of the winning company selects a girl (usually his O.A.O., if he isn't fed up with her by that time!), who is invited by the Superintendent to present the colors to his company. "After the regiment is formed with the company which is to receive the Colors immediately in front of the grandstand, the Color Girl is escorted by the Commandant of Midshipmen, and she steps forward onto the Field carrying a huge bouquet and followed by a plebe orderly chosen from the winning company."[4] The Color Girl makes a few congratulatory remarks to the winning company, then with the aid of the Midshipman Regimental Commander transfers the national and regimental flags from the old to the new color guard.

The new Color Company salutes the Color Girl with three cheers, then resumes its place in line. The Superintendent or the Commandant, with the Color Girl on his arm, takes a position in front of the pavilion. The Color Girl is really Miss America for the day! Photographers of all the leading newspapers and pictorial magazines will spread her picture from coast to coast, not to mention its final arrival on the Asiatic Station. The band plays "Anchors Aweigh," the companies swing into column, pass in review before the Superintendent and the Color Girl, and the parade is over.

On the evening of the parade, the annual "N" dance is held, and the First Class Hop in Memorial Hall.

GRADUATION

The four strenuous years of unremitting study and discipline followed by June week festivities have all led up to the final achievement of graduation. The Superintendent

[4] Kendall Banning, *Annapolis Today*.

makes his entrance, accompanied by the Commandant and the speaker of the day, who is either the President of the United States, the Secretary of the Navy, or the Chief of Naval Operations. Next the Admirals, Generals, and public officials escorted by gold-braided Naval aides take their seats on the platform according to precedence and rank. The graduating class is seated early in their shining white officers' uniforms without shoulder marks, with their Midshipman caps beside them. The honor or star men of the class are seated in the first row and behind the graduating class is placed the rest of the regiment in dark-blue dress uniform. Proud parents, interested relatives, and friends in gala attire comprise the large audience. The Chaplain of the Academy opens the exercises. Then the Superintendent introduces the speaker, who delivers the graduating address and later presents the diplomas.

After the honor men receive their Bachelor of Science degrees, the other members of the graduating class receive similar degrees in alphabetical order. No one knows, until the official list is published later, just who will be the "anchor man" or the "goat" of the class.

When the last graduate has resumed his seat, the cheerleaders conduct the class in singing "Navy Blue and Gold." Three cheers are given "for those about to leave us" by the undergraduates, which are returned by the graduating class "for those we leave behind." At the end of the third cheer, the graduates toss their Midshipman caps high into the air, whereupon ensues a vigorous scramble by relatives and girl friends trying to secure a cap for a souvenir. Often Navy Juniors get the coveted caps.

The Plebes have now become Youngsters. They make a wild rush into the Academy grounds, racing madly for the up to now forbidden Lover's Lane and diving for the Youngsters' Benches. As they run, they strip off their dress jackets and put them on inside out, opening their collars and putting on their caps backwards. This signifies their joyous freedom and abandon at being released from the restrictions, trials,

and tribulations which have to be smilingly endured by Plebes.
It is often said that of all the promotions throughout a naval
career, there is none which is received more ecstatically or
which constitutes so real an advancement as that of Plebe to
Youngster.

The graduates, after receiving the congratulations of their
guests, return to their quarters to obtain their officers' caps
and shoulder marks, thence to Bancroft Hall to a designated
office to be sworn in for their commissions. "Coming out into
the Yard with their shoulder marks in their hands, they pass
these marks to their sweethearts or nearest female relatives
by whom the shoulder marks are put in place. When Mother
and sweetheart are both present, often they divide honors
by each putting on one shoulder mark."[5]

Points of Interest at the Naval Academy

A brief tour of the Academy grounds will include the following points of interest:

The Chapel, a treasure house of memorials, always receives
its quota of visitors. Here are beautiful stained-glass windows
as memorials to Admiral Farragut, Admiral Sampson, and
other naval heroes. In the crypt under the chapel in a large
sarcophagus comparable to Napoleon's tomb rest the remains
of John Paul Jones, "the father of the American Navy," which,
having been lost for nearly one hundred years, were recovered
from a graveyard in Paris by General Lew Wallace and later
transferred to Annapolis with fitting ceremonies.

Many like to linger in Memorial Hall in Bancroft Hall to
pay homage to the brave men of the Navy who have given
their lives for their country. Here are memorials to these heroes
in portraits, bronze tablets, and busts, and on the walls a series
of murals depicting many famous naval battles. Here also is
perhaps the most priceless treasure of the Naval Academy, the
faded blue flag carried by Commodore Perry's flagship at the
battle of Lake Erie. On this flag, in white cloth letters, are

[5] Kendall Banning, *Annapolis Today*.

Captain Lawrence's immortal words: DON'T GIVE UP THE SHIP.

The Naval Academy Museum, a fine new building recently erected by donations from the Naval Academy Athletic Association and from the Naval Institute, claims the interest of many visitors with its huge collection of ship models, medals, papers, letters, and other historic relics of great value.

Then there is grizzled old Tecumseh, famous Indian chief, in feathers and war paint, an earlier wooden figurehead on the battleship *Delaware* of Civil War fame. For forty years Tecumseh stood guard over the Yard, but finally time began to take its toll. He needed more than a facial, so the class of 1891 decided to preserve the god of superstition in a casting of bronze. The important work was done at the Naval Gun Factory, and in the spring of 1930 Tecumseh was returned to his throne, but this time it was on a pedestal of Vermont marble. Great ceremonies and rites marked the occasion. In an iron box buried under the old Indian chief's statue were placed the biographies of each member of the class of '91 along with a complete Navy Register of all graduates of the Naval Academy. Tecumseh is called the "God of 2.5," and grimly he gazes upon the main entrance of Bancroft Hall. Midshipmen in going to and from their classes, and in leaving the Naval Academy on liberty, frequently salute him, thus seeking his spiritual assistance in whatever objective they have in mind. This is especially true during examination periods and before the annual Army and Navy game. On these occasions, in addition to the salute, pennies are cast in tribute. The small boys of Annapolis lie in wait in the shadow of the statue and reap a neat little sum which they immediately convert into candy, toys, and those odd things dear to a little boy's heart.

If you are a top-flight drag, you'll humor these childish customs and even fall in with them. Some day, if you're fortunate, you'll understand why they are important to Navy men.

Mahan Hall is the trophy hall. It is always the tower clock

of Mahan Hall that tolls the death knell of a lovely week end.
It strikes not the hours but the ship's bells. Everyone pays a
visit to the proud and haughty Japanese bell, just off Lover's
Lane. It hangs in its Oriental framework and is rung only
when Navy wins the Army-Navy football game—and then
with wild notes of victory.

Ten Don'ts for Drags

(From Kendall Banning's *Annapolis Today*.)

1. Don't keep Midshipmen waiting. (Liberty hours are too precious to waste.)
2. Don't chew gum in public.
3. Don't suggest anything that cuts into your host's bank roll.
4. Don't smoke in the Yard, on the street, or on the dance floor.
5. Don't bring liquor into the Yard.
6. Don't hold hands in public.
7. Don't indulge in loud or daring clothes.
8. Don't suggest your host take you places.
9. Don't commit the unpardonable sin of late dating with a St. Johnny.
10. Don't wear bunny wraps; meaning any kind of white fur. The hairs shed and mess up the blue uniform.

Midshipman Slang

(Taken from the *Lucky Bag, Reef Points,* and Kendall Banning's
Annapolis Today.)

Anchor: The last in a group; the unit rated lowest.
Anchor man: The Midshipman who stands at the bottom of his class academically.
Baltimore beefsteak: Calves' liver, so to speak.
Bear a hand: Sailor slang for "shake a leg."
Belay that: Stop; quit what you are doing.
Bilge: To flunk out of the Naval Academy.
Bilger: A Midshipman who has been dropped.
Bill: The perennial name of the Navy goat.
Blind drag: A femme invited by a Midshipman, sight unseen.
Bone: To study, to cram.
Brace: To assume a rigid military posture.
Brick: The girl with the thick glasses.

Bulkhead: A wall.

Can: A destroyer.

Caulk off: To sleep, particularly to sleep in the daytime.

Charlie Noble: The smokestack in the galley.

Collision mat: The uncomplimentary term applied to pancakes.

Com: A Commandant of Midshipmen.

Crab: A girl who lives in Crabtown, meaning Annapolis.

Crabtown: Annapolis, a fishing village on the banks of the Naval Academy.

Cruise: A practice trip on a war vessel during the summer. Time served on the *Reina Mercedes*, the station ship, in atonement for Midshipmen's sins.

Drag: A young lady guest of a Midshipman.

Femme: Any lady, but especially a young lady.

Foo foo: Perfume, scented talcum.

Gouge: To cheat.

Grass: Salads.

Grease: Influence or drag.

Gripe: To grumble.

Gyrene: A Marine.

Head: A toilet room on a ship.

Holy Joe: The Chaplain.

Java or Joe: Coffee.

Ladder: A stairway.

Man overboard: Your spoon is in your cup.

Moke: A colored mess attendant.

Pipe down: Keep quiet.

Pollywog: Anyone who has never crossed the equator or "line."

Reef Points: The Plebe's Bible.

River: An exam.

Sat: Passing 2.5 and better.

Scoffer: Inordinately rapid eater.

Scuttlebut: A drinking fountain; also a rumor of doubtful origin.

Secure: Knock off work.

Shellback: A person who has crossed the equator.

Shiverin Liz: The mess name for jelly.

Shiverin Liz in a snow storm: Same as above with whipped cream.

Sick bay: Headquarters of medical officers.

Skivvies: Underclothes.

Spanish athlete: Member of the Radiator Club.

Slum: Stew.

Swabo: Zero.

Wife: A roommate.

Yard engine: A young lady who lives in the Yard; a Navy Junior.

In regard to *Don't* No. 5: "Serving drinks to Midshipmen is a felony in Annapolis." Don't be guilty of even suggesting a drink.

Don't No. 9: Your Midshipman will glady explain this tip, and will take great pleasure in doing so.

One other thing: When does a drag leave Annapolis on Sunday? You are expected to leave between the hours of five and six in the afternoon because all Midshipmen report at formation at six-thirty. (Ten dollars including bus fare should generously cover all expenses of the week end.)

"As Long as There Is an Annapolis" Midshipmen will always look forward to week ends when the "One and Only" girl visits the Naval Academy. Youth will be youth; war seems only to make romance blossom, so there is no dampening of spirits among Uncle Sam's "embryo naval officers." These Midshipmen are the cream of American manhood. From every state in the Union they come, and tomorrow they will be officers of the United States Navy.

In time of war, it is customary to shorten the course to three or three and one half years; so, outside of a few minor curtailments such as June Week and other necessary changes, life for the Midshipmen goes on as usual. He will study and work harder than ever before, because he will be anxious to get into the Front Line, but he will also play harder—the week ends will be more appreciated than ever.

THINGS YOU MAY OR MAY NOT KNOW ABOUT THE U.S. NAVAL ACADEMY

The site of the present Naval Academy was once an old Coast Artillery post on the banks of the Severn. In 1845, during the term of George Bancroft as Secretary of the Navy, the Naval Academy was established. Bancroft was a scholar, historian, statesman, and experienced school administrator and organizer. At first the course was five years, of which the first and last years were spent at the Naval School, the other three being passed at sea. In 1850 the name was changed to the U.S. Naval Academy.

Also, it may interest you to know, Nancy Lee, in case Bill has not already informed you, Ensigns *are not* permitted to marry until two years from the date of graduation! There are two very sound reasons for this ruling: His first two years will be spent with the Fleet at sea, and his pay of $1500 per year will not cover his own expenses and those of a dependent. A young line officer, upon leaving Annapolis, is on probation more or less for seven years after graduation. At the end of two years' service he may marry.

THE TOWN OF ANNAPOLIS

Perhaps you have enjoyed the little bit of old Annapolis that you were able to see upon your first visit. If so, you will want to explore more and more of it upon succeeding visits, because Colonial Annapolis is one of the most picturesque, colorful, and interesting state capitals in the United States. Its names have been Providence, Town of Proctors, Town at the Severn, Anne Arundel's Town, and finally, in 1694, Annapolis, in honor of Princess Anne, at that time heir to the British throne.

Today Annapolis stands, still proud of its mansions of the Golden Age, but prouder still of the old families who built their homes here on the Severn. These old homes are gems of architecture with their Palladian windows, beautiful doorways, fanlights, and palatial interiors. The drawing rooms, ball rooms, and dining rooms are interesting with their imported marble mantels and fine hand-carved mahogany doors ornamented with sterling silver doorknobs and latchstrings.

Because of a decline in the fortunes of the descendants, much of the original furniture has been sold to collectors, but in some cases the fine old homes contain many museum pieces, and others are being restored.

The Hammond-Harwood House on the southwest corner

of Maryland Avenue and King George Street is perhaps the most outstanding home, though it has a close rival in the Chase mansion. The former was built by Matthias Hammond for his prospective bride, but at the last, as the story goes, the bride jilted him because she declared he cared more for his new house than he did for her. Shortly after the "love nest" was completed Mr. Hammond sold it, and finally it came down to Judge Chase who left it to his two granddaughters, the Misses Harwood. These old spinsters were desperately poor but terribly proud. Their house was filled with fine and priceless antiques, yet the elder sister, Miss Lucy, literally starved to death. They spoke to a chosen few on the streets, were haughty, defiant, proud, and went to their graves hating all "Damyankees."

The Chase Home or Lloyd House is now used as a home for old ladies, but its beauty may be enjoyed by the visitor for the small sum of twenty-five cents. There are two tragic incidents connected with the Chase mansion. In the old days, there was a great fireplace in the front hall, and as the story goes, Miss Mathilda Chase, a daughter of the house, fell asleep in her chair before the burning fire. A spark shot out from the fire, igniting her dress, and before she could be rescued she was burned to death.

The other incident was in regard to financing the Home for the Elderly Ladies. Mrs. Hester Ridout, after deeding the property to the church authorities, realized that an endowment would be necessary to maintain the home. She set aside $200,000 and sent for a lawyer to draw up a codicil to her will. At the moment the lawyer arrived, in walked a chatty neighbor. Mrs. Ridout requested her lawyer to call the next day, but Fate stepped in, and by the next day the generous Mrs. Ridout had passed to her reward. The badly needed endowment went to the estate.

Another of the finest houses is the Brice House, which in the old days had magnificent gardens extending down to the water. William Oliver Stevens in his charming book, *Annapolis,* describes the interior as noted for the beauty of its carving, plaster molding, elaborate fireplaces. Some of the interior is very similar to that at Mount Vernon. Brice House contains a secret stairway and has the unique distinction among Annapolis mansions in possessing real ghosts.

Paca House or Carvel Hall was built in 1763 by Governor William Paca, a signer of the Declaration of Independence. Since 1899 it has been used as the front of Carvel Hall Hotel.

Then there is the famous Randall House, once one of the show places of Annapolis and noted for its gardens.

The Lloyd-Dulany House on Conduit Street, along with the Chase home, is the only three-story mansion. George Washington was often a guest here. It is now owned by the Masonic Order.

Annapolis is laid out in two Circles, known as Church Circle and State Circle, from which the streets radiate. In the old State House, George Washington resigned his commission as Commander-in-Chief of the Continental Army.

Chapter II

NAVY WINGS

THE surprise air attack on Pearl Harbor convinced high-ranking Army and Navy officials that air power was to be one of the main striking forces in the present war. Of course, this arm must naturally work in conjunction with the Fleet and land forces, of which it is so definite a part.

Navy pilots were the pioneers in long-distance flying, since long-range flying is highly necessary in the Navy. Naval airmen are also proud of being the first to perfect dive bombing.

To be the wife or mother of a flying officer has its thrill, but each has a special work cut out for her. High morale among fliers is important. Domestic troubles and worries have killed more aviators than motor failure, high-tension lines, and low ceilings. Yours is a big job!

Even in time of peace there is an entirely different atmosphere in a regular naval air station from that in the average naval yard. There is an unspoken restraint—there is the ever present dread of "Crash Signal"—accident and death. To keep the shadow in the background, there is a certain tenseness, an almost hysterical gaiety at times. There is also an esprit de corps that distinguishes these flying officers. They are welded together by the high and constant seriousness of their responsibility.

Navy wives carry on despite the tension. To the less sophisticated eye aviators' wives do not stand out as being "worriers." However, the aviator's wife who says that she has not lived and worried over many crashes that never came to pass isn't a normal woman. The real aviator's wife would never think of admitting these unjustified worries even to herself, and last of all to her husband. It just isn't done in the Corps!

A favorite question that will often be asked you is this:

"Do you worry about your husband's flying?" THE AN-
SWER IS NO. Its sequel usually follows: "Doesn't it affect
you?" Maybe you can get around that one tactfully, but to
tell the truth, his flying will in time affect you, just as dropping
water on a stone finally wears it away. The high, emotional
tension under which a flier's wife lives will eventually break
her unless she is made of pretty stern stuff.

To begin with, most aviators are temperamental. Then be
prepared to adjust your social and home life to the odd hours
of your husband's vocation. All of these adjustments are vital
and necessary to his flying, and, as the real Navy wife, early
in your career you will find that they make for contentment
and real happiness.

Don't worry, my darling, if you stand by while Bill goes
through training at the Naval Station at Pensacola, Jacksonville, Miami, or Corpus Christi—then perhaps for extra good
measure through Randolph, the Army's aviation "West Point
of the Air"—you will feel very definitely that you have earned
your wings, too.

However, the way we learn to like it is this: It gets into
your blood, the men love to fly, and every wife is proud of her
flying husband, his wings, and what they represent. It is a
glorious life, fraught with danger but thrilling, devastating,
and soul satisfying. The present generation of young Americans is inherently air-minded, and to earn the right to wear
wings is the ambition of almost every young man who can
pass the rigid physical and mental examinations.

Pensacola, Florida, known as the Eagle's Nest in naval aviation, is the oldest training school. Additional training schools
have been opened at Corpus Christi, Texas; at Jacksonville,
and at Miami, Florida. At present, the Miami Air Station is
a sort of finishing school and is used for the advanced training squadron for students detailed to carrier squadrons. Just
as the production of planes has been stepped up for the
present emergency, so is the turning out of pilots keeping pace,
to meet the demands of the moment. Conditions and demands
are changing daily, almost hourly in some instances, so the

résumé of the life of an aviation student given here is based on the good old days when a naval officer had to serve two years with the Fleet before taking training at Pensacola.

Pensacola is affectionately referred to as "the mother-in-law" of the Navy, because so many of her daughters have become the wives of naval officers. There is something about those beautiful, soft-voiced Florida girls that seems to appeal to fliers. Every year Pensacola is the scene of numerous weddings. The course of training for students is so rigid and exacting that leave, even to attend one's own wedding, is impossible; consequently, many fiancées journey to Pensacola to be married. Regular Navy officers who are students have exciting experiences in getting married between flight checks and no leave.

Being an aviator's wife is a big job, and it is highly essential that a flier's wife understand and be cognizant of the importance of her husband's career. In every way possible she must keep up his morale. Flying is a highly specialized career; it takes more than just the ability to fly. The aviator's actions at the controls must be instinctive, quick, and subconscious, but his judgment in an emergency must be perfect. To do his best, he must have a happy, congenial home life. His mind must be free for the work in hand.

How very important it is for a wife to be enthusiastic during her husband's training, regardless of her own fears, her inhibitions, and her anxiety! These she must keep to herself. The instructors claim that married men, who have fewer distractions and lead more regular lives than do single men, make better aviation students than bachelors. That is a supreme compliment to the caliber of the wives of our Navy fliers.

Formerly, the course extended over a period from ten to fourteen months, and the students were assembled every six months and graduated individually, instead of in classes. Today, a new class of students is assembled every two weeks, they are graduated in classes, and the class is made up of men who have been selected from all of the thirteen Naval Districts

into which the United States is divided. Each class in turn is
divided into three separate groups: One consists of naval officers who have been graduated from the Academy; one is
composed of Naval Reserve aviation cadets chosen from civil
life by the Navy's selection boards; the third is composed of
enlisted men from the Navy. Each of the three groups is
designated by a letter: "O" is for the officer group, "C" for the
cadet group, and "E" for the enlisted group. All three groups
retain their separate identities throughout the course and are
separately quartered; but they all take the same course of instruction.

Aviation cadets graduate with the rank of Ensign in the
Naval Reserve, and with the official designation of "naval
aviator." The same designation is given to regular Navy officers who graduate, and the enlisted men graduate with the
designation of "naval aviation pilot."

It seems best to describe each group separately.

LIFE IN PENSACOLA FOR THE "O" GROUP

Pensacola is a coastal town situated on Pensacola Bay. The
harbor is guarded by old Fort Pickens and Fort Barrancas, and
the city has a rich historical background. Sighted by Ponce
de Leon in 1513, Pensacola has had the distinction of having
been under five different flags. During the War of 1812 the
British made it a center of operations. In 1824 Pensacola received its charter as a city and was selected as a site of the
Federal Navy Yard.

Consequently, it is a Navy town from way back, and,
though today the great expansion due to the present emergency has made it difficult, the people of Pensacola are and
have always been most hospitable to Naval officers and their
families.

The climate is that of north Florida, quite different from
that of Palm Beach. There are mild winters and hot, hot
summers, although in the afternoons a refreshing breeze
usually blows. Also, just because you are going to Florida,
don't expect to wear a bathing suit all winter. It gets plenty

cold, and a camel's-hair topcoat or even a light fur coat will be a welcome addition to your wardrobe.

Married student officers and their wives live in town. With the crowded conditions that exist in all naval and military concentration points, naturally, comfortable houses are at a premium. Rents range from $50 to $65 for a small bungalow or apartment, depending upon the location. Warrington is a near-by suburb, and many Navy people rent apartments there or live in the Bay Shore section near the Country Club. At the Naval Station there are quarters for the heads of departments. Some of these are old slave quarters that have been rebuilt. A building program is being carried out at present.

The popular San Carlos Hotel is located on Palofox Avenue, the main thoroughfare. The San Carlos cocktail lounge is a rendezvous for the Navy crowd. Around its walls is a frieze cleverly decorated with naughty Navy cartoons. In every way the San Carlos features naval aviation. Even the cocktail napkins have small planes on them. The food at the San Carlos is exceptionally good; especially famous is the deviled crab, and the sea-food plate.

Food is plentiful and reasonable in Pensacola. The fish markets are wonderful, with a wealth of sea food, including the delicious Bon Secour oysters. Everyone lives well, and at small cost in comparison with eastern and western stations.

Speaking of food, who is going to cook it? Well, if you noted the percentage of Negroes in Pensacola's census, you must assume that servants are plentiful and rather cheap. A good cook and all-round servant may be had for from $5.00 to $10.00 per week. Part-time servants who come after lunch, wash the morning dishes, clean, prepare dinner, and stay with children three or four times a week may be had for $4.00 per week. Of course they all "tote," thereby keeping up their usually lazy husbands and numerous offspring. But remember that food is cheap, you are in the South, it is too hot to do the work yourself, and if the toting includes only food, be thankful. Of course, if they start taking a fancy to your pet silver, that is a chicken of another feather. On the whole, however, they are honest, according to their own highly specialized code. It is wise to enjoy a good servant while you may.

The best clubs are: the Pensacola Country Club; the Osceola Golf Club; the Officers' Club. Naval officers who are bachelors live at Mustin Hall.

The Little Theatre group in Pensacola is very active and is eager to welcome Navy personnel into its ranks.

The Women's University Club is an active organization, the junior D.A.R. welcomes navy affiliates, and any sorority connections may prove valuable.

The "C" Group or Aviation Cadets

The physical requirements for aviation cadets are extremely rigid. The important educational prerequisite is two years of college or its equivalent.

Today, a "wishful flier" enlists in the Naval Reserve and for one month is sent to a Naval Reserve Aviation Base near his home for elimination flight training. During this period he is given the physical and mental tests, receives some preliminary instruction, solos, and in a small way is indoctrinated with Navy customs and traditions and the history of naval aviation. If he passes all tests satisfactorily, he will be sent either to Pensacola or to one of the recently opened training bases mentioned above.

About 60 per cent of those who enter complete the primary and basic courses. With the coveted wings goes a reserve commission and the flying cadet becomes an Ensign in the Naval Reserve or Second Lieutenant in the Marine Corps Reserve.

The classes are divided into two wings, the "right wing" and the "left wing." One wing attends classes in the morning and flies in the afternoon; the other reverses the order. This procedure alternates weekly.

The day of an aviation student starts early. Down along the water front and back on the flying fields the seaplanes and landplanes are tuned up. Before seven o'clock the station hums like a vast beehive.

The flight course is divided into five squadrons. Each squadron must pass its own stage requirements, i.e., instruction in primary seaplanes and landplanes, then in standard Navy planes, standard Navy seaplanes (especially the large patrol planes or flying boats and bombing planes), and finally the specialized training including night flying in formation, instrument flying, and advanced aerial acrobatics.

Every student in aviation is also given a short course of instruction in a one-story building known in nautical parlance as the "parachute loft."

The most spectacular part of the training is the brief phase of work known as "catapult training." The term is self-explanatory. Fliers are literally shot from a gunlike catapult, exactly the same type of machine with which all the cruisers and battleships are equipped. The spectacle is thrilling, but it is no stunt at all to the experienced flier.

The plane's propeller is turning over as the plane, nested in its cradle, waits to be shot off. The pilot "revs" up his plane before the take-off and holds his stick at a fixed angle. He and his observer put their heads back rigidly against the leather headrests to prevent the jerk of the take-off from injuring their necks (they go from zero speed to sixty miles an hour in about forty-five feet), and the plane is hurled off into the air. On returning from its flight, it lands in the water, usually on the "slick" or lee formed by the ship, taxies up alongside, and is hoisted aboard with a crane. Rough-water landings are spectacular and thrilling. The planes often nose over, washing out wing-tip floats and main pontoons. All heavy planes are equipped with flotation gear, and the pilot, in addition to his parachute, wears an inflatable life preserver.

At the training schools a special catapult is used—one that is fixed on the sea wall at about the same height above the water as the deck of a vessel. It operates on a pivot-like turntable, so that it can be pointed in any direction, and the pilot can take off over the water into the wind. It is said that the operation is so simple that only two catapultings are necessary to convert the student into an instructor. The first time, the student rides in the rear seat, the instructor in the front seat at the controls; then on the second trip their positions are reversed, and the student is in control of the plane.

The Link Trainer, also used by the Army and commercial lines for instruction in instrument flying—often miscalled "blind flying"—is employed in the last stage of Squadron 5.

THE CADET FLAME

If you are the O.A.O. back home in Vermont, Bob is your aviation cadet, and you plan to be married as soon as he receives his commission, you will do well to read the small bit that is given here in regard to his training. His letters will be filled with such terms as "flat-hatting" (low flying to scare the farmers and livestock), hedgehopping, and "gosport." (This last means a one-way communication device worn by an instructor with a tube which connects to the headgear of the student in the front. This enables the teacher to direct his pupil what to do and how to do it and criticize his errors, but does not enable the pupil to talk back, thus constituting a perfect alibi-proof system of education.) There will be long descriptions of emergency landings. He will probably expect you to know about the Link Trainer, and he will write of zooming planes, dogfights in the air, parachuting, catapulting, and many humorous stories about himself and his classmates, but all in his new lingo. Learn what the words mean.

There will be times during the course when Bob will be depressed. His fear of getting "washed out" will be apparent if you can read between the lines of his letter. That will be your cue to write him a cheerful, encouraging letter to let him know that you believe in him.

Some wag has said that "a cadet flame is of value only as a decorative background and a recreational outlet." That may be true in a measure, since the time of a cadet during his training is filled with flying and work; but if you are the O.A.O., that is something else. Write cheery, newsy letters with all the home-town news. If letter writing isn't one of your accomplishments, send him a subscription to his home-town newspaper. In return, he may send you *The Gosport*, a very clever magazine published at the Training Station by the cadets.

He will also appreciate a box of homemade candy or cake
now and then.

If you are "a cadet flame" in one of the four cities where
there are training centers, there are many little ways by which
you can make the life of a flying cadet happier. Invite him
to your home for family dinners. Cadets do not have much
money to spend on entertaining, although they are usually
generous with what they have. Be a good listener and "regard him as a hero," when he graduates to a new stage or
squadron and wants to do a bit of "hangar flying" and talk
about himself.

Of course you already know that no cadet can be married
while he is a student. In fact, upon entrance he takes an oath
that he is not married, or ever has been married; and should
he marry during the course of training, he automatically
would be washed out or busted. However a recent order of the
Secretary of the Navy permits a cadet to marry as soon as he
has completed his training and received his commission.

A naval aviation cadet receives $105 a month, $30 of which
is returned for his mess bill. His quarters are furnished, and
the government includes a $10,000 life insurance policy with
paid premiums during the training period.

OTHER TRAINING STATIONS

The Naval Training Station at Corpus Christi (recently
christened the "University of the Air") is located on Corpus
Christi Bay at Four Bluffs, a small settlement ten miles away.
The population of Corpus Christi is about 3,000. The tiny
town of Four Bluffs, which is now the Naval Air Station, was
formerly a land of brush and sand, of coyote and rattlesnakes
and chaparral. Before the flying field could be built, millions
of sand dunes had to be leveled. Today, large hangars replace
the sand dunes; the roar of giant bombers drowns the lonely
cry of the sea gull; the sleepy fishing village has been transformed into a great modern air training station.

The most desirable location for a home is between the air
station and the city.

Corpus Christi, the "Playground of Texas," has always been a tourist resort, and is famous for its fine fishing in summer and good hunting in winter. The climate is mild, and the spring and autumn are lovely seasons. The wild flowers in the spring, with Texas bluebonnets covering the countryside, is a sight you will never forget. The summers are hot, but there is a cool breeze which generally blows from the southeast.

Lightweight clothing is worn most of the year with tropical dresses for summer use. Lightweight woolens are comfortable during the intermittent cold spells called "northers," and a good warm topcoat is necessary. Warm blankets are needed for midwinter.

Servants, either Mexican or Negro, ordinarily are plentiful and reasonable.

The Naval Training Station at Jacksonville

Living conditions in Jacksonville are above average, and the people of Jacksonville are very proud of the Naval Air Station, which the government completed in 1940 at a cost of thirty-five million dollars. It is located on the site of old Camp Johnston of World War I days, about ten miles from the center of Jacksonville, on the beautiful St. Johns River. Two auxiliary fields are maintained near by, namely, Lee Field and Cecil Field.

Jacksonville is the largest seaport on the South Atlantic and the largest city in Florida, with a population of 200,000.

Spring clothes, consisting of light woolens or a silk dress and light topcoat, may be worn for about six weeks in the spring and practically all fall and winter, with the exception of the cold spells. In the summer, much time is spent at the beaches, so play suits, bathing suits, slacks are worn, also cotton spectator sports dresses for town wear, and cotton or some washable material, again, for evening and dinner dresses.

Not only does Jacksonville have a climate for healthful living, but because of its mildness very little need be spent for fuel and heavy clothing in winter. Negro servants are plentiful, but trained ones are scarce. The wages for women are from $8 to $10 a week, butlers get from $12 to $15, and laundresses from $1.50 to $2 per day.

Food is abundant, and the markets overflow with vegetables, although they are of rather poor quality. The prices are reasonable. Citrus fruits are plentiful except in summer.

Quarters

There is a very limited number of government quarters on the station at present. Actually, there are nine sets, with those under construction bringing the total number up to twenty-two. These are of course occupied by the senior officers and those officers whose duties require their presence at the station.

The quarters are of frame construction, Colonial in style, painted white with green trim, and are located on or near the river. They are surrounded by large oak trees and beautiful green lawns. There is a very comfortable B.O.Q. (Bachelor Officers' Quarters).

Riverdale Gardens

The government has built a housing project containing 164 houses. It is three miles from the air station and six miles from the business section of Jacksonville. At present, nearly all of the houses are occupied by naval officers.

Apartments and Houses

There are many small apartments and a few large apartment buildings in Jacksonville, with prices ranging from $50 to $100 per month depending upon size and location. Most of these are unfurnished with the exception of stoves, refrigerators, and hot water heaters.

The leading hotels are the Windsor, Roosevelt, George Washington, and Seminole. The rates are average, and special rates may be obtained on a monthly basis. The Martha Washington, a smaller family hotel, American plan, located in the residential section known as Riverside, is popular with Navy people, especially those with children.

There are a few beautiful old homes whose owners take paying guests for either overnight or more lengthy visits. Glanuska, three miles from the air station, is one of these.

Clubs

Jacksonville is a city of clubs, and a very sociable city. The private clubs are glad to extend membership to the officer personnel of the Navy and their families, and usually the initiation fee is waived and Service membership is given. The most popular clubs are the Timaquana Country and Golf Club, the Jacksonville Women's Cub, and the Cotillion Club.

The Jacksonville Junior League is always happy to welcome transfers from other Leagues.

The Bath Club at Ponte Vedra Beach, twenty-five miles away, is very popular during the summer months. Cabañas may be rented by the week or season.

Jacksonville's beaches, located eighteen miles east of Jacksonville, extend along the ocean front as far south as St. Augustine.

The Training Station at Miami

In addition to the regular training course, Miami gives advanced training at the Naval Air Station Opal Locker. The advanced school is located on the site of the old Naval Reserve Station. Pilots who are assigned to carrier duty are sent to Opal Locker for training.

There are about six sets of frame quarters for the heads of the departments, and also comfortable quarters for bachelor officers. Apartments in Miami may be had for as low as $60 or $75 per month, if one knows how to shop. It is said that there are two prices for homes in Miami; naturally, since Miami is a winter resort for wealthy tourists, the prices are exorbitant during the season.

An attractive Naval Club is being built. Miami is filled with luxurious hotels, and one can expect to find beautiful beaches, even lovelier bathing beauties, and all of the accoutrements that go along with America's most popular winter resort.

Prices keep pace; but fortunately, the course of training lasts only a short time and even Service people enjoy looking on for a short time to see how the other half lives.

INFORMATION—PLEASE!

Here is some general information about naval aviation that may or may not interest you upon your first perusal. But it is good data to have in the back of your mind in order to be what every man appreciates most in a woman, an intelligent listener.

1. Don't ever commit the unpardonable sin of airing your aviation knowledge; but HE will put you down with a better than 2.5 rating if you know the difference between a patrol bomber and a blimp. Remember, this naval aviation is a man's game and a man's world, and just about the time you think you know a little bit about the flying boats and can distinguish one, the model will change and you will be sunk again! About the only safe rule to follow is that of the wise old owl: Listen if and when you must, but give the impression of profound intelligence by keeping your knowledge to yourself.
2. Aircraft carriers are divided into two classes, namely, aircraft carriers and seaplane tenders.
3. Aircraft carriers are known as "the covered wagons" of the ocean. They are the mobile landing fields of the sea. Their flat-topped decks give them a distinctive and odd appearance. The decks are as level as a tennis court, and there is no superstructure except a single island of bridge. Stacks are set to one side and are sometimes folding. A carrier is always under way when the planes take off, thereby creating a wind. A carrier is supposed to give punishment but is not equipped to take it.
4. The aircraft carriers now in commission are:

U.S.S. *Saratoga*
U.S.S. *Lexington*
U.S.S. *Ranger*
U.S.S. *Yorktown*
U.S.S. *Enterprise*
U.S.S. *Wasp*
U.S.S. *Hornet*
U.S.S. *Bon Homme Richard*

Under construction are:

U.S.S. *Essex*
U.S.S. *Intrepid*
U.S.S. *Kearsarge*

5. Seaplane tenders are named for famous men: *Langley; Curtiss; Wright; Albemarle.*
6. Carriers are named for famous ships that figured prominently in the early history of the American Navy, and for famous battles.
7. The Navy's Flying Fleet is divided into four main groups: ship-based planes, patrol planes or flying boats, land-based planes, and lighter-than-air craft.
8. Ship-based planes can be carried aboard carriers, aboard large aircraft tenders, or aboard battleships and cruisers. Experiments have been tried out to fit a folding-wing plane into a specially constructed deck hangar aboard a submarine, but so far submarines do not carry planes.
9. The Lighter-than-Air Navy Base is at Lakehurst, N.J., and trains students in handling nonrigid, powered blimps. They are useful in coastal convoy work and coastal patrol.
10. Patrol planes are long-range flying boats and are built to patrol great areas of ocean.
11. The scouting plane is used for scouting out enemy positions. These planes are called "the eyes of the fleet."
12. The fighting plane is a small, fast, single-seater, flown by one pilot. Its mission is to attack enemy aircraft and it uses machine guns.
13. Torpedo planes carry torpedoes for horizontal attack, but these big planes must depend upon surprise, speed, and smoke screen to get within striking distance of an enemy ship.
14. Observation planes fly high over the target, observe the fall of shells, and radio back information for the change of elevation and for lateral displacement.
15. Naval aviators are well-trained pilots, and were the first to develop dive bombing and our famous bomb sight.
16. Navy aircraft must have greater strength than land planes to withstand the shocks of landing in a rough sea, of being flung at sixty miles an hour from a catapult, or of roaring in a dive bombing attack out of the skies at three hundred to five hun-

dred miles an hour. Also, their engines must be of special construction to prevent corrosion, as they are constantly exposed to salt spray.

17. The Distinguished Flying Cross is awarded to any person who, while serving with the U.S. Navy subsequent to April 6, 1917, has distinguished himself by heroism or extraordinary achievement while participating in an aerial flight.

Fighting Names Will Designate Navy Planes

Names with a belligerent ring hereafter will mark the fighting planes of the Navy and Marine Corps on orders of the Secretary of the Navy.

The orders supplant for popular use the prosaic letter-numeral designations heretofore characteristic of Navy plane identification. The new titles will be for popular use, the Secretary explained, and the old designations will remain in force and unchanged for all official correspondence and dispatches.

Fighters:
  Brewster F2A to be known as *Buffalo*
  Grumman F4F to be known as *Wildcat*
  Vought F4U to be known as *Kingfisher*

Observation scouts:
  Curtiss SO3C to be known as *Seagull*
  Navy PS2N to be known as *Kingfisher*

Scout bombers:
  Brewster 2B2A to be known as *Buccaneer*
  Curtiss SB2C to be known as *Hell-Diver*
  Douglas SBD to be known as *Dauntless*
  Vought 2B2U to be known as *Vindicator*

Patrol bombers:
  Boeing PBB to be known as *Sea Ranger*
  Martin PBM to be known as *Mariner*
  Consolidated PBY to be known as *Catalina*
  Consolidated PB2Y to be known as *Coronado*

Torpedo bombers:
  Douglas TBD to be known as *Devastator*
  Grumman TBF to be known as *Avenger*

HAPPY LANDINGS!

Chapter III

THE UNDERSEA NAVY

Our Four-Star Admiral swore, by the fine gray beard he wore
That his Fleet could lick Big John's scoutin' line.
So he formed protective screens, which were made of submarines
Of the fighting Roger type of Subdiv. Nine.

Swish, swish, swish, the craft is diving
Straight for a case of native wine.
Let's get boosted to the skies,
Then go down and never rise,
We're the cruisin', shootin' boys of Subdiv. Nine!

HAVING served his first two years in a surface ship with the Fleet, Bill will be eligible for the Submarine School if he has not elected to request training in naval aviation. These two services of the Navy vie with each other in esprit de corps, and each is necessarily within itself a closely knit group. There are several reasons for this: The submarine service is a small branch, and the officers and enlisted men are especially selected for very definite qualifications. The first of these requirements is dependability. The crew of a submarine is small, and each man has a special duty to perform. A submariner must also be a calm individual not subject to temperamental outbursts. He is preferably a quiet but cheerful fellow, without mannerisms that will get on the nerves of his shipmates in the crowded, close quarters of the submarine. Into every submariner is drilled the first law of underwater life: Decisions must be made and followed by immediate action. Constant drills train the men to secure the water-tight doors, in emergency, as reflex actions. Reactions must be timed to a split second, and they must be right the first time. Calm self-confidence is characteristic of the first-class submarine man.

39

THE SUBMARINE SCHOOL

If an officer asks for submarine duty and is accepted, he will be sent to the Submarine School located at New London, Connecticut. Formerly, a six months course of study was given, but owing to the expanded submarine program entailing the fitting out of recommissioned and newly constructed boats and the need for a larger number of trained officers and men, the training has been intensified and the period of the course reduced.

Submarine officers and enlisted men are trained to know thoroughly all parts of a submarine's equipment. They must be able to perform efficiently the duties at many stations besides the one to which they are assigned on board. The course of study includes the tactical operation of submarines, Diesel engines and lead-acid storage batteries, electricity, torpedoes, and communications. Together with these theoretical and practical studies, the students receive practical training on board submarines.

Officers who graduate are eligible, after serving one year in submarines, to take examinations for the merit designation of "Qualified in Submarines." This carries with it the privilege of wearing the "Dolphin," submarine insignia worn on the uniform in the same manner as an aviator wears his wings. A higher degree of excellence is reached when the submariner progresses to the stage where he is designated as "Qualified for Command."

LIVING CONDITIONS IN NEW LONDON

On the whole, living conditions are about the same as in other crowded Navy ports today. However, in some ways New London might be said to have the edge on some of the more expensive stations.

At present there are no government quarters for commissioned personnel, except for the Commanding Officer and bachelor officers. Apartments are few, but a number can be had at rentals from $45 a month up. There are many old-fashioned boardinghouses available and some of these are very comfortable. Unfurnished houses rent from $55 to around $90 and $100 for very indifferent accommodations. Every now and then a family may catch a windfall, some recently vacated family mansion. But such breaks are not to be gambled on.

The servant situation is acute. An average maid may be had for $60 a month and up; but at that minimum wage, you can expect only headaches in return for the battle. The majority of these servants prefer part-time work and are paid by the hour.

The social life is quite pleasant. New London society is conservative, but many agreeable contacts are open to Navy personnel. The U.S. Coast Guard and Navy groups are so large that these units are absolutely self-sustaining as to social recreation, yet relations are pleasant between all branches of the government service. The U.S. Coast Guard Academy and Connecticut College offer many improving opportunities as to music, literary programs, and athletic events. New Haven, with all of Yale's resources and advantages, is only fifty miles away. Social activity is very lively Navy-wise, and among civilians in and about New London.

There is a splendid Officers' Club, and an unusually active and able Navy Wives' Club for enlisted personnel. The hotels are good, but there are only two of them—the Mohican and the Crocker House. The base publishes a snappy weekly magazine or newspaper called the *Sub-Base Gazette*, in which is recorded social notes, important announcements, Marine Barracks' notes, and "everything that's fit to print" about the submariners at New London.

A VISIT TO A SUBMARINE BASE

For almost a year, on my frequent visits to the Pearl Harbor Navy Yard, I had been curious about that tall silo-looking building as high as a twenty-story skyscraper, that overlooked the harbor. I thought of it as a naval observation tower or look-out, but after much questioning, I was finally informed that it was a submarine escape training tank.

There is another one of these unique structures located at the submarine base at New London, I am told, and it is in these tanks that the training of a submariner begins. Before my visit, I had read up a bit on submarines so that I could listen intelligently and not ask too many stupid questions. Knowing nothing about Diesel engines or complicated machinery, I knew I would not make any faux pas in that direction if I kept quiet and listened with an eager, dumb, feminine look in my eye! But I really was interested in the ships themselves, in the escape tank, the famous Momsen lung, the diving bell, and the officers and men who manned these "pig boats."

One of the first points I noted was that submariners do not care for the title "pig boats," now that they have these large black beauties of death and destruction with their "high bows and their stately superstructure towering impressively above the water." I also learned that these death-dealing ships do not carry big guns or heavy armor. Their mission is to lurk beneath the waves with their deadly torpedoes, and to fire when they are at periscope depth or even deeper. They can imperil any vessel afloat, and they regard themselves quite legitimately as very nasty customers indeed for an enemy to tangle with in a close engagement.

The submarine is also an excellent long-distance scout, and it is used to locate enemy fleets, to observe enemy ports and coasts, and to disrupt enemy trade. I was intrigued by the distinctive black-hulled vessels lying mostly under water, and interested in their "toothpick" periscopes showing above the thin superstructure deck and conning tower.

The submariner believes that his ship is the safest type of vessel afloat because it is practically impossible to capsize it, and in case of a hurricane or typhoon he can submerge below the swirling waters and find peace in the quiet sea one hundred feet below the surface. As one crusty, somewhat henpecked petty officer explained in telling of the advantages of submerging: "When she's resting quietly on the bottom in forty fathoms, with killed motors, it's more than quiet, it's dead still, and you know *She* can't get hold of you, even by radio!"

First Steps to Becoming a Submariner

The Navy does everything thoroughly and efficiently, even to simply conducting a sightseeing tour around a sub base.

Anxious to see the various stages of training to which a submariner is subjected, we were first taken to the escape training tank located in the small examination room at the base of the tank. No chances are taken on the stamina and the physical condition of the men who must meet the rigorous emergencies of submarine life. The physical checkup covers eyes, ears, nose, throat, heart, and lungs. Special attention is given to the teeth to be sure they are in good condition for holding the mouthpiece of the Momsen lung apparatus.

The "Torture" Chamber

After the physical examination the men fit for underwater tests are placed in the compression chamber. This huge thermos bottle affair accommodates about fifteen students and two instructors. In it is given the real test to determine whether the men can take it!

We looked into it warily at first, then pulling our skirts together went through the hatch to investigate. I was thankful not to have to take the test, since the sight of this famous torture chamber gave me a violent attack of claustrophobia. It is often called the ear-cracking machine, and many dire and dreadful stories have had their beginnings in its interior.

This may or may not mean anything to you, my gentle reader, but "the normal air pressure at sea level is 14.7 pounds per square inch, and in this chamber as a test the pressure is stepped up to 50 pounds, which is the equivalent of the pressure at 110 feet below the surface of the water."

If a man can't take the pressure, and becomes ill or faints, he is removed from the inner chamber to a small escape chamber, where the pressure is gradually brought back to normal. The instructors tell some droll stories about the consternation and fright of the colored and Filipino mess attendants on their first tests; however, everyone who serves in a submarine must take the tests, even if his main job is making coffee and spreading sandwiches.

Meet "J. D. Jake"

After the students leave the decompression chamber, each is given a Momsen lung. Before experimenting with the lung, however, one should not miss paying his respects to "J. D. Jake," the dummy master-diver that so forbiddingly occupies one section of the room. What he is there for I never found out, but certainly he is there, attired in a heavy rubberized canvas suit weighing twenty pounds. On his head is a brightly polished helmet that weighs 31 pounds, on his chest a heavy metal breastplate that weighs 24 pounds, and on his feet enormous shoes weighing an extra 36 pounds. But the most imposing piece of equipment is an extra heavily weighted belt weighing 84 pounds. His canvas-gloved hands hang limply in front of him, as if to say, "Why must I support this 195 pounds of diving equipment on such a hot day?"

The Momsen Lung

The Momsen lung is so called after its inventor, Commander Charles B. Momsen, U.S.N. It was given the name "lung" because it really acts as a third lung. As the word is monosyllabic, it lends itself well for quickly conveying to the minds of the submarine crew, in case of accident, that they are to equip themselves with the device and be prepared for individual escape.

The lung itself looks like a large hot-water bottle made of stockinet with one strap which fits around the neck to hold it up, another strap which fits around the waist to hold it down, and two small metal clamps by which it is clamped to the trousers. The last-mentioned device prevents its floating upward on the wearer's body when he is submerged.

Have you ever had a basal metabolism test? Well, the rest of the apparatus, from the rubber lungs that fit in the mouth to the sturdy clothespin clamps that fit on the nose making breathing through the nostrils impossible, resembles that complicated piece of machinery employed in hospitals for such tests.

The explanation of the innards of the lung—and believe it or not, that almost human thing has "a heart which is a canister filled with soda lime" to absorb the carbon-dioxide generated in the lungs of the user—is much too complicated, with its various cut-off and flutter valves, for me to go into. Suffice it to say that "its function is to maintain equilibrium at all times between internal pressures and pressures of the surrounding water, thus keeping the bag at buoyancy irrespective of the depths of the water from which the ascent is made." Since the escape training was established in 1930, about 80,000 tank escapes have been made.

TANK TRAINING

Now for the diving tank!

Of course there is a spiral stairway winding around the tank, but the day was hot so we chose the elevator in the adjoining tower to carry us up the ten or twelve stories. Once on top, and crossing the narrow catwalk bridge into the tank, we found the wind velocity so great that my large cartwheel hat and I almost parted forever. After that experience I decided to check such a silly piece of headgear because I was told it would also interfere with my passage into the decompression chamber later.

Once inside the cylindrical tank, we walked around the enclosed circular platform at the top of the pool and stared down into the tube of fresh water one hundred feet deep. It looked very cool and inviting on such a hot day. The water is filtered through sand, chlorinated, and kept at a temperature of 85 degrees. A dozen or so students are sent to the tower at a time to begin lung training. This is one of the first steps toward qualifying as a submariner. Not cheerful, but a wise procedure.

The student must first learn how to make an emergency escape from a sunken submarine; and not only a student but every submariner from Admiral to the lowest-ranking mess attendant must repeat his training and "come up in the tank" to requalify once a year. The student is introduced to his escape training by easy stages. Standing by at all times are expert swimmers and divers, the instructors, and a medical officer.

A detailed explanation of every part of the lung, what it is for and how it is used, is given by the instructors. Demonstrations in the use of the lung are also given by the instructors. Preliminary ascents by students are made from various shallow depths, not greater than twelve feet. At some time during this stage of training the student is required to make at least one stop between twelve feet and the surface, for a period of about thirty breaths, to insure his proper breathing in the lung, all the time holding on to the ascending line. Having experimented, so to speak, with the lung, the student gains confidence when he finds how easy it is to breathe under water when wearing this device.

After having qualified in the use of the lung, all submarine personnel are required annually to make an ascent from the eighteen-foot depth. There are two side locks in the escape training tank which permit ascents from eighteen and fifty feet. There is also a submarine compartment at the hundred-foot level. All ascents from the fifty- and hundred-foot side locks are voluntary. The lung not only enables a man to escape from a sunken submarine but will support the wearer as a life jacket when he reaches the surface. The process of emerging from a sunken submarine is the same as that which submarine personnel experience in emerging from a side lock or compartment at the escape training tank.

To ascend too rapidly, even from a shallow depth of fifteen feet might prove fatal. In 1931 a sailor wearing a Momsen lung merely held his breath and allowed himself to shoot to the surface like a cork in a fraction over two seconds. The post-mortem report was as follows: "The deceased, after appearing on the surface, closed the shut-off valve and then reached for the ladder to ascend the float, but was unable to grasp it and fell backward. He breathed a few times and expired. The autopsy revealed numerous hemorrhages throughout both lungs, etc. The right ventricle of the heart was definitely dilated." [1]

All of which is a technical way of saying that his lungs exploded. Students are warned about the danger of making quick ascents, and also about the fact that their safety depends upon carrying out directions to the letter.

THE RESCUE CHAMBER

The submarine rescue chamber, another ingenious device, was responsible for saving the lives of thirty-three members of the ill-fated *Squalus* in 1939. It is an immense steel structure 10 feet high having a weight of 18,000 pounds. It is designed to be hauled down on to the hatch of a sunken submarine by a wire attached to the hatch. A total of nine men may be taken aboard the rescue chamber at one time. Once contact has been established, the chamber may make repeated trips from the surface to the submarine quite rapidly. To get a good idea of the prodigious job accomplished in rescue work and in raising a submarine from the bottom of the sea, I recommend to you the various works of Commander Edward Ellsberg, who is an authority on the subject. He has directed and taken an active part in the raising of several sunken craft.

DEEP-SEA DIVING

The movies have a way of making deep-sea divers very romantic and glamorous, but there isn't anything especially romantic about weighting oneself down with 195 pounds of

[1] Kendall Banning, *The Fleet Today*. Funk & Wagnalls Company, New York, 1940.

equipment and floundering about in the mud on the floor of
the ocean. After being lowered into the water, the diver
inflates his suit with air and floats, then slowly lets out the air
and settles to the bottom. There is no trick in sinking, but
great care is necessary when he is ready to make his ascent.

While the diver is at work, he is dependent upon the crew
above on the submarine tender. Someone is holding his life
line and air hose, and although there is telephone communication, the diver isn't very talkative. The heavy air pressure
makes it difficult to talk and also tends to make him a bit
groggy.

The great danger is a form of paralysis known as "the
bends" or caisson disease. It is the dread of all men who work
far beneath the water. Here is the way an old-timer describes
the bends:

Under air pressure the blood is full of air bubbles. If a diver
returns to the surface too fast, bubbles remain in the blood stream,
collect and settle in a certain area, such as the leg, back or arm.
The victim of the bends is stricken suddenly with severe pain
which may jump from one section of the body to another. One of
the men described it as an almost unbearable pain, as of needles
sticking in the body, or severe cramps. Oftentimes, the victim
loses consciousness. The only relief is to get under pressure in a
decompression chamber, where the pressure is built up as fast as
possible. In some cases, it is necessary for the patient to remain in
the decompression chamber for several hours. If the attendant has
to stay in the decompression chamber too long, he is apt to become
a victim of the bends himself—upon leaving. In a severe case of
bends, the diver's body remains sore for several weeks. The sore
muscles and tissues are like a sprain, caused by the expanding air
bubbles.

The world's record dive, without artificial breathing aids, was
made in Hawaii in 1915 at the time the F-4 was lost in 300 feet
of water about a mile from the docks in Honolulu. It was made
by Frank Crilly, a commercial diver, who located the F-4 nearly
a month after she went down.[2]

[2] Virginia Hill, "Workers under the Sea," in the Feature Section of
the Honolulu *Star-Bulletin*, Saturday, November 8, 1941.

and the room itself, aside from the necessary lubricating oil, is beautifully clean. But oh! the noise!

The torpedo room, with its torpedoes nestled down in their cradles, waiting only to be loaded into tubes and to have the firing key pressed to send them streaking through the water, was really not very interesting until suddenly I realized that here was the whole reason for this thing. Extra torpedoes were packed into converted space, and the crew had their bunks practically on top of the torpedoes. Nice little bedfellows! The men were busy preparing exercise torpedoes for firing. These practice torpedoes have yellow heads, so that after exercise runs, when floating on the water, they are more visible.

Submarines are named for fish. For example, *Tuna, Nautilus, Pickerel, Pompano, Salmon, Sturgeon, Trout, Sailfish, Triton* and *Gudgeon* are names of a few of the submarines in service today. Submarine tenders or auxiliaries are usually named for aquatic animals.

Chapter IV

THE MARINE CORPS

From the halls of Montezuma
To the shores of Tripoli;
We fight our country's battles
On the land and on the sea;
First to fight for right and freedom
And to keep our honor clean;
We are proud to bear the title
Of United States Marine.

Marine Hymn

THE Marine Corps is one of the most colorful branches of the United States Military and Naval Service. Captain Lovette has put it strikingly: "Marines have been landing as sea soldiers from ships of war on foreign shores since the dawn of recorded history. It is written that the Marines of Phoenicia, Greece, Egypt, Carthage and Rome had similar duties to the Marines of today, in that they were the soldiers on board fighting ships, and were usually the 'spear head' in landing operations."[1]

Today, the Marines are still the "spear heads," and in any landing operation on foreign soil, though operating under naval high command, they are the first to land. The Marine Corps is a two-fisted, hard-hitting organization. Their mobility and preparedness are an essential part of the very spirit of the Corps. Their timely intervention has nipped many a Latin-American revolution in the bud. A situation frequently reported in the United States newspapers reads: "The Marines have landed and have the situation well in hand."

The Continental Congress on November 10, 1775, au-

[1] Leland P. Lovette, *Naval Customs, Traditions and Usage.* United States Naval Institute, Annapolis, 1934.

thorized the raising of two battalions of Marines, and for that reason November 10 has been officially designated as the birthday of the Marine Corps and has been so observed by the Corps since 1921.

Marines played a vivid part in the War of 1812, and in 1846 they marched to Mexico and stormed the Castle of Chapultepec in the most spectacular battle of the Mexican War. Out of this encounter they brought home two mementos: the first line of the Marine Hymn, "From the halls of Montezuma," referring to the Mexican chief and his castle; and the red stripe, worn on the blue trousers of officers and noncommissioned officers, commemorating to this day service in that war.

Marines served in the Civil War. Under Colonel Huntington they took Guantanamo in the Spanish-American War in 1898, landing from the U.S.S. *Marblehead.* They were with Admiral Dewey the same year, and in 1900 in Peking they helped suppress the Boxer Rebellion. Since 1900 they have operated in China, Korea, Siberia, the Philippines, Hawaii, Cuba, Mexico, Nicaragua, Haiti, Dominican Republic, France, and Germany. They were ashore at Vera Cruz in 1914, and in 1915 they occupied Haiti, where they stayed until 1934. Many uneasy and volatile West Indian and Central American republics have become acquainted with them in a professional way.

In the first World War the Fifth and Sixth Regiments of Marines at Belleau Wood and at Château-Thierry established an enviable record for their corps. General A. W. Catlin tells the story of some distinguished visitors who were passing the cots in a military hospital in France. On one of the cots lay a man, quite still, with his face buried in a pillow. Something about him caused one of the visitors to remark, "I think this must be an American soldier." From the depths of the pillow came a muffled voice: "Hell, no; I'm a Marine!"

Every capital ship carries a detachment of Marines. The rank and file are good enough Latinists to know the meaning of *"Semper fidelis,"* which is their slogan, and they are proud to live up to it. The "gyrenes" are ready for frolic or fray in any part of the world.

The Fleet Marine Force has been organized into two divisions, and was established December 7, 1933. The home of the First Division is New River, N.C.; the home of the Second Division is San Diego.

The Marines' great specialty is landing operations on an enemy shore. They have developed a remarkable landing equipment, one element of which is the so-called "alligator." This is a flat-bottomed steel landing boat, a sort of oceangoing tank with the ability to swim through the sea at ten miles an hour and to speed across the land at twenty-five.

Tell It to the Marines

During war emergencies many expressions, both slang and otherwise, come into popularity; but "Tell it to the Marines" dates back to the days of Charles II of England. It seems that at the king's castle at Whitehall, a certain sea captain, newly returned from the Western Ocean, told the king of "flying fish," a thing never heard of in jolly old England up to that time. The king and court were vastly amused, but the naval fellow persisted. The Merry Monarch beckoned to a lean, dry Colonel of a sea regiment with a seamed mahogany face, and said: "Colonel, this tarry-breeches here makes sport of us landlubbers. He tells us of a miraculous fish that forsakes its element and flies over the water like a bird." "Sire," said the Colonel of Marines, "he tells the truth. I myself have often seen those fish in your Majesty's seas around Barbados." "Well," decided Charles, "such evidence cannot be disputed. And hereafter, when we hear a strange thing, *we will tell it to the Marines,* for the Marines go everywhere and see everything, and if they say it is so, we will believe it."

The exploits of the Marine Corps are justly celebrated in popular fiction. One of the best-known writers of such historical fiction, is Colonel John W. Thomason of the Marine Corps. Some rainy dreary afternoon, if you want to read entertaining stories about Marines and their experiences, hie yourself to the nearest library and read *Fix Bayonets*, from which the above story was taken, or *Red Pants*.

Another popular writer of Marine stories is the late General Frank E. Evans. His experiences as a Marine Officer with the A.E.F. and as a military observer in Morocco with the Foreign Legion, and his five years in Haiti in command of the native troops, gave him a wealth of material for numerous short stories. While in France he wrote a charming group of Marine stories for his then small son entitled *Daddy Pat of the Marines*.

MARINE CORPS ORGANIZATION

The Marines are essentially soldiers but are blessed with the sea habit. They arc organized as a corps under the Secretary of the Navy, and for purposes of administration, discipline, and training in land warfare, constitute an independent branch. Marines normally serve with the Navy, but as in the first World War, by direction of the President they may be assigned to service with the Army. Except when serving with the Army, the Marine Corps is governed by the regulations for the government of the Navy.

The Marine Corps Headquarters is in the Navy Department in Washington, D.C. The Commandant has the rank of Lieutenant General. The troops are organized into two divisions plus many defense battalions and detachments for ships and shore stations.

Young men are attracted to the Marine Corps from all walks of life. The standards of the Corps are high as to physique, intelligence, and character. And a Marine loves to say, "It is *still* possible to become a Marine, if you're *Man* enough." Their esprit de corps is excellent and their morale is always high. There was a time when the Marine was looked upon as a mere handy man for the Navy, a sort of web-footed policeman who was neither soldier nor sailor. But discipline, training, experienced leaders, and fine personnel have altered all that. A Marine believes with all his soul that no man can

lick him, and his motto is "To kill—or be killed." He has no
equal as "an international policeman."

THE LEATHERNECKS

What a name! Perhaps you wonder why Marines are so
called. Well, it dates back to the early days of the Revolution
and to the black leather stocks which were adopted as part
of the uniform. Even as late as thirty-odd years ago, the inner
lining of the collar of the full-dress coat was of leather, to
make it stand up.

THE MARINE UNIFORM TODAY

The field uniform of the Marine Corps is forestry green
for winter and khaki for summer. The insignia of rank for
commissioned officers corresponds with the relative rank of
officers of the Army. The campaign hat is similar to the field
service hat of the Army. The hat cord worn by officers is of
gold and scarlet, with ends finished with gold-and-scarlet
acorns. The Corps device of bronze is worn on the front of the
hat by officers and men. The globe which forms part of their
Corps device has been their stage; it is surmounted by an
anchor, with the American eagle poised on top of the world.
The uniform differs from that of the Army and Navy, of
course. The dress uniform is the famous dark-blue blouse
(known as serge-blue) with the yellow-and-red sleeve markings and chevrons, the light-blue trousers (known as sky-
blue), the white cloth belt with highly polished buckle, the
black shoes and visored cap.

The rank of N.C.O. (or noncommissioned officer) is
shown by the chevrons worn on both arms of the blouse and
overcoat, and on the sleeves of the khaki shirt. No chevrons
are worn on combat coveralls. None are needed! In the Marine
Corps an N.C.O. is known by his bark and his bearing.

WITH THE HELP OF GOD AND A FEW MARINES

This saying has been attributed to nearly every naval hero
from John Paul Jones to Admiral Dewey; however, it ex-

presses the very spirit of the Marine Corps. The late General Evans used to say: "With the help of God and a few other Marines."

The second stanza of the Marine Hymn seems apropos here to express that splendid spirit:

> Our flags unfurled to every breeze
> From dawn to setting sun,
> We have fought in every clime and place
> Where we could take a gun.
> In the snow of far-off northern lands
> And in sunny tropic scenes,
> You will always find us on the job,
> The United States Marines.

THE MARINE WIFE

This topic is in itself well worthy of a special book, but suffice it to say that the wives of all Marines are made of pretty stern stuff! They have to be, in order to be good helpmates to the men they marry. Definitely, the Marine Corps is no place for the hothouse-plant type of wife. A Marine officer's wife must accustom herself to "carrying on" for long periods alone, just like the Navy wife and the Army wife of today. Marine wives have always had to adjust themselves to sudden moves and departures, and today nothing in the way of unexpected and secret orders surprises them.

LIFE AT QUANTICO FOR THE MARINE WIFE

The Marine barracks at Quantico, Virginia, are located on a reservation of approximately six thousand acres near the village of Quantico. There are available on the post about 256 sets of married officers' quarters of various sizes, which are furnished except for rugs, mattresses, and draperies.

There are no hotels available in the vicinity, and only a few small unattractive houses (furnished) in Quantico. There are a few tourist homes at Dumphries, three miles from the post, but most people who do not have quarters prefer to live in Fredericksburg and commute.

The climate is very much like that of Washington, except that the summer heat is less oppressive. Except for short periods, there are no extremes of temperature.

Servants (mostly Negro) are scarce and very unsatisfactory, even though each set of quarters is equipped with servant's room and bath. Mostly, the few trained servants prefer to go to Washington where wages are higher.

Schools

A modern brick school is located on the post with grades from kindergarten through high school. There is also an excellent nursery school. The schools are supervised by the Virginia Public School Board. Transportation problems are solved by school busses.

GENERAL LIVING CONDITIONS

The Post Commissary is splendid, and food is less expensive than in Washington.

Owing to the size of the post, a car is almost a necessity. In addition, a "jalopy" or "second car" is desirable, as the quarters are scattered and the distances are great. The commissary does not deliver unless one is ill.

There is a government hospital on the post which takes care of the officers and enlisted men, who in turn maintain a Family Hospital by means of very nominal dues. Membership entitles dependents to such medical care and hospitalization as may be necessary, at low costs.

One of the outstanding buildings at Quantico, and a model for the other services, is a three-quarters-of-a-million-dollar Hostess House. It serves as a hotel, is equipped with a cafeteria, a gymnasium, bowling alleys, a well-stocked Post Exchange, a cobbler and tailor shop, and an excellent library, also a thrilling museum of Marine uniforms on wax figures, and relics and documentary history dating back to 1775. The center of the building is occupied by an air-conditioned auditorium with a seating capacity of about 3000. There is a large stage on which the latest movies are shown, besides plays, radio programs, and road shows.

Recreation

All officers stationed on the post are expected to belong to the Officers' Mess, for which the dues are $2.50 a month. The mess is located in the Club House where regular meals are served. The Club House also is available for private parties. The mess likewise operates a bar where liquors and wines may be purchased.

It also operates for no additional fee a golf course, golf clubhouse, swimming pool, and skeet range. Tennis courts, bowling alleys, movies, riding horses, and a modern gymnasium are available for the use of officers and their families without charge. The Post Exchange Recreation Fund has furnished several sailboats. Reservations may be made for these by seeing the dock master at the marine dock.

THE MARINE BASE AT SAN DIEGO

San Diego is the principal training center on the west coast, just as Parris Island and Quantico are on the east coast. Camp Elliott, the home of the Second Division, is located near San Diego. There are only five sets of quarters available in San Diego, and these are reserved for the heads of departments. The hundreds of officers attached to the base live in or near San Diego.

General Living Conditions

Loma Portal and Mission Hills are popular suburbs. There are few apartments, but many small houses of the bungalow type are available. It is advisable to get one with heating facilities. Remember the old saying of the tourist who "went to California for the winter—and *got* it."

Food is less expensive than in any other section of the country, though sea food and good cuts of meat are rather high.

A car is most desirable, although there is good bus service. The Bank of America furnishes an excellent map, which is an absolute necessity, as you will find when you try to ferret your way around the numerous canyons on your way to call or to shop.

There aren't any servants except for those persons who can afford to pay California taxes and are down to their last *yacht*. Truly, as has been said, there is no servant class in California. The best most people can do is a part-time maid. Wages are high even for these, and a trained general servant's wages are exorbitant. If you have a good servant, by all means bring her with you.

There are two excellent service clubs, one at Coronado and one at the base in San Diego, and several popular hotels in San Diego.

WHERE IS NEW RIVER?

New River Marine Barracks is located in Onslow County, North Carolina. The reservation consists of about 85,000 acres and has a water frontage of eighteen miles on New River and fourteen miles of Atlantic Ocean with a continuous stretch of beautiful beach.

Jacksonville, the nearest town, has a population of less than 1000 and at present there is no railroad passenger service in operation, though of course this situation will be remedied in the near future. The following towns are near Jacksonville:

Morehead City, a town of 3700 population, is 45 miles east and at present is the center of Marine Corps social activities. Quite a few officers have rented homes there, since it has a good public school, several very good stores, and a lovely water setting near Bogue Sound and Atlantic Beach. Being more or less a summer resort, accommodations during the winter months are fairly plentiful. Furnished houses and apartments rent for from $50 to $80 a month, depending upon size. There is an attractive Beach Club and two hotels: the Morehead Villa which is the social hub and the Fort Macon Hotel with rates $2.50 and $2.00 per day respectively.

Kinston, N.C., is 42 miles north of Jacksonville. Its population is 15,000. Since Kinston is one of the large tobacco markets in the world, houses and apartments are at a premium during the season, from September to December, when the tobacco buyers are in town. The city has a good public school system, excellent markets and dairies, two movies, a country club with a good golf course, and excellent hunting and fishing in the vicinity. The leading hotel is the Kinston, at $2.50 per day.

New Bern with a population of 12,000 is 38 miles northeast of Jacksonville. It is one of the oldest settlements in the state. Living conditions here parallel those described for Kinston, except that houses and apartments may be rented throughout the year. The leading hotel is the Queen Anne at $2.50 per day.

Wilmington is 50 miles southwest of Jacksonville and has a population of 50,000. It has excellent railroad service, being on the Atlantic Coast Line R.R. route, and is also a bus terminal. There are good schools, a country club, two golf courses, and several libraries. Its leading hotel is the Cape Fear with minimum rates at $3.00 a day.

Since the completion date of officers' quarters is at present unknown, it is likely that you will make your home in one of these near-by towns or cities.

LIVING CONDITIONS AT NEW RIVER

Most of the reservation is wooded, and every effort is being made to preserve as many trees as practicable so as to retain the natural beauty of the place. The officers' quarters will be located on Paradise Point, and 133 sets are contemplated. These will be completely furnished, except for mattresses, linen, dishes, and kitchen utensils. An Officers' Club, and a B.O.Q. with a capacity for quartering 350 officers, are in the blueprint stage. Construction began at this base in April, 1941. It is hoped that the barracks and main part of the base will be completed during the spring of 1942.

The post is definitely in the making, but the following yarn shows the fortitude and adeptness of the individuals of "the leatherneck corps":

By way of an official communication it was reported that a recruiting officer in the field, one chilly day last week, came across a recruiting sergeant who took his duties seriously. The recruiting officer, feeling the chilly weather, noticed that the sergeant was not wearing his blouse. Upon inquiring he was informed that the sergeant, in line with recruiting duty, had loaned his blouse to a local merchant for a window display. "I'm glad that he (the sergeant) had an extra pair of trousers," the officer wrote, "otherwise I would have probably found him home in bed."[2]

Recreational Facilities

A private car is a necessity at New River. In addition to being your chief means of transportation, it will be a great source of pleasure since there are many interesting places within easy motoring distance.

Bird and squirrel hunting are allowed on the reservation (with shotguns only). No deer or bear hunting is permitted. Service personnel enjoy resident hunting and fishing privileges, the license costing only $3.10 annually.

THE MARINE CORPS FUTURE

There is a popular belief among many Americans that when the Army and the Navy finally gaze on heavenly scenes they will find the streets are guarded by United States Marines! The following verse of the Marine Hymn signifies this prophecy:

> Here's health to you and to our corps
> Which we are proud to serve;
> In many a strife we've fought for life
> And never lost our nerve.
> If the Army and the Navy
> Ever gaze on Heaven's scenes
> They will find the streets are guarded
> By United States Marines.

[2] *Army and Navy Journal*, October 11, 1941.

Chapter V

THE COAST GUARD

When the old storm signal's flyin'
Every vessel seeks a lee,
'Cept the Cutter, which ups Anchor
And goes plowing out to sea.
When "the hurricane's a-blowing"
From the banks to old Cape Cod
Oh, the Cutter with her searchlight
Seems the messenger of God.

(From Evor S. Kerr, *United States Coast Guard.*
Robert W. Kelly, New York, 1935.)

THE United States Coast Guard is one of the oldest of the government's services. When President George Washington appointed Alexander Hamilton as first Secretary of the Treasury, there was little money in the government's coffers because a lot of citizens evaded customs and in devious ways managed to avoid paying taxes and duty on imported goods. This wholesale smuggling was robbing the Treasury, and it was Alexander Hamilton's duty to solve the problem. He took his headache to Congress, and immediately that worthy body of lawmakers appropriated money for ten cutters, which were to be used to suppress smuggling and piracy. They were small craft, but they patrolled the Atlantic seaboard from New Hampshire to Georgia and managed to "put a crimp into the smuggling business."

Today, the duties of the Coast Guard are divided into two main classifications: law enforcement and humanitarian supervision and assistance. In time of war the Coast Guard, like the Marine Corps, comes under the jurisdiction of the Navy. "As a matter of fact," Lieutenant Roy S. Horn, U.S.N., has said, "the Coast Guard doesn't have to wait for war to have a

63

battle on its hands. It is fighting all the time, with Nature if not with Man."[1]

It was created and exists for the sole purpose of protecting the public—saving their lives and protecting their properties. There are various other duties assigned to the Coast Guard including the enforcement of navigation laws, neutrality patrol, safe anchorage of craft, oil pollution, sea patrol, halibut patrol, whaling patrol, and a watch over sponge fisheries off the Gulf Straits of Florida. Just try running your yacht or speedboat without proper running lights, or anchor a cargo of gasoline or dynamite in the wrong spot in New York harbor— you will have to explain and answer to the Coast Guard. Shoot a fur seal in the water anywhere and the Coast Guard will arrest you—they are the "legal keepers of the royal seal."

The ultimate aim of the United States Coast Guard, whether in the frozen wastelands of Alaska, the ice-strewn waters of the North Atlantic, the flooded areas of Mississippi, the hurricane-swept shores of Florida, or the patrol of "an international regatta," is "To serve."

In time of peace this branch operates under the Treasury Department and is an independent service headed by a Commandant with the rank of Rear Admiral. All ranks, rates, pay, general routine, and regulations are patterned after the Regular Navy with certain necessary deviations.

Headquarters are located in Washington, D.C. Similar to the Navy's organization, the United States is divided into sixteen districts, most of which dovetail nicely with the operations of naval districts in the same area. Today, the Coast Guard is an integral part of the Navy.

The Life Saving Service grew up in the early days of sailing vessels when bad storms wrecked ships. In England, just a few years prior to the organization of the Revenue Cutter Service, the Royal Humane Society had been organized for the purpose of saving lives at sea, and it is reported to have been the first organization of its kind in Europe.

[1] "Semper Paratus," *National Magazine*, August, 1941.

The Coast Guard

China is known to have created, many centuries ago, an organization to rescue those in distress on the water. In the old romantic
days of sailing ships, there were no radios and of course, many of
the vessels were less seaworthy than our large liners of today;
however, marine disasters still occur. The tragedy of the Morro
Castle burning, and the ramming of the Mohawk are recent
enough in all of our memories to recall the wonderful work performed by the Surfmen in bringing the injured and drowning
victims ashore.[2]

THE COAST GUARD ACADEMY

There is something very glamorous about the Coast Guard.
The stories of heroic rescues performed on the sea by seamen,
surfmen, and airmen appeal to young Americans. Appointment to the Coast Guard Academy is entirely by competitive
examination, and only the best men win. An average of 2000
candidates take the examinations and about 250 pass; of these,
125 to 150 are appointed and about 50 are commissioned. You
can't get rich in the Service, as the pay is the same as the
Army and Navy, yet there are enough applications on file to
fill the Coast Guard for the next ten years. So, it must be the
glamour and the desire to serve that appeals to youngsters.

Formerly, officers in the Coast Guard were obtained from
the Merchant Marine and detailed from the Navy. This
proved unsatisfactory, for the maritime officers did not get
along with the Navy personnel. In 1876 a law was passed
for cadet training, and the bark *Chase* was built as a floating
academy. It must have been fun for the twelve students, at
that time, to cruise around the Atlantic while studying, then
as a diversion and to get their land legs to attend a few shore
classes in Baltimore. In 1912 the cadet corps moved to Fort
Trumbull, New London, but the Coast Guard Academy of
today is practically a new plant made necessary by the additional duties assumed by the Coast Guard and the greater part
played as the maritime law-enforcement force of the nation.

Located on the banks of the Thames River, it has its cadet

[2] Hickman Powell, *What the Citizen Should Know About the Coast
Guard.* W. W. Norton & Company, Inc., New York, 1941.

barracks, armory, gymnasium, laboratories, engineering hops. The Academy's seven main buildings were opened as a unit in 1932. They are built on a beautiful slope of countryside overlooking the Thames at New London, Connecticut. In front of the administration building stands a flagstaff that was once the mast of the fine old revenue cutter *Hamilton*.

THE CADET AT WORK

The four-year course is a stiff one, and the cadets are under the military control of instructors twenty-four hours a day for eleven months a year. They study French, English, chemistry, physics, radio, electrical engineering, mathematics through calculus, naval construction, navigation, ordnance and ballistics, seamanship, and surveying. A well-rounded course in physical training and athletics completes the program.

When a new cadet joins the corps he is called a Swab, which corresponds to the lowly title of Plebe used at Annapolis and West Point. Upperclassmen instruct the raw recruits, and in a few weeks they become proficient in the elementary drills. At all times a cadet leads a military life. Discipline is strict.

Life for the Coast Guard cadet is not all work by any means. For the present, gone are the interesting and enjoyable sea-terms known as the three-months' practice cruise visiting such foreign ports as Gibraltar, Alexandria, Athens, Stamboul, Marseilles, and the Canary Islands, or such southern ports as St. Thomas, Rio de Janeiro, Buenos Aires, Bahia, and Trinidad.

New London and Connecticut College with their respective quotas of attractive girls add to the social life of the cadets. Throughout the year there are formal and informal dances which culminate in the famous Ring Dance, similar to the one held at Annapolis.

The summer months are filled with informal parties over the week ends. Sailing parties, beach parties, clambakes, and picnics are popular forms of entertainment, and many pleasant Saturday afternoons are spent at Rocky Neck Park and Devil's Hop Yard. In winter, skating, hockey on the College

Pond, and terrific snowball wars are enjoyed. Occasionally, some ambitious group hires a big sleigh, and what fun to go riding along the frozen country roads.

After four years of study, grind, and hard work, graduation finally arrives. Graduation week is indeed a gala time with the baccalaureate and commencement ceremonies, the presence of the Secretary of the Treasury, the Commandant, and other notables. On the stage are assembled high-ranking Coast Guard officers and visiting dignitaries, while in the audience are proud families and friends. Awards of prizes to members of the graduating class are made, and following the graduation address diplomas and commissions are presented. The ceremony is completed as all join in singing "Alma Mater," dearest of all Academy songs. The cadet is now an Ensign in the United States Coast Guard and is glad to exchange the narrow stripe of the cadet for the stripe of the commissioned officer.

All of this ceremony, like every other Navy ceremony, has today taken on a crisp conciseness, for the grim business of war dictates that there be no dallying about the business in hand. A graduate is immediately, by virtue of his training and of the pressing need, an officer on serious errands bent.

Normal Duties of the Coast Guard

Several years ago the public became acquainted with the Coast Guard through press accounts concerning liquor patrol activities. The famous *I'm Alone* case, in which a vessel of British registry was sunk by a Coast Guard cutter in the Gulf of Mexico, and other captures in the prevention of smuggling gave the false impression that the Coast Guard existed solely for the purpose of enforcing the Eighteenth Amendment before that law was repealed.

Prohibition had a great effect on the development of the Service. Congress cut down appropriations for the Navy at this time, but lavished funds on expansion of coastal patrol for war against the rumrunners. For ten years a force of 24 destroyers and 300 vessels were operated for this purpose as well as for carrying on the humanitarian assignments. It was an uncongenial, unpopular, and difficult job, requiring all the ingenuity and initiative that only a military force could display, but out of it grew a very fine Intelligence Service. The men learned to decipher code messages, track down outlaw radio stations, and trace liquor shipments before their arrival. In other words, they outsmarted the smuggler.

SMUGGLING

Smugglers' boats are usually spotted by Coast Guard stations or by patrol boats whose duty it is to scout for them and radio information of their movements. In the old days suppression of piracy, enforcement of neutrality and the stopping of slave traffic were some of the duties; but today prevention of the smuggling of narcotics and Mexican gold, enforcement of neutrality laws, and patrolling the borders take up the time of the Coast Guard in addition to their other duties. They are on the alert for smugglers of dope. There is a continual campaign going on to prevent narcotics from passing our borders. The Coast Guard knows most of the tricks of smuggling. "One very neat device for smuggling dope is to drop the buoyed package overboard at a prearranged spot, to be picked up later by a motor boat. Since the Coast Guard is on the alert for this, the smugglers very cleverly resort to putting a small light can of dope in a heavy sack of salt, so that it sinks at first and does not rise to the surface until the salt is dissolved."[3]

ICE PATROL

The International Ice Patrol is another work of the Coast Guard. This service was established after the sinking of the *Titanic* in 1912 as the result of striking an iceberg. It is estimated that several hundred icebergs go into the North Atlantic off the Grand Banks of Newfoundland each year. In some years the number may total a thousand. The Coast Guard

[3] Hickman Powell, *What the Citizen Should Know About the Coast Guard.*

keeps track of the big bergs, warns great ocean liners so that they may stay clear and use the recommended ocean lanes.

As the cutter today enters Alaskan waters in late spring, on Bering Sea Patrol, it may be greeted by all kinds of signals. Here a stranded hunter on shore signals that he wants to be taken on board and returned to civilization. There a couple have hoisted a man's coat and a woman's dress on a high pole, signifying that they wish to be married by a Coast Guard officer. At another point on the coast a man who has committed a crime is taken on the ship to be tried in the ship's court, or kept in the brig until he can be tried in regular courts on land. Sometimes an injured person is brought on board to be given medical attention in the ship's sick bay. Still farther along at a native village a tooth is to be pulled or a funeral service read. All along the way mail is left and picked up, supplies are delivered. The Coast Guard is a popular branch of the Service in Alaska, and has done much for the people and their development.

WEATHER PATROL

This service is one of the most vital importance. Were it not for the detailed weather reports sent out by the Coast Guard, transoceanic aviation would never have made the degree of advancement that it has today. "Weather is, above all other things, the great uncontrollable hazard of aviation." When Lindbergh and Byrd were preparing for their transoceanic flights, they hung eagerly on the words of Weather Forecaster Kimball of New York, and commercial air navigation today is very dependent upon the weather reports of the Coast Guard. These reports are also of great interest to mariners. Along the coasts the Weather Patrol collects and broadcasts hurricane and storm warnings. Inland they issue storm and flood signals, thereby saving many lives and often property.

On the Atlantic Patrol, two cutters equipped as floating weather bureaus are continuously stationed between Bermuda and the Azores to assist the weather bureau in preparing fore-

casts for ocean commerce and especially for transatlantic
planes.

An account by the skipper of the cutter *Pontchartrain*
gives a rather good idea of what it is like to be at sea twenty-
six days, during twenty-two of which the wind blew a gale,
sometimes ninety miles an hour. If you have ever experienced
a bad storm at sea or had an extremely rough crossing you may
have some idea of what it would be like to be on a small cutter such as the *Pontchartrain*, 250 feet long and 2000 tons.
And she wasn't going anywhere; her job was to stay in one
spot, to record the weather. Her station was near the Gulf
Stream, where warm and cold water close together meant continual disturbance, cumulus clouds piling up and breaking
loose in nasty squalls. The Captain says, "it was nothing unusual to roll at any angle of 40 degrees or more, and as for
pitching, . . ." well, he doesn't say, but the cutter actually
took dives into the rough seas. "A man could hardly stand up
on the cabin floors, except with a footing of the new fangled
sponge rubber carpets. The most difficult task was trying to
eat, with chairs lashed to the heaving table, although a good
many of the 150 men on board did not bother trying."[4]

He further remarks that

During the first summer that the weather patrol was new, men
embarked on it in anticipation of adventure. They took fishing
tackle along, and some brought expensive books on strange deni-
zens of the sea. But when they dropped their hooks they never got
a bite, and reading was too uncertain a pleasure to be enjoyed.
After the second week of pitching and tossing about, the whole
adventure got to be quite a bore. Weeks passed with never a ship
in sight, never a sail on the horizon, nothing except an occasional
floating bunch of sargasso weed.[4]

NEUTRALITY PATROL

Coast Guard officers were designated under the Espionage
Act as captains of the port in all leading United States har-

[4] Hickman Powell, *What the Citizen Should Know About the Coast
Guard.*

bors, so as to assure safety of shipping and movements of vessels. Most important in port supervision was control of the movement and loading of explosives, as increasing amounts of war munitions were shipped from this country. The greatest danger in this job is sabotage. Another not too pleasant duty in regard to this detail is the sealing of radios of belligerent ships when in port, checking armaments, and checking on shipyard work being done on belligerent vessels in our ports.

Neutrality patrol today consists of keeping an intensive surveillance over all shipping and watching for enemy vessels on the high seas.

AIR PATROL

Many exciting rescues are made by the Coast Guard Service in the flying lifeboats. These are large seagoing planes adapted for general coastal service on water or land and especially suited for rescue work. They are the guardian angels for the small craft operating along the coast, and many a yachtsman owes his life to the aircraft of the Service.

This class of super-seaplanes is named for bright stars beloved of the navigator, such as *Arcturus, Antares,* and *Altair.* In case of desperate illness or injury at sea a doctor may board the plane and give treatment to the stricken person, and in a short time the victim may be resting in a city hospital.

Stationed at El Paso, Texas, is a permanent Air Patrol Detachment, with jurisdiction to enforce all federal laws relating to customs and revenue. It brings aid to the sick, transports patients, carries serums if an epidemic is spreading, and searches for lost planes. Each plane carries food, a stretcher, blankets, and medical supplies ranging from first-aid kits to rattlesnake and tarantula bite antitoxins. It is really a hospital on wings.

Most spectacular of all the activities of Coast Guard aviators is their practice of taking emergency medical cases from vessels at sea and rushing them to hospitals. Landing or taking off a big plane from a smooth harbor or concrete runway is one thing, but handling a big ship in a heavy sea with waves running eight or ten feet high is something else. The Coast Guard practices take-offs and landings in the open sea. They make rough-water landings at night by the light of flares. Their work is endless and they take it in their stride. It is all in the day's or night's work to them. They have earned a reputation as a fine government military force without fanfare of publicity and headlines.

Beach Rescues

Now we come to an important and primary function of the Coast Guard Service, that of promoting safety at sea. Today its activities spread over 40,000 miles of coastline and rivers. "Rescue" is the word most closely associated with the Coast Guard. The war to save lives is never at an end for these valiant men.

The surfman is usually an entirely different type of man from the sailor. He is practically an acrobat when handling his small boat in the high waves. Everything is said to depend upon timing, speed, and balance. To be a master Waikiki surf-board rider is play compared to the trick of bringing a lifeboat thundering in on a big roller. Timing the big waves that usually come in groups of three, and being ready to rush his boat into the "slatch," a stretch of slack water, requires practice and expert handling of small boats, and when the United States Navy goes on maneuvers in the Caribbean it takes along a hundred Coast Guard surfmen to handle small boats for landing parties.

One of the first requirements of a surfman is that he must be a strong swimmer. He must also be able to dive straight down to a target seven feet under water and bring up a ten-pound object. In addition, he learns to shoot straight, is an adept at first aid and in resuscitation of the apparently drowned.

George Frieth is considered one of the greatest life guards

who ever lived. He was part Hawaiian and part German, and the ocean was like his home. He worked on a difficult part of San Diego beach and saved dozens of lives on the mile stretch which was his post. One day eighty-five soldiers from a near-by training camp got caught in the rip tide and were swept seaward. They were crying for help, when after a mile run Frieth was among them. Not pausing for rest, he brought in three or four men at a time from the grip of the mad current, rescuing forty-six of the 85 soldiers, a truly superhuman feat.

Thousands of lives are saved every year by coast guardsmen at the many stations that outline the lakes and seashores. In 1927, when the levees on the Mississippi gave way, it was the Coast Guard that answered the distress signal. Again in 1938, when the Ohio River got out of control, the surfboats cruised over flooded cornfields and rescued distressed families from rooftops, helped evacuate refugees, and assisted the Red Cross in caring for the injured and homeless.

Discipline comes first in the training for rescue work. There is a heroic story told of a guard who in answering a call for help found that among the five drowning bathers in the rip tide was his own wife. Naturally his impulse was to carry her to safety and let the rest go, but his powerful sense of duty and responsibility gave him the strength to support all five until help arrived. His wife was one of the three victims who needed resuscitation when shore was reached. There was only one resuscitator at the station, and this was used on an aged woman, while the guard applied artificial respiration on the limp form of his wife. He said afterwards that only his experience of many years prevented him from collapsing. He was, however, unable to keep the proper cadence necessary for successful artificial respiration. He turned the job over to someone else and sat holding his wife's hand in dumb misery. Later on a groan from the loved one, the usual preliminary of return to consciousness, reassured him that perseverance to his duty had not been in vain. The creed of all coast guardsmen is: WE MUST SAVE LIFE.

The Cutter Service

The Coast Guard's greatest military value to the Navy is that it relieves the latter of a great deal of detail, in shore and patrol work, and thus leaves the fighting force free to concentrate on matters of combat. In comparison with the Battle Fleet, the Coast Guard is no great sea power, yet its speedy armed cutters can be used to advantage against submarines.

What is a cutter? Well, it is something between a naval vessel, a seagoing tug, and a private yacht. It is a small craft but sturdy, and there are various classes. The largest ships are named for former Secretaries of the Treasury as before mentioned, such as the *Hamilton*, *Bibb*, *Duane*, *Ingham*, *Spencer*, and *Taney*. Another group is named for cities and lakes, including the famous *Tampa*. Others carry names from Greek mythology. Then there are the Picketboats, built to combine strength and durability with lightness. The tenders, though, take the prize for names. These heavy vessels are built for drudgery, and they are tough craft, yet ironically they bear the names of flowers and flowering trees. Someone with a peculiar sense of humor must have christened the *Violet*, the *Arbutus*, the *Jasmine*, *Lilac*, and *Orchid*.

Coast Guard ships are ever on the lookout for trouble. When the signal of distress comes over the radio, the "cutter thrills to the call of the supreme test." SOS—SOS comes the message, then the disabled ship's name and position. Hurry! Hurry! Hurry! Full speed ahead! The cutter is off, beating her way through the blackness of the night and the swirling waters. At last she arrives and finds the distressed vessel in a bad way. Her bridge is gone, shot away by the submarine that gave the mortal blow, she has listed to starboard, her boats have been carried away in the heavy sea. One by one the half-frozen crew is rescued and revived on board the cutter. The seas are breaking everywhere around the disabled ship. Someone has said, "the death of a ship is a sight to stir the soul," but the work of the Coast Guard is not done. Its men must not only watch this valiant craft in her death struggle but salvage or sink her so that she may not become a menace to navigation. Of all the dangers at sea the derelict is one of the most dreaded. Sometimes it drifts along entirely submerged and is difficult to see in daytime; at night, it is even more dangerous.

A boat is lowered from the cutter with a deadly charge of TNT as cargo, and the boat's crew row to the derelict and board her. When all is in readiness, the crew returns to the cutter and the timed explosive heaves the derelict high into the air, a mass of splinters, fragments and shreds of wood, rope, and steel amid ocean spray. A once gallant ship has gone to the bottom.

WIVES OF COAST GUARD OFFICERS

Coast Guard personnel unless on duty at the Academy live more or less the life of the average civilian. The Coast Guard officer's wife makes her friends among the civilian community in which she lives. Also, if stationed near an Army post or a Naval station, she has a social life with both Services. With a leaning toward the Navy, she observes the laws of the Navy, and no one is more cognizant of the slogan "Silence today may mean safety tomorrow."

As explained before, the officers of the Coast Guard have the same rank and title as those of the Navy, with one exception!—that of Commodore, an honorary title given to those of over forty years' service. It corresponds to the grade of Rear Admiral. Familiar to most old-timers is the story of the Lady Commodore (reprinted by permission of the U.S.C.G. Academy *Alumni Association Bulletin*, June, 1941). Since the tale has a good moral, recounting it will not be amiss, especially at this time.

Back in the days when the title of Commodore indicated the next senior active rank above a Captain, a certain mild-mannered Commanding Officer left his vessel one afternoon, for a brief visit ashore. Reliable motorboat transportation was then unknown, so he had to cross by oar-propelled gig. Arriving at the landing, the Captain instructed the Swedish-born coxswain to hold the gig there until his return. Shortly, the wife of a junior officer arrived at the float and jumping into the gig, requested to be rowed to the ship. In halting jargon the embarrassed Swede tried to explain, but the impatient lady thrust him aside, took the tiller herself, and gave the commands for getting under way. Returning to the landing the Captain found his gig out of hailing distance on its way to the ship, and being admirably handled by a skirted figure in the sternsheets. At a conference of all officers the next morning the Captain spoke as follows: "Gentlemen, a lady is perhaps the fairest flower in her garden, in her proper garden. As you know, gardens are impracticable aboard ship. A search of the Regulations reveals no authority for any, nor any authority for the appointment of Lady Commodores. I trust you will be guided by these remarks."

Bear in mind that this story is not meant especially for Coast Guard wives, but for all Service wives, because Lady Commodores have flourished since the days when captains took their wives to sea. They still flourish today, but their ranks are few. Women folk should give strength, aid, and comfort to their husbands, not be Lady Commodores who lessen the efficiency of officers by family squabbles, financial worries, rumors, and taking over the helm.

You seldom hear of heroes in the Coast Guard. Not that there aren't plenty—the Service is full of them—but service is everyday bread-and-butter stuff in this life-saving business. Nor do you see the wives of Coast Guard officers wearing any special medals, but theirs is also a life dedicated to service, with waiting and long hours of anxiety at times. The motto of the Coast Guard, *Semper paratus*, meaning "Always ready," is one that we should all adopt.

The magnificent work of the Coast Guard is well known, and constantly brings forth the admiration of the American people. Theirs is a double duty of defending our shores in time of war and of serving humanity in time of peace. Lieutenant Victor Blakeslee, U.S.N., says that "in time of emergency the Navy knows that its sister service can be called upon for all manner of sacrifice and can carry out any mission, however dangerous."

Chapter VI

ENGAGEMENTS AND WEDDINGS

> Sweethearts and wives! Fill up the glass
> with crystal clink and clatter
> And drink the liquid jewels down ——
> May the former become the latter.
> When raging winds and waves unite
> to form a mighty chorus,
> We know that loving hearts at home
> are nightly praying for us.

NANCY LEE, you and Bill are two of those fortunate young people who had a prewar wedding; so we have decided to leave the chapter unchanged . . . even to the honeymoon at the Royal Hawaiian Hotel in Honolulu! War never seems to stop weddings; in fact, it appears to promote or encourage them.

In Manila during the battle of Cavite in the thickest of the firing a prominent wedding was in progress, and the ceremony continued despite falling bombs and flying shrapnel. Nothing can stop Dan Cupid, once boy meets girl and a wedding is in the offing!

It was a custom in the old Navy previous to prohibition days, when ships were at sea, to drink a toast at dinner on Saturday night to sweethearts and wives. This toast dates back to Lord Nelson's day, and the second stanza continues:

> Sweethearts and wives, those precious names
> That make our hearts grow warmer
> Through every storm on sea or shore ——
> May the latter remain the former.
> When lightnings flash and billows roll
> And straining hawsers sever,
> Our thoughts upon the reeling deck
> Are with them both forever.

Engagements made at the Naval Academy are necessarily of long duration because of the present Navy regulations with regard to marriage. Naval Academy graduates must defer marriage for two years after graduation. On first thought this may seem unfair, but in time of peace there are two very good reasons for it. The first is professional; the second, economic.

Upon graduation from the Naval Academy, an Ensign is assigned to two years of duty at sea with the Fleet. After all, the government educated Bill to be a naval officer. Financially, his small pay is sufficient for his own needs as most of his time is spent at sea; but no amount of stretching the budget can make it adequate for two. The answer for every Ensign is to forget about marriage until he has served his apprenticeship of two years.

A good idea of the general situation can be gained from the yarn told in Commander Hockey's fascinating book, *The Navy's Best Stories.*

A young Ensign one time asked the Admiral for the hand of his daughter in marriage. The Admiral asked him, in no uncertain terms, how in the hell he ever expected to support a wife on an Ensign's pay. The young officer thought awhile and then said, "Well, Admiral, you married when you were an Ensign." Quickly, and in tones most terrifying, the Admiral replied, "I lived on my father-in-law, but I'll be damned if you do so."

The O.A.O. who is willing to wait is the girl worth having. Waiting is a real test of character and love, and it is far better to find out if one or the other is fickle before marriage than afterwards. Of course this does not mean that either the Ensign or his bride-to-be should make foolish promises and refrain from enjoying the society of others. The Navy Department may be hand in hand with Cupid in delaying marriage for its officers. Deferred marriage has much in its favor, although at times it may seem cruel.

It is still customary in the best circles, and particularly in the Service, for an officer to call on the girl's father or mother or whoever is head of the family and ask for the girl's hand in marriage. Generally speaking, it is no surprise to the girl's family, if the young Naval officer has been particularly attentive over a period of two years.[1]

If the parents of the girl approve the engagement, the young officer should acquaint his parents with his intentions if he has not already done so. He breaks the news of his happiness to his parents by a personal visit, a letter, or a wire, choosing the method best suited to his purse, and considering the distance involved. One enthusiastic young Ensign wrote ecstatically to his mother and father: "Dear Parents: Hang on to your hats! I'm going to be married." Then he told them all about Sally and her family. He was even thoughtful enough to send along a good picture of his "dream girl." The letter glowed with happiness, and his mother and father each wrote to Sally a cordial letter welcoming her into the family. They also wrote graciously to Sally's mother and father, since it was impossible for them to call personally. The family of the young man must always welcome the bride-to-be. It is customary for them either to call upon or to write to the future daughter-in-law.

If the young officer is an orphan, his nearest relative should welcome his fiancée into the family. A definite understanding should be reached before a formal engagement is announced.

THE ENGAGEMENT RING

The Annapolis graduate usually gives a miniature of his class ring for an engagement ring. Generally it contains a diamond, although any precious stone is perfectly proper. In the early days of the Academy the engagement ring was not worn in public until the engagement was announced. Today the miniature ring is worn all during the years of a "secret" engagement.

If the young officer is especially affluent, he may choose

---

[1] In time of emergency or war, the two-year regulation is subject to change by the Navy Department. Aviation Reserve Ensigns must wait two years after being commissioned.

to give a solitaire as an engagement ring, in which case the miniature may be worn as a little-finger ring.

There is no set rule about engagement rings, but all Army and Navy wives are proud to wear a miniature of their husbands' class ring. Often it stands them in good stead as an unofficial passport, especially if their full name is engraved inside!

THE ANNOUNCEMENT

The announcement is always made by the parents of the bride-elect. Several days before the announcement of the engagement is released to the press, the bride's mother either telephones the various daily papers or sends a written, signed notice to the society editors. The latter method is the approved one, as many papers require a signed statement in order to avoid future trouble in the way of law suits that may be brought by jilted brides or discarded grooms. If the families concerned are prominent, the society editor will usually ask the bride to have her photograph made by the paper's photographer. Often the bride-elect may have a favorite photograph on hand, and it is quite correct for her to offer this one to the paper. Of course she will never think of proffering the photograph unless one is requested.

A signed copy of the engagement notice should be sent to the Service periodicals, *The Register,* 511 Eleventh Street, N.W., Washington, D.C., and *The Army and Navy Journal,* 1701 Connecticut Avenue, N.W., Washington, D.C.

The following is the proper form:

Mr. Howard Calhoun Patterson and Mrs. Patterson (or Mr. and Mrs. Howard Calhoun Patterson) announce the engagement of their daughter, Nancy Lee, to William Satterlee Tyler, Ensign, United States Navy, son of Mr. and Mrs. James Lewis Tyler of Baltimore, Maryland.

Miss Patterson attended Holton Arms in Washington and was a member of the 1941 graduating class from Wellesley.

Ensign Tyler is a graduate of the United States Naval Academy, class of 1939. The wedding will take place in the late fall.

Local papers may carry a much longer announcement; oc-

casionally, however, a brief three-line announcement may
seem quite sufficient. The engagement of a widow or divorcée
is always announced as quietly as possible. She either tells her
friends or writes a brief note to them; but the announcement
of the marriage itself should appear in the papers and Service
journals.

Should an engagement be broken, regardless of the circumstances it is always broken by the girl—at least as far as the
public is concerned! In these uncertain times it is often best
not to announce the exact time of the wedding, especially if
the event is planned for a distant date. The Navy Department
takes no account of the best-laid personal plans, and sometimes
complete arrangements have to be changed because of a change
of orders.

Your Trousseau!

If there is time between the announcement of your engagement and the day you go to the altar, Nancy Lee, there will
be parties given by your friends. These usually take the form
of luncheons and showers. Regardless of how insistent your
friends may be, by all means limit the showers to two and no
more. It is truly an imposition to have more, because the same
intimate friends are invited to each shower, and the quality of
friendship has to be pretty good to survive the strain. Then
a wedding present as a climax really runs into money, and
often into unkind words as well.

An appropriate shower for a Navy bride would be a linen
shower or a personal shower, should the hostess consult you.
By all means, tactfully veto a miscellaneous shower, crystal
shower, or a kitchen shower. Whether you realize it or not,
my darling, you are entering a life of eternal gypsying. There
will be times when you will need to set up for real housekeeping, but the dime store will be the solution to your problems
because you will either sell or give the utensils away when
orders come. Now is the time to become accustomed to
traveling light. Learn to keep yourself mobile. Don't start out
by burdening yourself and your handsome Ensign with valu-

able though useless gimcracks. A set of Spode china is a glory to look at, a delight to eat from—and an invention of Satan to pack.

Showers usually take the form of a tea, after which the gifts are presented in some novel fashion. In smart circles showers are not as popular today as formerly; however, it is a matter of personal taste.

Personal Trousseau

You can have as elaborate a wedding as you choose. After all, this day of all days comes only once in your life, and all brides "naturally should be pampered." However, regardless of your income, limit your personal trousseau to the present necessities!

The happiest solution of the matter is to consult a Bridal Secretary or the Bridal Service of one of the large stores in your nearest city. These consultants have a list of trousseau needs, and nothing pleases them more than to work out a knotty problem such as the needs of a Navy bride who plans to lead the life of a glorified gypsy. Explain your position honestly, tell exactly what part of your budget you wish to allot to the wedding, then the amount for your trousseau and all that goes with it. This service is free, believe it or not; but if you are skeptical and still wish to plan your own trousseau, here are a few suggestions:

The safest rule to follow is perhaps to have a nucleus of substantial clothes, using what you have on hand in the way of the more expensive items such as a fur coat and good tailored tweeds. Today a bride usually limits her trousseau to clothes for a single season. If her income is very restricted, she may have just a few frocks besides her bridal gown and a few sets of lingerie and linens.

An Adequate Trousseau

1 classic suit, or a 3-piece suit with various types of blouses and
   sweaters

2 evening dresses (with boleros or jackets—suitable for dinner)
1 dinner skirt with 2 evening blouses and an evening sweater
    blouse
2 active-sports dresses
1 restaurant dress, short and suitable for a P.M. dress, cocktail
    party, or informal dinner
1 good daytime dress for luncheons
1 dressing gown
4 negligees (the prettiest, most glamorous one you can afford)
1 hostess gown or hostess pajamas
2 bed jackets
4 nightgowns
3 jersey slips
4 jersey panties
4 brassieres
6 pairs of stockings, various weights
2 pairs of day shoes
1 pair of evening shoes
1 pair of walking shoes or golf shoes
2 bathing suits
Beach clothes, shorts, slacks, sandals, etc.
1 raincoat, umbrella
3 play suits (washable, attractive ones to wear around the house
    while cooking)

If you have a rich father with a generous disposition, by
all means include a fur coat. If you're really smart, you'll take
also a fur-lined coat and bank the remainder of the check.
From the first, establish a clothes budget and be adamant
about spending it for anything except clothes. A good appearance is most important. Remember also that not many people
will see your clothes a second time, because you will always
be on the move.

In buying evening clothes, choose noncrushable materials
such as lace, jersey, or crepe chiffons. Often after driving all
day, say from Long Beach to San Francisco, you will arrive
just in time to dress for dinner. In addition to the fact that
hotel valet service is expensive, it will save time if your dinner
dress needs no pressing.

Many Navy wives include a miniature ironing board and iron in their luggage, and no traveling outfit is complete without its box of soap flakes and an adjustable clothesline. You will soon learn to be an expert laundress in a 4 x 6 bathroom, along with your other accomplishments.

It is far more fun to buy a dress when the occasion demands than to buy everything at once, so bank your trousseau check and forget you have it until a real wardrobe need presents itself. Don't worry, it will upon your next move! Somehow, the clothes you have on hand never seem to be quite the answer, and you will enjoy freshening up your wardrobe. Then, too, there will come the day when you get lonesome, blue, and homesick. Buying a frivolous new hat does wonders for the feminine morale on such an occasion. Try it and see for yourself!

HOUSEHOLD LINEN

Here again your trousseau linens will differ from those of your Army sister or your little cousin who married her home-town beau and settled down in a pretty vine-covered cottage where she expects to spend the rest of her life. At any rate, the happy way in the Navy is to travel light; yet you would not be a real bride were you not to have some household linens to bring to your new home.

Your little *trousse*, French for bundle, of which the word *trousseau* is the diminutive, must be extremely light. Here is a minimum list which may seem extremely sketchy to your mother and grandmother as they mentally take stock or recall their own well-filled linen closets when they were brides. However, I assure you the list offered will be adequate for the needs of the average young itinerant Navy couple.

Buy the best linens you can afford because good linens last indefinitely. You'll be disillusioned with a bargain sheet the first time it is laundered. Its starchy beauty that so attracted you in the store washes away with the sizing after its first trip to the laundry. When it returns from its third or fourth trip, you'll want to use it for mosquito netting.

The minimum list should include:

6 sheets, linen or good grade of percale, 72" x 108"
8 sheets, if equipping twin beds
8 bath towels, large absorbent ones, 22" x 44"
6 small turkish towels, easy to launder, 16" x 27"
6 small linen towels, guest size
8 pillowcases
2 bedspreads
2 Kenwood blankets
6 washcloths
2 chenille bath mats
3 attractive bridge sets, with napkins for informal luncheons and suppers
1 beautiful (the most elaborate you can afford) luncheon set—12 place doilies, napkins, and runner
6 dish towels
4 dishcloths
2 luncheon sets for everyday use

Be sure to provide yourself with a "packing trunk," one of the rugged old-fashioned variety in which to carry linen and silver. Later you will acquire camphor chests and lockers as you need them.

LUGGAGE

One of the MUSTS in your trousseau is attractive, durable luggage, preferably of the airplane variety. Some of your moves may be by airways, and even if you are landbound, airplane luggage is the lightest and most sturdy being built today.

A good, strong wardrobe trunk of a standard make is the first necessity. A combination shoe and hat trunk, the large size for large hats, is a good buy. These usually come with a tray to be used for lingerie or accessories. A wardrobe suitcase and an overnight bag or train-box for make-up completes the ensemble.

NAVAL WEDDINGS

Naval weddings differ but slightly from the usual formal wedding, except that they are probably more elaborate. In fact, a naval wedding, with the officers in full-dress uniform with their dazzling epaulets and glittering gold lace, their gay cocked hats and shining swords, presents a striking background for the beautiful bridesmaids and the exquisite bride in her traditional white gown. For once the groom almost outshines the bride. It is the nearest approach to the glamorous court life of bygone days that remains today.

However, under present conditions, a formal naval wedding is a bit hard to plan, unless an officer is on shore duty, and even then, he may suddenly be ordered to sea. During war periods naval weddings are often quite impromptu affairs. It is remarkable how lovely some of these informal weddings really are. Certainly they have that quality so dear to a Navy wife: adaptability. Large, formal weddings often have to be postponed indefinitely owing to ships' movements, sudden orders, or cancellation of leave; and the complications may be so great and involve so many people that the bride will finally arrive at the altar a haggard wreck of her former self.

Since it is almost impossible at present to set a definite date, many brides consider it wiser to send out announcements rather than invitations. Of course an invitation is a nicer compliment than an announcement, and the words are self-explanatory, but *that's the Navy.* Invitations should be sent out three weeks in advance of the wedding—but, oh! what a chance the Navy bride of today is taking! Very likely about three days before the wedding her parents will have to put an announcement in the social columns to the effect that the wedding has been indefinitely postponed. Those in Navy circles will understand, but your other friends may not.

At any rate it is nerve-racking to wonder if the groom and the ushers will be able to be on hand for the wedding, and a worry that the bride should not have during the happiest days of her life. So perhaps it is best to bow to the inevitable and settle upon announcements rather than the more formal and correct invitations.

The bride and her mother should consult a good stationer and place the order with him. Printed invitations or announcements are in very poor taste. Be firm about having them engraved, and avoid any fads in styles of engraving, quality, and shape of stationery.

The wedding invitation should read:

Mr. and Mrs. Howard Calhoun Patterson
request the honor of your presence
at the marriage of their daughter
Nancy Lee
to
William Satterlee Tyler
Ensign, United States Navy
on Saturday evening, the tenth of June
at eight o'clock
St. Michael's Cathedral
Charleston, South Carolina

The invitation to the breakfast or reception is enclosed in the wedding invitation and reads as follows:

Reception
Immediately following Ceremony
South Battery

R.S.V.P.

The announcement of a wedding should read:

Mr. and Mrs. Howard Calhoun Patterson
have the honor of announcing
the marriage of their daughter
Nancy Lee
to
William Satterlee Tyler
Ensign, United States Navy
Saturday, the tenth of June
One thousand nine hundred and forty-two
Charleston, South Carolina

In Army and Navy circles the invitation should read:

Lieutenant General and Mrs. Adair McGinley
request the honor of your presence
at the marriage of their daughter
Phyllis Anne
to
Ralph Searles
Lieutenant Commander, United States Navy
on Wednesday evening, the fourth of May
at five o'clock
Post Chapel, Hickam Field
Honolulu

Reception
Immediately following Ceremony
Hickam Field Officers' Club
R.S.V.P.

Or an announcement:

Rear Admiral and Mrs. Dawson Hale
have the honor of announcing
the marriage of their daughter
Margaret Jean
to
Mason Davenport Haynes
Lieutenant, United States Army
Saturday, the tenth of June
One thousand nine hundred and forty-two
Coronado, California

On formal invitations, announcements, or calling cards the full name and title should appear. Abbreviations are not correct.

Calling Cards

In the rush of wedding plans you may forget about calling cards, so a good time to order them is when you decide upon your invitations or announcements. You will need them in returning calls as soon as leave is over and you are settled down to life in the Navy. Officers always have their own personal cards. Ask Bill to send you one of his so that when you order yours the engraving will match. Your personal visiting cards should read simply: Mrs. William Satterlee Tyler. Avoid using abbreviations or initials, such as Mrs. William S. Tyler or Mrs. W. Satterlee Tyler. Neither form is in the best taste. The entire name, regardless of its length, should appear.

Joint calling cards are growing in popularity, although formerly they were used only when sending gifts or in sending flowers for funerals. While officers of junior rank in the Navy are always introduced as Mister, up to the grade of Commander, nevertheless it is quite correct to use the following form on your joint calling cards: Ensign and Mrs. William Satterlee Tyler, or Lieutenant and Mrs. William Satterlee Tyler.

THE FORMAL NAVAL WEDDING

Assuming that it is a time of peace, or that your fiancé is on shore duty and it is possible for you to have an elaborate church wedding, let us follow a formal wedding through its various stages. This is given in detail only as a guide. A smaller or less formal wedding may be fashioned after it quite easily.

We will assume that the bride-elect is from a very wealthy, socially prominent, civilian family. The setting is a historic old cathedral, at which the bride's family has always worshiped. Perhaps a Bishop will officiate, or some other high prelate assisted by several clergymen. A vested choir with a renowned soloist will furnish the music, and the entire church will be elaborately decorated by a florist. The chancel will be a bower of flowers, and the pews for the families and distinguished guests will be designated by ribbons or sprays of flowers tied to pew ends.

This seems a good place to stress the importance of a rehearsal. By all means, have a rehearsal "if only to get an estimate of the situation." One thing about naval and military weddings is that the officers are usually more at ease than the feminine members of the wedding party; a wedding pageant is to them just another dress parade. The bride always directs the rehearsal but rarely takes part in it, as it is considered bad luck. Someone else is her proxy. The organist, who takes a very important part, should most certainly be present. After many repetitions, the entire party should master the art of walking to the wedding march. The head usher will set the tempo for the organist and the ushers will march in with military precision, but bridesmaids and especially the bride and her father must not give the impression of scurrying up the aisle or of lingering on "leaden or wobbly feet." The bridesmaids should understand the advantage of walking on a single line, placing the heel at each step on an imaginary mark running down the aisle. Once mastered, this will insure an easy flowing movement instead of the "walking on eggs" gait that so often mars a beautiful wedding.

All the officers will be in full-dress uniform, epaulets, cocked hat, and sword. If it is a summer wedding, they will wear white full dress. A recent order from the Navy Department announces the discontinuance of swords, but for those who have them or can borrow them "the arch of steel" continues.

The wedding day dawns! The marquee is up at the church, the ruby-red carpet is covered with the white aisle strip to protect the bride's train, and the old cathedral where the bride was christened twenty years before has become a thing of indescribable beauty. An experienced florist has transformed it into a perfect Eden, and everything awaits the bride and her wedding party.

After collecting their bouquets at the bride's home, the bridesmaids proceed to the church. There they assist the bride in any way possible, and await their entrance cue in a room off the vestibule.

The ushers arrive a half-hour before the ceremony begins. The officers, having deposited their capes in a room off the vestibule, don white gloves and assume their posts at the different aisles. One officer should take charge as head usher in order that he may be free to escort distinguished and elderly guests, as well as to co-ordinate the duties of the ushers.

An usher asks everyone whom he does not know whether he is a guest of the bride or of the groom (reminding one, somehow, of the old game of London Bridge). The bride's family and friends occupy the pews on the left side, and the groom's family and friends are seated at the right. Flag Officers, Commanding Officers, and Executive Officers, such as should be given seats of honor, should always be seated according to their rank. Other officers may be seated according to the friendship with the families. When an usher escorts a lady down the aisle he offers her his arm. If a gentleman has come with her he walks behind them. When a gentleman is alone, the usher walks beside him.

The parents of the bride always sit in the first pew to the left, facing the chancel. The parents of the groom always sit in the first pew on the right. The immediate families occupy the pews behind these. The honor guests and especially invited friends, who should have pew numbers, sit within the ribbons of the first twenty pews. If the groom's Commanding Officer and his wife are present, they should be seated as honor guests immediately behind the groom's parents.

It is a nice gesture to send cards denoting seating the day before the wedding to closest friends or most distinguished guests ("Second Pew, Left," etc.). These are presented to the groomsmen.

When all the guests have been seated, the head usher escorts the bride's mother to her seat. She is the last lady to be seated. Then the doors are closed and no one is seated during the ceremony. The ushers march in in pairs, carrying their hats fore and aft at an angle, and station themselves beside the first pews in the nave. The pairs divide, the ushers on the right turn right, and those on the left turn left. The bridesmaids do likewise. Where the bridesmaids and ushers stand during the ceremony depends upon the size and arrangement of the church. In a large church, it makes a pretty picture if the bridesmaids and ushers alternate and stand on the steps leading up into the chancel; or it is equally effective if they proceed to the chancel and await the bride.

After the ushers come the bridesmaids in pairs, followed by the maid or matron of honor. She stands on the left at the top of the steps opposite the best man. If there are flower girls, they precede the ring-bearer and separate at the chancel steps, standing in front of the groomsmen and bridesmaids.

The bride drives to the church with her father. They wait with the bridesmaids until it is time for them to join the procession.

The bride enters on her father's right arm, so that poor Dad doesn't have to stumble over a mess of train and veil to get to his seat. Authorities disagree on this point, and for the bride to enter on her father's left arm is equally correct, but at the rehearsal try out both entrances. Father will agree with the first plan, whether you do or not. But after all, it is up to you! It is your wedding.

The proper wedding marches are: Processional, Wedding March from *Lohengrin*, by Wagner; Recessional, Mendelssohn's Wedding March. Handel and César Franck have written some appropriate wedding music, so consult your organist in case you are dubious about "Oh, Promise Me."

On the first note of the Wedding March, the clergyman, followed by the groom and the best man, steps from the vestry into the chancel. The groom removes his right glove, holds it in his left hand, and stands at the head of the steps to await his bride. If there are several steps to the chancel, the groom goes down the steps to meet her, which seems more gallant. The guests like to see him smile as he watches his bride come up the aisle. Some bridegrooms look glum and scared.

When the bride and her father reach the steps of the chancel, the bride is met by the groom. She does not take his arm. When her father has given her away, he steps back into the left front pew and joins her mother.

At this point the bride and groom, maid of honor and best man, move forward to the altar. The bride hands her

bouquet to the maid of honor, and the best man passes the
wedding ring to the groom, who in turn hands it to the clergyman. During the ceremony the clergyman returns the ring
to the groom, who places it on the bride's finger at the words
"With this ring." In a double ring ceremony, the maid of
honor hands the groom's ring to the bride, who places it on
his finger as soon as she has received her ring.

The ceremony over, the handsome groom kisses his lovely
bride, the clergyman says a few congratulatory words wishing
them happiness, and the triumphant organ music begins. The
bride and groom turn, the bride receiving her bouquet from
the maid of honor, who also adjusts her train. Then the happy
couple leave the chancel, but at the head of the steps they
pause for a moment.

The ancient and traditional ceremony of the bride and groom
walking under the arched swords of the officer ushers is always
expected. At some weddings you will see this ceremony performed in the church, but never in a Roman Catholic church.
Would you like to know the reason for this? The practice of
drawing swords at the altar or in the chancel of the church is entirely wrong. Because of the old law of right of sanctuary and
refuge, as well as the very nature of a church, it is considered a
flagrant breach of military etiquette to draw a sword in church.
The "arch" should be made outside the church if possible, but if
inclement weather or street traffic should prevent this, then the
crossing of swords may take place in the vestibule near the door.
Civilian ushers line up with naval ushers. The senior usher should
give the order "Draw swords."[2]

Only the bride and groom may pass under the traditional
arch of steel; it is not proper for any other members of
the wedding party to have this honor.

The bride should appear sweet and serious but not in the
least self-conscious. While she does not, obviously, walk with
downcast eyes, she meets none of the many eyes focused upon
her except, for a fleeting moment, those of her mother.

[2] Leland P. Lovette, *Naval Customs, Traditions and Usage.* United
States Naval Institute, Annapolis, 1934.

94 THE NAVY WIFE

After the bride and groom have passed under the arch of swords, the best man escorts the maid of honor. The ushers return to escort the bridesmaids or they walk out in pairs. Unless they prefer to walk out with their husbands, it is a nice custom and adds a military touch if two ushers return to escort the bride's mother and the groom's mother to the door of the church before the ribbons are released. Even if there are no ribbons, the guests wait for the families to leave. There is ample time for this courtesy. The ushers form in two lines facing each other at the entrance of the church and stand at attention until the guests have filed out. At a recent wedding, the bride and groom retired to a room off the vestibule until the guests had left the church. Then the wedding arch of swords was formed, and they walked under the arch to their waiting automobile. The bride told me that those five minutes with Jack alone immediately after the wedding were a time she would always treasure.

Everyone loves to see the bride enter her new life under an arch of swords. Service weddings are always romantic, all brides are beautiful, but this year's Navy brides are more than beautiful—they are brave!

The bride's father, if he is not in the Service, wears a morning coat or a cutaway and dark-gray striped trousers. Very light-gray buckskin gloves are usually worn.

The bride's mother, although she has all the responsibility of the wedding, often does not appear to take an active part. She is the last person to enter before the procession, and she should be becomingly and beautifully gowned. The groom usually sends the bride's mother and also his own mother a corsage. Perhaps a pale gray-blue or lavender chiffon or lace dress, or a velvet dress of any becoming color, with a small matching hat may be worn.

A Service Wedding

Should the bride be an Army junior and the groom a Naval officer, Service traditions may highlight the occasion.

THE INFORMAL WEDDING

With officers' dress blues or the full-dress uniform stored away in moth balls for the "duration" and the impossibility of getting leave, informal weddings will probably be the vogue for the immediate future. Naturally, every bride wants to be married at her home church or in her own house, but to those young women who have pledged their troth to a naval officer this wish is next to impossible of fulfillment. Parents and grandparents shake their heads and wonder what the world is coming to when a bridegroom cannot come to claim his bride and the girl goes off to some foreign port to be married. If the family is wealthy, perhaps her parents accompany her to where HIS ship is in port, but more often the brave young bride goes off alone. And these girls have courage! To go from comfortable homes, where they have been accustomed to certain luxuries, pretty clothes, servants, etc., to a boardinghouse room or a tiny apartment where they must learn to cook, sew, wash, iron; to be away from their families, then on a few hours' notice to pack up and move—well, it requires more than puppy love. Whatever you wish to call this type of stamina, these young brides have it.

THE WEDDING AT A STRANGE CHURCH IN A STRANGE PORT

Before you arrive, if possible, your fiancé should make all arrangements for the wedding unless you are to visit friends and the wedding is to take place several days after your arrival. In this case, you may help with the plans or make your own arrangements. Every woman loves a wedding, and your hostess will like to help with the arrangements and take part in them. If she is a seasoned matron she relives her own wedding. If she happens to be a young bride herself she enjoys the responsibility and gets a thrill out of appearing matronly.

Sometimes it may happen that a young officer has not had an opportunity to make any close friends among the officers' wives. Then the simple thing is for him to go to the church of your mutual choice and lay his problem before the minister.

Clergymen in coastal towns have these calls every day. "It's happening all over the country, this tender spectacle of love, even Cupid's in the Navy now!"

Your fiancé may, in your absence, make all the arrangements and plans with the help of his Navy friends and a sympathetic minister. There may be music, a soloist, floral decorations, and a small reception afterwards, but remember, all of these expenses should be borne by the bride's family.

If time permits, letters as to plans should be exchanged, and along with her trousseau the bride should be given a check by her family sufficient to cover the expenses of the wedding. It is assumed that the young officer will have some idea of the financial status of the bride's family, and if appropriate, the decorations and entertainment should be kept simple. The groom will arrange to have several of his classmates or shipmates act as ushers, and his best friend among his brother officers will serve as best man.

If a Navy Chaplain performs the ceremony it is not customary to offer him a fee, but if the ceremony is performed by a regular minister, ten dollars is the usual offering. This amount is placed in an envelope which the best man gives to the clergyman in the vestry immediately after the service.

THE HOME WEDDING

For sentimental reasons the bride may wish to be married at home or in the home of a relative or close friend. Should she be fortunate enough to live near a naval base, it may be possible for her to plan a home wedding that will be most attractive and at the same time economical.

This type of wedding, no matter how simple, is always lovely. At dusk, and lighted by pale candlelight, the house can be particularly lovely. Spring flowers used in profusion or autumn leaves artistically arranged as a background may take the place of an expensive florist's creation. An old-fashioned garden also makes a perfect setting for a beautiful wedding. The note to strive for is intimacy and informality— always missing in a church ceremony.

A home wedding may be as simple or as elaborate as you choose; but try to keep it from freezing into a stiff pattern. Home should stand for gracious and affectionate living. The dining room table pushed into a corner and the kitchen range draped with bridesmaids' wraps are poor aids to an overly formal service. Don't try to turn a duplex apartment into a Paris cathedral!

Marriage at a Rectory or Magistrate's Office

In a magistrate's office or a rectory the groom may wear uniform, though civilian clothes might be less conspicuous and preferable. An elaborate wedding dress does not seem appropriate. A small breakfast, luncheon, or dinner is in perfect taste following the ceremony.

What the Bride Wears

The traditional white wedding gown dates back to Anne of Brittany, who said "no" to the customary scarlet costume of her day and started a trend in white wedding gowns. Today, the bride in a formal wedding wears white, but there is a tendency in modern fashion for brides to choose delicate shades, such as shell-pink and ice-blue. This is a matter of personal taste. The bride may, and indeed often does, wear just about what she pleases.

She may choose to look like the lily maid of Astolat and, in a gown of white, glowing chiffon, drift down the aisle on her father's arm, or she may prefer to look like a nun, with her face veil arranged fold after fold like that of a saintly bride of the church. Many girls like the idea of being married in their mother's or grandmother's bridal finery, with the bridesmaids in corresponding old-fashioned dresses. The veil may be long and flowing or short and fluffy. A lace mantilla arranged with a Spanish comb or natural flowers is always lovely. Never has a bride had a freer rein, which is as it should be, for after all it is her day of days!

Satin is the conventional material for bridal dresses, but again the bride is free to choose her own style. For the informal wedding she may wear taffeta, velvet, jersey, lace, crepe, chiffon, mousseline de soie, organza, dotted swiss, or any summer material. The conservative bride, marrying a naval officer, with an eye to the future should choose a material and a style of dress that with slight alteration can be converted into an extra evening dress.

Of course, if the bride wishes for sentimental reasons to keep her dress inviolate, she may make it as elaborate as she wishes. Wedding dresses are often handed down in families, and it is a nice old custom to perpetuate.

THE BRIDESMAIDS

The bride decides on the number of bridesmaids, their costumes, and flowers. Everything should be planned to blend in with the general theme of the wedding. The material of the bridesmaids' costumes should complement in color or be of material similar to that of the bride's dress.

It is customary if the bride has a sister to choose her for the maid or matron of honor. If there are several sisters all of them may be included in varying capacities, even as junior bridesmaids.

If the bride has no sisters she usually chooses her most intimate friend. It is a nice gesture to invite the groom's favorite sister to be a bridesmaid. A bride may have one attendant, or if she is a festive person she may have eight or twelve. She seldom has more than six, however, as more than that borders on the theatrical and begins to make it look like a triumphal march. The maid or matron of honor is dressed a little differently from the bridesmaids, though the entire cortège is always a harmonious whole.

"Bridesmaids have practically nothing to say about the dresses they are asked to buy and wear, but inwardly they hope that the bride will be conservative as to style and cost. They want a bridesmaid's dress that they can do this to and that to, and one that when they appear in it a second time will not mark them as a member of so-and-so's sextet."[3]

[3] Helen Ewing, "The Bride Wore," *Mademoiselle*, September, 1941.

It is customary for the bride to give each bridesmaid a small gift or remembrance, although this is not at all obligatory. Depending upon the bride's circumstances, she may give some little trinket; but it is nice to give something lasting, no matter how small. Charm bracelets are popular gifts, compacts are always acceptable, and one recent bride gave each of her bridesmaids a miniature silver pin in the shape of a spoon that was a replica of her own pattern of silver.

The groom usually gives to his best man and ushers some small gift, such as studs, links, or a cigarette case, if he can afford it.

Flowers

Although a bride may select the flowers and make arrangements with the florist, the groom pays for:

Flowers sent to the bride
Corsage sent to the bride's mother
Corsage sent to his mother

The bride's family pays for:

All flower decorations for church and home
Flowers for bridesmaids
Flowers for flower girls
Flowers for maid of honor or matron of honor
Fee for the organist
Fee for the soloist

Receptions

When the guest list is large, and the bride wishes to ask more friends to the reception than can be accommodated at her home, the party is usually given at a club or hotel. Home receptions have a more definite charm, however, if they can be managed.

Properly speaking, the only persons in the receiving line are the bride and groom and the wedding attendants, but often at a large reception at a club the line is formed with the mother and father of the bride first, then the bride and groom standing between the two families, and the attendants following the groom's parents.

A simpler arrangement for the home reception is for the bride and groom to receive alone. The party may be as elaborate or as plain as one desires, but it is customary to have a wedding cake. The bride cuts the first slice with her husband's sword, his hand on hers. The cake is then cut and distributed to the guests by an attendant. It is also customary to drink a toast to the bride.

If there is to be a seated wedding dinner, then the caterer or the club steward will be glad to submit menus and make suggestions. The center table should be the bride's table, at one end of which she and the groom are seated. The wedding cake is the centerpiece, and all the guests receive little white boxes of wedding cake which they may take home to dream on.

At last, after the dinner, the dramatic moment arrives when the bride whispers to the maid of honor to assemble all the bridesmaids in the hall. They all gather at the foot of the steps and, like any white-gowned and veiled bride out of Godey's *Lady's Book*, she tosses her bouquet to them with these words, "Hail, there, pretty maidens, standing all a-row, the one who catches this, the next bouquet shall throw." The bride hurries upstairs, accompanied by her mother and her bridesmaids, to change into her going-away costume. Her whole trousseau is packed in two pieces of airplane luggage—in her mother's day it would have taken four large trunks to hold her wardrobe, which was planned to see her through two years at least. The modern bride buys her trousseau for a season, and the clever Navy bride buys it only for her first station.

Then comes the quick getaway with the rice and old shoes thrown after the departing couple!

Wedding Presents

If wedding invitations have been sent out (three weeks before the wedding date), gifts will begin to arrive soon thereafter. If announcements are sent, the gifts will arrive probably before you return from your wedding trip. In either case, provide yourself with a gift book, which can be bought at any good stationer's. As you open each gift, fill in the date the present is received, the article, where it was bought, the name and address of the donor, and the date the gift was acknowledged. Make it a rule to acknowledge each gift as soon as it is received. If several arrive at once, play a little Santa Claus game with yourself by opening one at a time and acknowledging it with a written note of thanks before opening another. Your note of thanks will be more enthusiastic if you write immediately to the person who was kind enough to remember you. A bride must write a note of thanks to every person who sends a gift. The omission of this is the one thing that the sender may forgive but never forget, and your youth will not excuse you.

To telephone is not enough, although in your enthusiasm you may express your first thanks in this manner; the WRITTEN NOTE MUST FOLLOW, no matter how simple it is. But use a little thought on the wording. There is nothing more disappointing or deflating than to receive a line or so of thanks for a sizable silver salad bowl on which you have spent your all:

Dear Commander and Mrs. Brown: Thank you so much for the dear little silver bowl you were so sweet to send us.
Sincerely,

Perhaps the persons who sent it sacrificed something they wanted very much, in order to give you a present they hoped would add to your happiness.

Try to write a gracious and appreciative note to each one who has remembered you, and particularly avoid using the word "little." Of course, a typewritten note or letter should never be sent, and worst of all is the engraved card of thanks. Do not let any beguiling salesman entice you into buying a printed card which will be a permanent admission on your part of not knowing the social graces; you are the one who has the gift, not the engraver. Do your own composing, even though you are no poet.

Displaying the Gifts

Wedding gifts are sometimes displayed at the wedding reception, and sometimes a bride shows them to intimate friends she invites in to tea. There are definitely two schools of thought on the subject: One considers it a vulgar display to show one's popularity; the other thinks it quite proper. Let your conscience be your guide. The card of the sender is left on the gift, though in former days it was carefully removed.

Checks (the most welcome gift a Service bride can receive) are never displayed, though it is quite all right to refer to the convertible coupe that you and Bill plan to buy with his grandfather's check, or to the check that Aunt Mamie sent you for an electric toaster.

White-covered tables should be arranged, and special tact should be used in displaying the presents. Don't place a gorgeous silver epergne from rich Aunt Harriet next to the chromium cheese dish from your favorite Aunt Ellen, who hasn't much of this world's goods. Silver should be placed on one table and china on another (though heaven forbid that the Navy bride receive very much of this lovely commodity).

General Information on Gifts

Before the present emergency the average junior naval officer spent the first seven years of his service at sea—and he probably will again! Your lovely wedding presents will be stored, either in your mother's attic or in commercial storage. The latter will cost you money. At any rate, you won't be settled and keeping house if you follow the Fleet. After seven years at sea, your young Lieutenant is due for two years shore duty. If he is ambitious and has worked hard, he may be sent to a postgraduate school for one to three years. There you will have your first opportunity to unpack and really get acquainted with your wedding presents.

Flat silver, which is really a necessity, will be the most useful present you can receive, next to a check. Insist upon sterling, even if you can only manage four of the necessary pieces. You can continue adding to it until you have a dozen of everything. Happy the young bride whose far-seeing mother or grandmother selected a pretty pattern of silver and has been adding to it through the years. It is never too early for a girl to begin collecting her silver.

Your flat silver will go along with you on each move, either in your wardrobe trunk or in your packing trunks. A non-tarnish silver chest is a nice thing to have, but the usual flannel containers are easier to pack. Here is a list of what you should get with the checks you receive, or if relatives ask you frankly what you need in silver.

Flat silver in sterling:

 4 luncheon-size knives and forks
 4 bouillon spoons
 4 butter spreaders
 4 salad forks
12 teaspoons
 3 large table or serving spoons
 1 steak or carving set

Later you can build your service up to twelve, also filling in with cream-soup spoons, iced-tea spoons, ice-cream forks, after-dinner coffee spoons, and the large-size dinner knives and forks.

In a good, heavy plate you can use:

1 silver meat platter
1 silver vegetable dish with 3 compartments
1 silver bread tray
1 or more silver sandwich trays

Of course, if some fairy godmother presents you with a sterling silver tea service, and you receive in addition a beautiful silver tray and a large portion of Tiffany's stock, don't throw it away; but if you are a wise child you will put it in storage and not try to carry it around with you. The excess weight and the burglar and fire insurance that you will pay won't be worth it.

With the list given—plus an electric toaster, a silex coffee maker, a waffle iron, and a grill, all of which should be small enough to fit into spare corners of your packing trunk—you should be able to set up housekeeping in the average furnished apartment. If the dishes, glassware, and cooking utensils aren't furnished, then you must patronize the dime store, and either sell or give away what you have bought when you move. After a few moves you will have your packing down to a system—the blankets and household linen will protect the silver, and when dispatch orders come in to "proceed at once," the silver and linen will practically leap into their accustomed places in your packing trunk. It is all very simple, when you learn how to plan and pack.

How to Mark Linen and Silver

Formerly, only the bride's monogram or initials were used, but today it is deemed proper to use the bride's future initials. Don't go in for fads if you expect to enjoy your silver in the days to come. The best plan is to choose a conservative pattern with a simple marking. Very plain silver, which was so popular a few years ago, scratches easily; so choose something that you really like that isn't too expensive when you are ready to add to it. Simple block letters are considered smart, or a single Old English initial.

The Wedding Trip

If you are lucky enough to have one, this is the event of your life. There will never be another trip to compare with it; so forget everything, and be happy. If Bill has to go back to duty immediately after the wedding, don't feel sorry for yourself but plan on a deferred honeymoon! Whatever fate has in store for you, be a good sport, and try to adjust yourself to present conditions. Above all, don't forget ——

"You're in the Navy now."

This is a secret, but Bill has orders to report to a ship at Pearl Harbor, in Honolulu. This is almost too good to be true, because it means government transportation for himself and Nancy Lee, with a glorious honeymoon in romantic Hawaii. After all, the Navy has its compensations.[4]

---

[4] Alas, no Hawaiian honeymoons for Navy brides for a while! After the war—well, who can say?

Chapter VII

NAVAL TRADITIONS AND CUSTOMS

Sing me a song of the Service
 Of our brotherhood tried and true,
Of the faith we hold with the men of old
 Of a creed that is ever new.
A creed of honor and courage,
 Of loyalty, even to death,
Of a simple steadfast devotion
 To the last expiring breath.

Song of the Service
—W. J. DIMITRIJEVIC, '32

NOW that the rice is out of your hair, Nancy Lee, and Bill is reporting for duty in his new ship, it is time for you to learn something about Uncle Sam's Navy, something about the Service with which you must learn to share Bill's interest—yes, even his love and his life if need be. No officer can be successful who does not love the Service and give to it his finest loyalty, a loyalty that comes even before his home ties.

You can count yourself as one of those fortunate prewar brides who was able to have the kind of wedding you had always dreamed about and a honeymoon de luxe with a trip to Honolulu thrown in by the government just for luck. Wedding checks and Bill's careful budgeting as a benedict also made a honeymoon at the Royal Hawaiian Hotel a real possibility. That will be something to tell your grandchildren about, my sweet, along with the Battle of Pearl Harbor and a few other trying times such as the trip back to the mainland when you were evacuated on two hours notice and zigzagged across the Pacific dodging enemy submarines.

Well, the memories of the Royal are pretty nice, aren't they? And didn't Bill act like a real millionaire? Perhaps you have learned by this time, Nancy Lee, that all Service men are more than gallant to their sweethearts and wives and spend money as if they had it until they are down to their last sou. Well, it is a jolly forgivable fault, for like the Blue-jackets they go back to their ships at sea, and while it may be hard on you to adjust yourself to the penny-pinching days ahead—still you had a honeymoon in the most beautiful place in the world, in the "Paradise of the Pacific," so be thankful!

No doubt you wondered as you read the heading of this chapter what bearing naval traditions and customs could have on the happiness of a Navy wife. Be assured, my darling, that they do have a most important bearing and will continue to influence Bill's character and his manner of living as long as he is in the Service and even if he should be retired. It may make your path easier if you know something of these tradi-tions and customs and some of the essential characteristics of naval officers, so brace yourself for some pretty stiff reading by John Paul Jones, the Father of the American Navy.

ESSENTIAL CHARACTERISTICS OF NAVAL OFFICERS

The education, training, and indoctrination of naval offi-cers with naval traditions and customs have as their objective the development of officers whose essential characteristics were so well expressed by John Paul Jones in a letter to the Continental Congress in 1775. A portion of this letter, as quoted by Buell in his book, *Paul Jones, The Founder of the American Navy, a History,* reads thus:

It is by no means enough that an officer of the Navy should be a capable mariner. He must be that of course, but also a great deal more. He should be as well a gentleman of liberal education, re-fined manners, punctilious courtesy, and the nicest sense of per-sonal honor.

He should not only be able to express himself clearly and with force in his own language both with tongue and pen, but he should also be versed in French and Spanish.

The naval officer should be familiar with the principles of international law, and general practice of admiralty jurisprudence, because such knowledge may often, when cruising at a distance from home, be necessary to protect his flag from insult or his crew from imposition or injury in foreign ports.

He should also be conversant with the usage of diplomacy and capable of maintaining, if called upon, a dignified and judicious diplomatic correspondence; because it often happens that sudden emergencies in foreign waters make him the diplomatic as well as military representative of his country, and in such cases he may have to act without opportunity of consulting his civic or ministerial superiors at home, and such action may easily involve the portentous issue of peace or war between great powers. These are general qualifications, and the nearer the officer approaches the full possession of them the more likely he will be to serve his country well and win fame and honor for himself.

What Are Naval Traditions and Customs?

(Various notes taken from a pamphlet published by the Office of Public Relations, Twelfth Naval District.)

Now, exactly what do we mean by naval traditions and customs? Naval traditions are unwritten rules of conduct for naval personnel based on historical precedent and mutually accepted by them for their guidance. Naval customs are ceremonies or procedures designed and used in the Navy to inculcate respect for authority, to enhance morale, to strengthen discipline, and to promote uniformity of action throughout the Navy.

The customs and traditions of our Navy are hoary with age. They date back to the early days when "iron men went down to the sea in wooden ships" (some facetious young Ensigns like to reverse this quotation). The value of tradition and custom to military or naval service is incontestable. The worth of ceremony rests mainly upon the fact that it binds us to the past while at the same time lending an air of dignity and respect to all official relations, at home or abroad. Ceremony is said to be the cement of discipline, and upon discipline the Naval Service rests.

A Thumbnail Naval History

The early history of the American Colonies is largely the story of a maritime people. All the original settlers faced the perils of the deep to reach their new homes, and in those days transatlantic passage was certainly most uncomfortable and perilous. From over the sea came all the crude necessities of life except the plainest food and the logs with which to build and heat their simple dwellings; back over the sea in trade went the products of their skill and toil.

Even between the different Colonies the sea was the quickest and safest means of transportation. With the early development of a shipbuilding industry fostered by the excellent timber from the forests of New England, by the rapidly expanding fishing industry, and by the gradual increase in trade, the people of the Colonies early became sea-minded. By 1775 more than one-third of Great Britain's sea-borne commerce was carried in vessels built in the Colonies.

George Washington was among the first to recognize the important part that sea power might play in gaining the independence of the Colonies. Soon after he took command of the Army near Boston in July, 1775, he arranged with some Massachusetts shipowners to arm and man their ships and to send them to sea in hopes of capturing some British ship from which might possibly be obtained powder and other supplies badly needed by his army. These vessels have sometimes been called "Washington's Fleet." They captured one or two small vessels, but on the whole their operations were of little importance.

From the Colonial merchant ships came most of the officers and men who manned the fleet later built for the Continental Navy.

Among those who came into the Navy from merchant ships, most of which ships were operating as privateers or under letters of marque, were many men who later became naval heroes: Hopkins, Barry, Truxton, Decatur, Porter, Biddle, Preble, and Perry.

During the Revolution there took place one of the American Navy's greatest exploits, a foundation stone of its traditions. This was the defeat of the British frigate *Serapis* by the *Bon Homme Richard*, the latter an old converted merchant ship in the command of Captain John Paul Jones. It was in this battle—with the ships foul of each other and lashed together, the *Bon Homme Richard* torn by shells, on fire, and leaking badly—that John Paul Jones, upon being hailed by the British Captain and asked if he had surrendered, made the never-to-be-forgotten reply, "I have not yet begun to fight!" and proved it by winning the battle. What a glorious example!

As soon as the War for Independence ended the Navy was allowed to disintegrate, and in 1785 the last of the ships of the Continental Navy was sold. Upon the inauguration of President Washington in 1789, the administration of the Navy was placed in the War Department, but by act of Congress of April 20, 1798, the Navy Department was created as a separate administrative branch of the government. Benjamin Stoddert was appointed the first Secretary of the Navy.

In the Mexican War and in the Civil War the operations of the Navy were largely confined to bombardment and blockade.

The war with Spain was primarily naval. The actual state of war was precipitated by the blowing up by a mine of the U.S.S. *Maine*, at anchor in Havana harbor. The war was brought to a successful conclusion by the destruction of the Spanish Fleet by Commodore Dewey at Manila, and by Admiral Sampson off Santiago, Cuba.

In World War I the activities of our Navy, because of the inferiority in the number of surface ships of the German Navy compared to its opponents, were restricted chiefly to antisubmarine and escort operations. However, there was ample evidence that the officers and men of the modern Navy are of the same material as those in the days of "wooden ships and iron men."

The attack on Pearl Harbor on December 7, 1941, was the scene of the start of the Pacific conflagration. For history students of the future there will be a new and glorious page in the records of the United States Navy. They will read about and remember Pearl Harbor as a story of the daring bravery, cool-headedness, strength, and skill of the Navy. An American Admiral gave his life in giving help to brother officers; four young Reserve Ensigns manned a destroyer and fought like veterans in the thickest of the fight; a dying Captain, disemboweled by flying shrapnel, continued to give orders and refused to be moved, but ordered his junior officers to leave the burning deck; scores of enlisted men swam from sinking ships through oil-burning waters trying to reach safety as the enemy machine-gunned them. Once ashore, those who survived manned small boats, reported to other ships, and continued to fight.

In such a short review of our Navy's history it is impossible to mention more than a few of the incidents upon which its traditions are founded. Use some of your spare time, Nancy Lee, to read a detailed naval history. It will make you proud to be a Navy wife! As a suggestion—keep a record of the war today.

The Navy is proud of its history, with its many brilliant examples of courage, determination, professional skill, and self-sacrificing devotion to duty. It is proud of its traditions, founded upon these examples and upon those of the British Navy from which the Colonial seafaring men learned so much. Our record has to date been excellent, for the United States has never lost a war, nor the Navy a fleet action. Perhaps this can be attributed in part to the teamwork and training of our armed forces and the effect of customs and traditions as handed down to us by the founders of the Navy. True, some mistakes have been made, some examples of selfish ambition have been noted, some professional jealousy has gone beyond conventional bounds. Nevertheless, morale has been uniformly high, our record is clear of mutinies, and officers and men of today stand ready to emulate the best of the heroic traditions of the past.

You can never really know Bill until you understand, and fully realize, the high standard of honor, loyalty, and performance of duty required of him in his daily life. Perhaps nothing can so impress this upon your mind as an example of the formally worded Articles for the Government of the Navy.

Parts of two articles are quoted.

Article 1. The Commanders of all fleets, squadrons, naval stations, and vessels belonging to the Navy, are required to show in themselves a good example of virtue, honor, patriotism, and subordination; to be vigilant in inspecting the conduct of all persons who are placed under their command; to guard against and suppress all dissolute and immoral practices, and to correct according to the laws and regulations of the Navy, all persons who are guilty of them; and any such Commander who offends against these articles shall be punished as a court-martial may direct.

Article 4. The punishment of death, or such other punishment as a court-martial may adjudge, may be inflicted on any person in the naval service

(1) Who makes, or attempts to make, or unites with any mutiny or mutinous assembly:

(2) Or disobeys the lawful order of his superior officer:

(7) Or, in time of war, deserts, or betrays his trust, or entices or aids others to desert or betray their trust:

(8) Or sleeps upon his watch:

(9) Or leaves his station without being regularly relieved:

(10) Or intentionally or willfully suffers any vessel of the Navy to be stranded, or run upon rocks or shoals, or improperly hazarded:

(12) Or strikes or attempts to strike the flag to an enemy or rebel, without proper authority, or when engaged in battle, treacherously yields or pusillanimously cries for quarter:

(13) Or, in the time of battle, displays cowardice, negligence, or disaffection, or withdraws from or keeps out of danger to which he should expose himself:

(18) Or fails to encourage, in his own person, his inferior officers and men to fight courageously.

Naval Customs

Some naval customs have come down to seafaring men of today from the seamen of Greece, Phoenicia, Carthage, and Rome; others are of more recent origin. Naval customs are so numerous that it will be necessary to consider them by classes if one is to appreciate their full significance. The most important customs are designed to inculcate

1. Respect for God
2. Respect for the nation
3. Respect for authority
4. Respect for the individual.

Respect for God

The Commanding Officer of each ship to which a Chaplain is attached, by Regulations is required to hold divine service every Sunday unless conditions make it impracticable to do so.

During divine service on board a ship of the Navy, a pennant called the Church Pennant, a white triangular field with a blue cross, is hoisted on the same halliard with, and above, the national ensign. This is the only occasion on which it is ever permissible to hoist any flag or pennant on the same halliard, or at the same staff, above the national ensign.

For centuries, since flags were first used to indicate nationality, the hoisting of one nation's flag below another's has indicated a capture by the force of the nation whose flag is flown above. The hoisting of the Church Pennant over the national ensign during divine service is the Navy's way of indicating its recognition of the supremacy of God.

Divine service is held, weather permitting, on the quarterdeck under an awning. The portable altar is draped with the national ensign. At the beginning of the service the bugler sounds "Church Call"; the ship's bell is tolled; and the Boatswain's mate passes the word, "Out smoking lamp! Quiet about the decks!"

No smoking, card playing, or other games are allowed on deck or in officers' messrooms, no loud talking or boisterous behavior. But the rights of the individual are recognized, and no person except the members of the band, who supply the music as part of their duty, is forced to attend the service.

The only times it is permissible to half-mast the national ensign are: during funeral services of naval personnel; during the transfer of the body of a deceased officer or man from ship to shore; while the body of a deceased Captain of a ship, or that of a Flag Officer, is on board the ship in which he died, except when at sea; and when so ordered by higher authority during periods of mourning, or as a memorial for the dead. In the case of the death of the Captain or of a Flag Officer, such Captain's pennant or Flag Officer's flag is half-masted until sunset on the day of the transfer of the body to shore or burial at sea. All Navy ships at anchor within sight of the ship which half-masts her colors follow her movements in half-masting and hoisting colors. The custom of half-masting colors is in recognition of the power of God over life.

RESPECT FOR THE NATION

To all seafaring men the national ensign is symbolic of the nation. The colors constitute the only mark which distinguishes the nationality of a ship. Hence when at sea another ship is in sight during daylight (except another ship of the U.S. Navy of the same fleet), or when within sight of inhabited land, the colors are hoisted so long as there is light enough for them to be seen.

A merchant vessel, upon passing a warship, dips its colors (lowers them to half-staff) and hoists them only after the dip has been answered by the dipping of the warship's colors. The custom is in recognition of the status of the warship as a representative of the power and dignity of the nation.

During battle, ships always hoist their colors, and the striking, or hauling down, of a ship's colors is a recognized token of surrender. When the colors are hoisted upside down, it is a signal of distress indicating that the ship is in immediate need of assistance.

When the ship is not underway, the colors are hoisted at

8:00 A.M. and hauled down at sunset. The ceremonies at these times are designed to bring to the minds of officers and men the respect due the colors as the symbol of the nation, and as a mental renewal of their oath of allegiance. The jack, similar to the blue field of the national ensign, is hoisted simultaneously with the colors at a staff at the stem of the ship.

Morning colors: At morning colors the guard of the day (usually Marines) and the band are paraded on the quarter-deck facing the flagstaff. As the ship's bell strikes eight, the bugler sounds "Attention," all officers and men on deck face aft and stand at attention. The Marine Guard presents arms. The band plays the National Anthem, at the first note of which all officers and men raise their right hands to their caps in salute. The colors are run smartly to full staff, meaning to the top of the staff. Upon completion of the National Anthem officers and men drop their hands to their sides; the bugler sounds "Carry On" and the ceremony is completed. When no band is available a bugler will sound "Colors" in lieu of the playing of the National Anthem.

When a United States warship carrying a band is anchored in a foreign port, or when in a United States port there is a foreign warship anchored in the same port in close vicinity, the band plays the national anthem of the nation of such port or ship after "The Star Spangled Banner."

Evening colors: The ceremonies at evening colors (at sunset) are the same as for morning colors except that the colors are started down at the first note and lowered slowly so as to be completely down with the last note. Great care is observed that the colors do not touch the deck.

You may be interested to know that a national ensign when unfit for further use *must be burned* in order to prevent its desecration by use in any other form.

Full Dressing Ship

When a ship of the United States Navy is at anchor or moored, on national holidays, 4th of July and 22nd of February, it is full dressed from 8:00 A.M., to sunset. National ensigns are flown from the mastheads and a rainbow of signal flags runs from stem to stern, passing high up on each mast. When a foreign nation is honored, its national ensign is flown at the mainmast head. Boats in the water of a ship which is full dressed carry colors.

Saluting the Quarter-deck

When an officer or man reaches the upper platform of the gangway ladder in boarding a ship, or steps onto such platform in leaving a ship, he faces aft and salutes the quarter-deck. Also during daylight a similar salute will be given upon reaching the quarter-deck by way of a hatch or from any other part of the ship.

The origin of this custom is uncertain. It apparently existed before nations had flags. Some consider that it originated as a recognition of the Captain's authority. Today it is considered more as a salute to the colors, which can usually be seen from the quarter-deck, but this custom is carried out when boarding or leaving.

RESPECT FOR AUTHORITY

In the conduct of war unquestioning obedience is essential. Such obedience can be obtained only by inculcating respect for authority. Authority means responsibility. It is for this reason that throughout the ages a Captain of a sinking ship has been the last to leave the ship. He accepts the responsibility for the condition of the ship and before he leaves must insure that all other persons precede him in seeking to save their lives.

In order to establish an order of precedence in succession to command it was necessary to establish ranks, and seniority within each rank. To inculcate respect for authority as indicated by rank, its honors must be rendered not to the holders of the rank as individuals, but in recognition of the authority and responsibility conferred upon them. Hence there is a table of honors, indicating from President to Ensign the honors to which each is entitled by virtue of his election, appointment, or commission.

An examination of this table will show that the honors to be rendered include the ceremony of "piping the side," the variation being only in the number of side boys. Beginning with Commanding Officers, the ceremony includes a guard of honor. Commencing with Flag Officers, the band is paraded, and under certain circumstances a salute is fired. For the ruler of a nation (or a member of a royal family as a potential ruler) there are included "manning the rail" and the national salute. Of these various ceremonies only manning the rail and piping the side are exclusively naval.

Manning the Rail

Manning the rail consists of stationing men along the rail of all weather decks, facing outboard, an arm's length. In most navies, at a given signal all men extend their arms reaching to the shoulders of the men adjacent on either side. In the days of sailing ships the men instead of manning the rail manned the yards—the large booms extending horizontally across the mast from which sails are suspended. Presumably such practice came from a desire to show off the proficiency of the crew and to indicate to the sovereign that his men were willing to take risks in his honor.

Gun Salutes

Gun salutes are fired only by ships equipped with a saluting battery of small guns carried solely for the purpose—battleships, cruisers, and a few others. The internationally accepted national salute is twenty-one guns.

National salutes are fired by ships of the United States Navy at noon on the 22nd of February and the 4th of July. At noon on the 30th of May, Memorial Day, a salute of twenty-one guns is fired at the rate of one gun per minute. Minute guns are a customary form of salute to the dead.

Upon entering a foreign port where there is a saluting station, a saluting ship fires a national salute in honor of the nation of the port, the national ensign of such foreign nation being flown at the mainmast head during the salute.

The President, rulers of other nations, and members of royal families are saluted with the national salute. There is an established scale of salutes, less than twenty-one guns for various public officials, members of the diplomatic corps, "Flag" Officers of the Navy and Coast Guard, and the "General" Officers of the Army and Marine Corps. All salutes are given in an odd number of guns. Why, no one knows, but in early times it was considered that an even number of guns fired meant that the Captain or Master was dead. Not so today in our Navy. Should an even number of guns be fired, it would merely mean that the gunner couldn't count or that some error had been made.

Salutes between nations are given and answered "gun for gun." In the days of Queen Victoria, Commodore Joe Fife, who commanded our Asiatic Fleet, sailed into Hong Kong on the occasion of a visit there by Queen Victoria. He fired a salute which should have been twenty-one guns but instead was twenty-two—a terrible error.

Immediately after this he received a message from the British Admiral, as follows:

"The British Naval Commander is unable to return any such salute and desires explanation and reason for the extra gun."

To this Joe Fife flashed the following reply: "Twenty-one guns for Queen Victoria and one for Commodore Joe Fife, by Gad!" (I shudder to think of the poor gunner who couldn't count in this case.)

Another story is told of the old Commodore, who is by now almost a legendary character in the Navy. It seems that his vessel, disabled in a storm, was being towed into San Francisco Harbor by a British ship. Another storm came up and the English Captain, fearing that he might lose his own vessel, sent Commodore Fife a signal which happened to rhyme. "If wind and tide do not abate, I cannot tow you through the Gate."

At this the old Commodore was exceedingly wroth and, not to be outdone, signaled back also in rhyme. "As long as you have steam and coal, you'd better tow, dad-blast your soul."

Piping the Side

The term "piping" is derived from the use of the boatswain's pipe during the rendering of the honors. A boatswain's pipe is a special type of whistle—a metal tube about six inches long, at one end of which there is a hollow metal ball without a top, an opening for the escape of air when the other end of the tube is blown into. The escape of the air produces a sharp, piercing sound whose tone, within limits, can be varied by changing the pressure of the fingers over the escape hole.

Pipes of this type have been used by seamen for centuries to call the attention of the crew to an order about to be given by word of mouth, to synchronize the efforts of men hauling on lines with the sound of the pipe, and in more modern days as a form of salute rendered to officers or officials boarding or leaving a ship. It is because of the similarity in sound between the boatswain's pipe and whistling with the lips that the latter is banned on board ship.

The present ceremonial custom of piping the side evolved from a practical custom of sailing-ship days, when ships carried no gangway ladders. The means of reaching the deck in those days was by a rope ladder hung over the side of the ship or by a sea ladder consisting of metal strips attached to the ship's side as steps. Such a climb was difficult at times, especially if the ship was rolling. Frequently it was necessary to provide a boatswain's chair. This was merely a flat seat of plank with lines from each end meeting overhead, at which point they were attached to a line which passed through a pulley block overhead and then to deck. By this means a person sitting in the seat, pushing against the side of the ship with his feet, could be hoisted to the ship's rail with little danger to him.

When the boatswain's chair was used, men were stationed to haul on the line to hoist the chair. The Boatswain, watching over the side to note a favorable moment for hoisting, gave the signal by a blast on his pipe. The chair was used more often by elderly officers who had grown stout with the years, so as a rule the higher the rank of the officer to be hoisted on board the larger the number of men required. Hence today we have the Boatswain or Boatswain's Mate piping the side and the number of side boys increasing with the officer's rank —two for an officer up to and including Lieutenant Commander, four for Commanders and Captains, six for Commodores and Rear Admirals, and eight for officers and officials of still higher rank.

Hand Salute

Hand salutes are exchanged between officers and between officers and enlisted men, except when under arms or in formation, on every occasion of their meeting, passing near, or being addressed, except:

1. Men at work, except when addressed, do not salute.
2. Men seated at work, at games, or at mess are not required to rise or to salute except in the case of a Flag Officer or Captain.
3. Officers seated in boats shall salute without rising except when a senior enters or leaves the boat, or when acknowledging a gun salute.
4. Officers of one's own ship other than the Captain, except during inspections, are to be saluted only on their first daily meeting and upon addressing or being addressed by their seniors.

The hand salute is a friendly greeting and acknowledgment of membership in a military service. It is a dignified and military gesture. It is just as incumbent on officers to salute their seniors as it is for enlisted men to salute officers; it is equally incumbent on the senior to return the salute. In the Navy the hand salute is not made when the head is uncovered.

Official Calls

Official calls are visits of ceremony or courtesy. Flag Officers, upon assuming command, at the first opportunity pay official calls upon seniors in the chain of command. Com-

manding Officers and unit Commanders call only on seniors
in the type of ship to which assigned.

Officers junior to Commanding Officers are required to call
upon their Commanding Officer in his cabin on board ship
within forty-eight hours after reporting for duty.

Respect for the Individual

Respect for the individual can be demonstrated no better
than by the attitude of seniors to juniors and by the manner
in which correction and punishment is administered. John
Paul Jones in the before-mentioned letter written to the Naval
Committee of the Continental Congress expressed his ideas
on these subjects so well that he set a standard which today
is the ideal for officers of our Navy. He said in his letter:

> Coming now to view the naval officer aboard ship and in rela-
> tion to those under his command, he should be the soul of tact,
> patience, justice, firmness and charity. No meritorious act of a sub-
> ordinate should escape his attention or be left to pass without its
> reward, if even the reward be only one word of approval. Con-
> versely, he should not be blind to a single fault in any subordinate,
> though at the same time he should be quick and unfailing to
> distinguish error from malice, thoughtlessness from incompetency,
> and well-meant shortcoming from heedless or stupid blunder. As
> he should be universal and impartial in his rewards and approval
> of merit, so should he be judicial and unbending in his punish-
> ment or reproof of misconduct.
>
> A Navy is essentially and necessarily aristocratic. True as may
> be the political principles for which we are now contending they
> can never be practically applied or even admitted on board ship,
> out of port or off soundings. This may seem a hardship, but it is
> nevertheless the simplest of truths. Whilst the ships sent forth by
> the Congress may and must fight for the principles of human
> rights and republican freedom, the ships themselves must be ruled
> and commanded at sea under a system of absolute despotism.

Discipline

Navy discipline in the old days was much stricter than at
the present time. The following story is told to show how

Captains behaved in the past. A sailor named Gallagher fell overboard from the frigate *Columbus* during a blow in the Straits.

In a well-regulated frigate such as the *Columbus* it was only a short time before the ship was hove to and a boat lowered. Naturally, in the performance of this maneuver, a certain amount of noise occurred, and the Captain, sleeping below, awoke at the tramping of feet over his head and hurried to the deck.

It took but a few minutes for him to mount the poop and size up the situation. Leaning over the rail, he saw the lifeboat returning and rasped out to the Midshipman in charge, "Have you got your man?" The Midshipman's piping voice returned the cheerful "Aye, aye, sir."

Turning to the Officer of the Deck, the Captain said in a curt but incisive voice, "Light the battle lanterns; beat to battle."

Before the drums had ceased beating, the ship was alive with half-dressed officers and men rushing to "general quarters." The Executive Officer reported the ship ready for action. The Midshipman, followed by the cold and dripping Gallagher, climbed up the sea ladder and over the side on the quarter-deck. The Captain received the report of the Executive Officer and, with a grim look at the shivering Gallagher, said, "Call all hands to witness punishment."

The crew and officers marched aft and paraded in their accustomed places on the quarter-deck. The Master-at-Arms with the inevitable "cat" stood waiting orders. In the tense stillness of the night, accentuated by the creaking of the yards of the heaving ship, the Executive Officer reported: "All ready to witness punishment, sir." The Captain stepped forward. The stillness was painful.

"What's your name, my man?"

"Gallagher, sir."

"Master-at-arms, trice him up to a grating and give him a dozen of the cat."

When they got through the Captain asked, "Gallagher, you would like to know why you are punished, I suppose? Well, it's because you *left the ship without permission.* Pipe down."

Discipline today, while nothing like as severe as in the past, still has plenty of bite to it. Even our recently enlisted men sometimes feel the lash of their Captain's humor. A story has been circulating concerning a Bluejacket who obtained ten days' leave to visit his home on the other side of the country and bought a round-trip sleeper plane ticket. When he left the ship, his parting instructions from the Officer of the Deck included a warning to return on time and to refrain from asking for an extension of leave except in case of dire emergency. Requests for extension, he was told, would be carefully investigated and if matters had been misrepresented, the Captain would punish the offender with a period of confinement in the brig.

Our young sailor arrived home, had a wonderful leave, and presented himself at the airport in time to get the last plane which would take him back to his ship on time. Just as he and the other passengers were about to go aboard, a young girl rushed toward them, waving a ticket and a telegram. She explained that her mother was very ill and that she must get passage on that plane in order to reach her mother's bedside at the earliest moment. The ticket agent had informed her that all space was sold, but allowed her to appeal to the passengers for an exchange of tickets. The young Bluejacket stepped forward and traded tickets. The plane departed.

Glowing with satisfaction at his good deed, the gallant sailor suddenly remembered the instructions of the Officer of the Deck—there must be no requests for extensions. However, he would be overleave unless he asked for an extension, so he telegraphed his Captain, "Urgently request one day's leave. Just gave berth to a girl," to which his unsympathetic Captain promptly replied, "Congratulations. Extension not granted. Your next confinement will be in brig."

OTHER CUSTOMS ON BOARD SHIP

Day's Duty

The officers and crew of a ship other than the Captain, Executive, and on large ships heads of departments, are organized into two watches, starboard and port, and each watch into two sections. Normally at least one section must remain on board; a section so designated is, for the day, the Duty Section. So, Nancy Lee, when Bill tells you he will have the duty every fourth day you will understand.

Watches in Port

In each section there are usually four or more line officers who in turn take watches as Officer of the Deck. The Officer of the Deck remains on deck during the period of his watch. All watches are of four hours duration, starting at midnight, except two, from 4:00 P.M. until after dinner (6:30 to 7:00 P.M.), and from after dinner until 8:00 P.M. These two short watches are called "dog watches." Why? Well, I have heard but one plausible reason: Because they are curtailed!

The reason for "dogging the watches" is easier to explain. It permits the watch to be relieved in order to obtain its evening meal at an appropriate hour. Were the watches continued from 4:00 P.M. to 8.00 P.M. it would be necessary to give the men of such watch their evening meal at 3:30 or at 8:00 P.M., both of which hours would be inconvenient. There previously was also another good reason. In the old sailing ships approximately half the crew was required on deck at a time in order to work the sails. There were but two watches, on duty alternately. If each period were of four hours duration then a watch would always be on duty during the same periods each day. In order to cause the periods on duty to alternate daily, the one from 4:00 P.M. to 8.00 P.M. was split into two.

One head of department, a line officer not restricted to engineering duty only, must be on board at all times. Such officers rotate in taking the day's duty.

Wives Visiting the Ship

In normal peacetime when the ship is in the home port, officers' wives frequently go on board after 4:00 P.M. to see their husbands, and stay for dinner and the movies, returning to shore about 9:00 P.M. Except by special invitation a wife should never go on board ship during working hours, nor should she go on board or remain on board while her husband is on watch as Officer of the Deck. So, Nancy Lee, when Bill's section has the duty you will be welcome on board between 4:00 P.M. and 9:00 P.M., except during the periods in which Bill is actually on watch as Officer of the Deck.

Navy Time—The Enigma

Perhaps we have misled you a little by our use of P.M. above. In the Navy there is no A.M. or P.M. Time is reckoned in twenty-four-hour periods beginning at midnight, and is expressed in four figures. The first two figures represent hours and the last two, minutes; thus one minute past midnight is 0001, noon is 1200, and your 4:00 P.M. is the Navy's 1600. When Bill tells you to take the boat that leaves the landing at 1610, you must remember that such hour is 4:10 in the afternoon, by your watch.

Time by the Ship's Bell

In the days of sailing ships the only real reason for indicating time by the ship's bell was to inform those on watch of the period of time they had to wait before they would be relieved and at liberty to turn in again, or the time to wait until the next meal. There were no watches and few clocks in those days so the marking of time by the ship's bell was of great importance.

It was therefore desirable that each time the bell was struck it should give positive information as to the time. One stroke to represent the half-hour as is used in most striking clocks was insufficient, as that does not identify the half-hours. A system was therefore devised by which each stroke of the bell would indicate the passage of one half-hour since the watch began. By this means each person was able to measure the progress of his watch by the strokes of the bell, except in the dog watches which as I have explained were shortened.

The day is divided into four-hour periods beginning at midnight; one bell may be 0030, 0430, 0830, 1230, 1630, or 2030. If you were on watch you would have little difficulty in identifying which. One of the happiest sounds a sailor ever hears is eight bells at the end of a cold and cheerless watch. He doesn't care whether it is 0400, 0800, 1200, 1600, 2000, or 2400 (or 0000).

Each hour in this system is indicated by an even number of strokes, the half-hours by an odd number. The two strokes representing an hour are struck in rapid succession, with a pause before the next two, or before the last single stroke in the case of a half-hour.

The rapid ringing of the ship's bell is a fire signal and, when the ship is at anchor in a fog, a warning signal to other ships or to boats.

It would be possible to write many chapters on minor customs which have an important bearing upon the life of a naval officer. Should you care to know a few more, read the poem entitled "The Laws of the Navy" by Captain Hopwood of the Royal (British) Navy. In its various stanzas he discusses many features of Navy discipline and various Navy customs and ends with the stanza quoted below. The advice given therein should be thoroughly comprehended by every Navy wife.

> Now these are the laws of the Navy,
> Unwritten and varied they be;
> And he that is wise will observe them,
> Going down in his ship to the sea.
> As the wave rises clear to the hawse pipe,
> Washes aft, and is lost in the wake,
> So shall ye drop astern, all unheeded,
> Such time as the laws ye forsake,
> Now these are the laws of the Navy

And many and mighty are they,
But the hull and the deck and the keel
And the truck of the law is—OBEY.

CEREMONIES PERTAINING TO THE SHIP

Before a ship is ready for operations there are three ceremonies to be performed: the laying of the keel, the launching and christening, and the commissioning.

By "laying the keel" is meant the securing on the building ways of the first strips of metal to form a portion of the ship's keel. The time required for construction is reckoned from the laying of the keel. For large important fighting ships it is the practice to make a minor ceremony of this act by requesting some important official or high-ranking naval officer to drive the first rivet. Even for small ships this act receives some notice, and the time and date of the driving of the first rivet is carefully recorded.

The next ceremony is the launching and christening. Ships are normally constructed on building ways on land and when adequate hull work is completed to insure her being watertight, the ship is permitted to slide down the inclined ways into her natural element. This day is a gala day at the building yard. The Secretary of the Navy invites a lady to sponsor the ship. She selects a maid or matron of honor. On this day, only less than on her wedding day, the sponsor is the center of all eyes and attention. Her duty is to christen the ship—to give it a name just as it starts sliding down the ways.

The christening, or naming, of ships dates back long before the Christian era. Since the earliest days of recorded history ships have been named, partly for identification, of course, but more perhaps because ships seem to have life and personality.

Launching ceremonies have not always been happy occasions with flowers, flags, and pretty speeches. In olden days, it was customary to offer up human sacrifices when the new ship first entered the water. The Vikings and early Norsemen attached human victims to the rollers over which the ship glided into the water.

A much nicer but rather extravagant custom was to drink prosperity to the ship out of a silver cup which was then thrown overboard. This practice seemed too expensive, and in 1690 the British decided to break a bottle on the bow instead.

The following is the story of a launching of a submarine written by the sponsor.

On a high staging my Matron of Honor and I stood with several men who were to make the ceremonial speeches. Just below us was a platform on which there were gathered to watch the launching and christening about fifty honored guests, officials and my personal friends. The staging and platform were gaily decorated with blue and gold bunting. Still lower, on the ground were gathered several hundred spectators, many of them workmen who for the past few months had labored strenuously to prepare the ship for her first plunge into her native element.

As soon as the speakers had finished I was introduced as the sponsor and handing my large bouquet to my Matron of Honor, I stepped nervously closer to the stem of the submarine and seized the ribbon bedecked bottle.

Looking at the trim submarine, outlined in small waving flags, her bow draped in Navy colors, I felt that no God-child was ever more proudly bedecked. What a thrill to know that this ship was about to take the water for the first time and that she would carry the American flag all over the world!

Suddenly there was a whistle beside me. The ship started sliding down the ways. I lunged forward exclaiming as clearly as I could, "I christen thee, *Gudgeon*"!—and swung the silver encased bottle against the vessel's stem. The champagne flew all over my face and clothes. What a relief! I knew I must have hit the perforated part of the casing. Congratulations upon the successful baptism, the breaking of the bottle, poured in from the people on both stands, as amidst the cheers and blowing of whistles the *Gudgeon* gracefully took the water. Excitedly I thanked every one as best I could, and casting one last look at my submarine now coming to rest on the river, I climbed down from the staging.

Following the ceremonies there was a luncheon at the Navy

Yard Club, for seventy-five of the Christening Party, during which I was presented with a beautiful silver tray. My emotions were deeply aroused but I managed some sort of a speech of gratitude.

May that tray go on down to posterity, the glorious symbol of my happiness and pride in having been a Navy Sponsor.

—ANNE BRISCOE PYE

Today, the Navy has decreed seven-minute launchings, minus the pomp and ceremony of prewar days.

The new wartime tempo was set with the launching of the U.S.S. *Bogue* at Tacoma. The only part of the old tradition retained was the smashing of a bottle of champagne across the bow, speeches, band music and other pomp being eliminated.

The "crossing the line" ceremony, a custom still observed, began as an act of worship of a deity. The present ceremony of a fictitious Neptune on board is a relic of the Middle Ages when it was performed not at the equator but upon arriving in the tropics, passing certain landmarks, entering the Arctic Circle, and so on. In these rituals those members of the crew who had not previously visited the spot were thrown from the yardarms into the sea, unless they chose the alternative of giving money to the older sailors.

During the early part of the seventeenth century the custom arose, and is carried out to this day on board ships crossing the equator, of dressing a member of the crew in the garb of Neptune, complete with crown, trident, seaweed hair (made of rope-yarns), and having a large retinue of mermaids, mermen, and other mythical inhabitants of the deep. Appropriate ceremonies are held when the vessel crosses the equator, and all of the novitiates, or pollywogs, pay their forfeit or find themselves thrown into a tub of water on the forecastle, lathered with salt-water soap, and shaved with a huge wooden razor.

Perhaps the greatest single offering that Father Neptune has received took place in the spring of 1936 when the entire United States Fleet crossed the equator and no less than forty thousand pollywogs were initiated into the mysteries of the deep and could thereafter proclaim themselves to be salty shellbacks.

THE ARMY-NAVY FOOTBALL GAME

Annually on the last Saturday in November, usually at the Municipal Stadium in Philadelphia, Pennsylvania, the football teams of the United States Military Academy from West Point and the United States Naval Academy from Annapolis meet in a game which creates intense interest from Washington to Manila and from Alaska to the Panama Canal Zone.

The Cadets from West Point and the Midshipmen from Annapolis are transported en masse to be present at this game. The respective academies alternate in being "host." The Corps of Cadets and the Regiment of Midshipmen march from their trains on to the playing field, the organization acting as host marching on first. The spectacle of these fine stalwart young men in the gray or blue uniforms is stirring.

During the emergency, these games will probably be discontinued. This nation will be busy playing a different type of football, but your son and your son's son will play again in Army and Navy games and the friendly rivalry between the Services will always carry on the old Annapolis-West Point tradition.

NAVY DAY

Navy Day has been celebrated annually since 1922. The idea of having one day of the year designated as a day on which to know the Navy is credited to Mrs. William H. Hamilton, founder of the National Navy Club of New York. This idea was approved by the Navy Department, and upon its request, the President of the United States proclaimed October 27th as Navy Day. This date, the birthday of the late President Theodore Roosevelt, was selected because his belief in sea power and the development of the Navy during his administration were so great that he has been called the "Father of the modern Navy."

The Navy, for its part, in normal times distributes ships in various ports of each coast to make them available to visitors. The ships are full dressed, and all ships and naval shore establishments hold open house to the public. On board ship, various types of drills are held, airplanes are catapulted, and visitors from miles around are shown through many parts of the ship in order to see how and where sailormen live and work. The people of the nation have their best opportunity to learn at first hand something about the men and material of their Navy. With each such celebration thousands of people board a Navy ship for the first time, an experience that few will ever forget.

It is natural that the Service will ever hold dearest the deeds of its own, but it is most profitable for the sea officer to turn to other navies and to learn something of their great seamen. Nelson, Rodney, and Suffren all impressed their genius on the saga of naval warfare. The daring of Von Muller in the *Emden* as he roamed the Pacific and Goodenough's work in command of the Fifth Light Cruiser Squadron at Jutland will give the officer of any Navy accounts of courage and daring that are worth remembrance.

Who are the most outstanding officers in the United States Navy? Carved on the amphitheater at Arlington are the following names: John Paul Jones, Thomas Truxtun, Edward Preble, Isaac Hull, Stephen Decatur, Oliver Hazard Perry, Thomas MacDonough, Charles Stewart, David Glasgow Farragut, David Dixon Porter, Andrew Hull Foote, John Lorimer Worden, George Dewey, and William Thomas Sampson. These names were selected a few years ago as the most distinguished American naval officers by a committee of admirals, captains, and college presidents. The names comprise a great composite tradition. All of these officers reached an eminence in the Service that few will attain.

However, every man in the Navy of today can look back upon the glorious records of the past and feel proud of the Service to which he belongs. In the dangerous times to come, in the fight for freedom which lies ahead, who knows what opportunities for gallantry may occur, what chances there may be to add his name to that honor roll of men who fostered the traditions and established the customs of our Navy.

Chapter VIII

BUSINESS OF THE NAVAL HOUSEHOLD

It's not leaving Old England we care about,
Not sailing for shores far away.
It's the blooming monotony wears us out
And the prospect of Botany Bay.

SUCCESSFUL Service women are probably, as a group,
the most resourceful, efficient, and brilliant generals in
the entire field of homemaking. Although there are
certain basic problems in any household, the wife of a Navy
man has an entirely different set of housekeeping problems
from those of her Army sister or civilian friend.

Hers is an itinerant household. What she calls home is
literally the place where she hangs her hat. It may be a room
in a modest hotel, or it may be a tiny "efficiency" apartment.
Again, it may be a furnished bungalow with which she will
hate to part. A wonderful offer may even present itself in
the form of the lease of a luxuriously furnished estate, staffed
with expert servants. At some time her husband will probably
be attached to the Naval Academy, to a Navy yard, or to
a naval station. There she may be furnished quarters, and
will enjoy for a time the compensations of a pleasant, pre-
dictable social life.

During her husband's many years of service, she will probably run the gamut of living conditions. If she starts where
most Navy wives do, her first abode may be a boardinghouse,
or a tiny apartment in the purlieus of Long Beach, San Diego,
or Norfolk; if she is very lucky, her husband may finally
reach the post of command of a Naval District, with a large,
well-appointed home and usually a fine vegetable and flower
garden. But whatever the location, whatever the difficulties,
her job is to make the place into a home.

131

To do this the Navy wife must be nothing short of a genius. First of all, she must be a financier. This is a requisite, what with the Army, Navy, Marine Corps, and Coast Guard still carrying on and trying to keep up a standard of living necessary to the morale of the armed forces. With the base pay the same as that established in 1908, this is indeed a trick. In 1922 a new scale of allowances was added, but the base pay remained the same. Consequently, with the increase in the cost of living in the past twenty years, the present pay scale has resulted in a gradual reduction in the standard of living of service personnel as compared to that of most civilians. Somehow, the Navy wife manages!

In many foreign services, an officer is not permitted to marry unless he or his prospective bride has an outside source of income or unless he has attained a rank and age at which his pay is considered adequate to support a wife. As has been stated previously, there are some restrictions upon early marriages in our regular services. Such restrictions are not based upon financial grounds, however, but on professional grounds.

Unless there are outside resources, the maintenance of a suitable standard of living and the making of adequate financial provision for the future necessitates scrupulous care and efficient planning. In other words, in addition to being a financier and a business manager, the Navy wife must be a culinary expert, an interior decorator, an expert in marketing and buying, a finished chauffeur, a perfect hostess, a devoted wife and mother, a social success, and a woman who can make an Ensign's pay stretch from the east coast to the Asiatic Station without ever breaking. A rather large order, isn't it?

However, it has been done and is being done every day by Navy wives—this living and getting along on a shoestring! When you see a group of Navy women at a social affair, they are always well-dressed and beautifully groomed. In diplomatic and civilian circles experienced Navy wives are as much at home as among the members of their own set. More than that, they know what to say to Lord Montrose, how to en-

courage Congressman Smith to indulge in his own favorite
monologue about "what I am going to do for the Navy," and
how to listen interestedly, intelligently, and flatteringly to
the most stodgy old-timers, be they civilians, Generals, or
Admirals. She gets along well with servants and speaks the
kitchen lingo. She has a perfect treasure store of foreign
recipes for dishes which she can prepare and serve herself.
She loves to travel, enjoys different peoples, change of scene;
but most of all, she loves the Service. She is truly a cos-
mopolite!

You, Nancy Lee, when you became a Navy wife, accepted
a definite share of responsibility for the success of your husband's naval career. You cannot meet this responsibility solely
by bestowing upon him your love and kisses. You must have
married for love; no one could be so ignorant as to marry a
naval officer for his money. You may, of course, have been
influenced in your decision by the glamour that surrounds
the Navy, or by a desire for a life of travel and adventure.

Youth is carefree, frequently impatient, prone to resent
official requirements as intrusions on personal rights. Often,
through lack of foresight and planning, and failure to estimate
the ultimate results of its actions, it plunges itself into difficulties whose consequences cannot be eliminated by sorrow,
repentance, or regrets. A wife's carelessness in financial matters or disregard of social proprieties not only reflect upon the
character and intelligence of her husband, as evidenced by his
selection of a wife, but also produce a state of anxiety and
disappointment which cannot but divert his mind from his
work, thereby reducing his efficiency and beginning the wreck-
ing of his career. Those who are old in the service can name
many once promising, efficient young officers whose naval
careers were early blighted by the actions of unworthy wives.

There is, however, also a bright side to the picture. Most
officers who attain high rank concede to their wives a large
part of the credit for the success of their careers. Every favorable impression a Navy wife creates reflects credit upon the

Navy and adds to the prestige of her husband and to the
esteem in which he is held as an officer and a gentleman.

The following suggestions should be helpful to a young
wife who wants to do her share of the Navy job.

THE VALUE OF SYSTEM

To a bride, or to the average newcomer into Navy life,
the realization of future responsibility is a bit bewildering.
She wonders perhaps if she ever will become one of the
charmed circle of successful Navy wives. You will, Nancy
Lee, if you learn to play the game. You are going to find it a
difficult game; but it isn't all hard going, and the joyful
periods are so wonderful that they make up for the trying
ones. It's a life of great possibilities, and it will be just what
you and Bill make of it together.

Every successful business in the world is built upon the
foundation stones of system and records. Without these a
business cannot continue to thrive. The Navy household is
a business, and since Bill will be at sea a large part of the time,
you necessarily are the business manager.

Be Your Own Executive

One of the wisest and best investments for a portion of
your leisure time is a good secretarial course. Enroll in a
short course if there is a possibility of your having to pick up
stakes and move; then, if there is more time, continue your
study. In such a course you will learn not only typing, but
the value of system, methods of filing, and the use of records.
Such a course will make your Navy life easier going. This is
merely a suggestion, but it is one based on the experience of
hundreds of women who have tried it out. Some will always
prefer the trial and error method. They have to learn the
hard way. If that is your disposition, go to it.

To accomplish the maximum in assisting your husband to
complete a successful naval career, it is essential that you
keep certain records. Some of the records herein proposed

must be kept with absolute accuracy; for others their extent and the degree of accuracy depends upon conditions which you will learn only by experience. The records you are advised to keep may seem at first unduly extensive, but none is recommended which will not prove to be worth while in insuring against financial embarrassment, in preventing neglect of social obligations, in increasing your future happiness, and in retaining your husband's respect, love, and devotion.

The materials recommended for use in keeping your records are: a loose-leaf binder to hold paper of standard dimensions, 8½″ x 11″; a card index, with alphabetical guide cards, contained in a small metal box; cards of small size, say 5″ x 3″; a small notebook with pencil, to be carried in your handbag; a small notebook for automobile operation records, to be kept in the glove compartment of the car; a large engagement calendar; and a lightweight metal lock-box of a size large enough to hold your loose-leaf binder. It is desirable that in the top of this box there be a compartment to hold papers which you may find it necessary to keep with you, as noted later.

In addition it is desirable to have a second tin box to hold materials which you constantly require in your daily work. Among such articles you should have the following:

stationery	pencils	scissors
post cards	pens	tape measure
stamps	clips	paste
scratch pad	thumbtacks	checkbook
	account book	

By setting up a bridge table or clearing the dining table in a small apartment, with your material for your records and your work box at hand you will be ready to proceed.

In your loose-leaf binder there should be at least six heavy paper separation sheets, each with a tab to show the nature of the records on the pages immediately following. These tabs should be labeled, in order, Log, Social, Financial, Legal, Automobile, and Dates (calendar, not social).

Your Log

Your log should be a record of events to which, in the future, it may be necessary or desirable to refer in order to refresh your memory. A log is in no sense a diary; it is a record of facts and should be kept free of sentiment and mental wanderings. It is not essential that a log contain daily entries, but the items hereafter noted, if scrupulously recorded, will prove to be of inestimable value.

Your log is especially important when you are moving from one station to another, or for any day in which there occurs any important or unusual event. Notes may be made in your notebook in pencil but should be transferred to your log in ink at the first opportunity. The log should contain data for at least five years; it may be that length of time before your husband's income tax return is finally audited, and during such period you are subject to a call for verification of statements made in your joint income tax returns.

The following items, at least, should be recorded in your log:

1. Departure from a permanent station, stating date and hour of departure, means of transportation used, and names of dependents making the trip. *Such data are required* in making a claim for reimbursement by the government for the transportation of dependents.

2. Expenses during a trip by automobile, from one permanent station to another, for gas, oil, tires, spare parts, and repairs to car, etc. If your husband, traveling under orders, makes the trip with you in the car, he is entitled to claim as deductions from income his actual travel expenses, i.e., the cost of gasoline, oil, etc., for a mileage equal to that between stations, and the cost of his food and lodging for the number of days required to make the trip; but not to exceed the normal period for such a trip. If the wife travels without her husband in the car, travel costs are not deductible from income. They should nevertheless be recorded to form a sound basis for estimating the cost of automobile trips which she may consider making in the future.

3. Arrival at a permanent station after a trip from the last per-

manent station from which transportation at government expense has been authorized, including date and hour of arrival. *These data, likewise, are required* in making a claim for reimbursement.

4. Lodging places and eating places used en route. It is surprising how often some article of value is left in a place where one has eaten a meal or spent the night. If the name of each place is noted, such lost articles frequently may be recovered. Especial note should be made of any place which is particularly desirable; no telling how soon you, or a friend, may pass along the same route.

5. Interesting places visited, or sights seen. Part of life's pleasure is in enjoying previous pleasures in retrospect. Recording of such data will provide a source of much future pleasure. When you are not on the move, entries in your log will be less frequent but possibly not less important. Some of the data hereafter recommended for inclusion in your log should be duplicated in other records, but by placing them in your log you have a more complete record.

6. Leases, or other written agreements made. A record of all matters which may at any future date result in legal complications should be recorded in general terms in your log and in more specific terms in the legal section of your records.

7. Interesting or prominent people met. One of the greatest pleasures of Navy life is the making and renewing of friendships. The round of ports visited by Navy ships varies little from year to year, but months, even years, may pass between your successive visits. To recall past friendships, nothing is more important than records. You should record in your log names and addresses of people you would like to remember, in order to bring their names into association with other events there recorded.

   In addition, names of such people should be filed in your card index, both alphabetically and under the city in which you have met them, and, if not the same, the city in which they live. Much pleasure is lost to many people, especially in the Navy, by failure to contact people who have previously shown a friendly interest.

8. Social obligations incurred and returned. For the sake of association, social obligations incurred or returned should be listed

in your log as well as recorded in the social section of your records.

9. Important events in family life. These will include engagements, weddings, births, illnesses, injuries, and deaths. Dates and hours of births and deaths may frequently in later years be of *unexpected legal importance*.

10. Employment or discharge of any servant, including date and hour. Many states now have an employer's responsibility law, which makes the employer responsible for the support of a servant injured while in his employment. It is important upon discharge of a servant and upon final payment, where such a law exists, to require the servant to *sign a paper*, stating that no injury has been received while in your employ.

Social Records

Your social records in your early life may not be numerous, but they are important and should consist of:

1. A list of initial calls which you and your husband should make, each checked off when made.
2. A list of calls to be returned, checked when made.
3. A list of social obligations. It is desirable that separate lists be made, one for occasions on which both you and your husband were jointly entertained, and one for occasions on which you alone were entertained.
4. A list of social obligations returned. This may consist of a statement of the occasion, its nature, and the list of guests. When obligations are returned, be sure to check them off the list of outstanding obligations.

Financial Records

Your financial records must be accurate and complete. An exact budget is most difficult to figure out and more difficult to live up to under the varying conditions of Navy life, and is not recommended. You and your husband must decide upon a definite financial plan. In this plan you will have a definite monthly allotment, and definite financial obligations to be met. Nothing can more quickly cause a rift in your marital happiness, or more quickly have an adverse effect on your husband's career, than for you to be careless in financial matters. Your records, therefore, should contain, at least, records of the following transactions:

1. Opening or closing of any bank account.
2. A check of your bank balance at the end of each month. Don't forget to consider outstanding checks which may not yet have reached the bank.
3. A statement of all bills paid, dates of payment, and amounts of each. This does not apply to cash purchases. A wife must be especially careful never to leave a port without making adequate provisions to cover all outstanding financial obligations.
4. Although using checks to pay bills costs a few cents per check, such method is desirable in payment of final bills in any port, and in any case where the bill exceeds a few dollars. All canceled checks should be kept in a compartment of your lockbox. In some cases, notably checks which have a bearing on income tax return, canceled checks should be retained at least three years.
5. Payment of any taxes. Certain taxes are legitimate deductions from gross income in income tax returns.
6. Charitable donations. Such donations are deductible from gross income on income tax returns. Any donation should be recorded, and if of $5.00 or over should be made by check.
7. Purchase or sale of any income-bearing stocks, bonds, or other securities or property.
8. Commissions or fees paid to any agent or broker.
9. Money spent on repairs or improvement of any real property owned. When such property is rented, some such expenditures are authorized deductions from income derived from rental.
10. Sums received from any source except your husband. Money received as interest, dividends, etc. must be accurately recorded as to nature, source, amount, and date received.
11. Any insurance premiums paid, such as car insurance, employer's insurance, etc., with name of insurance company, amount, and date.
12. Any money lent or borrowed. Both lending and borrowing are bad practice and should be considered only as an emergency procedure.

13. Notation of any monthly payment such as that on a car or on F.H.A. loan on a mortgage on a house, which must be continued by you in event of your husband's death.

Legal Record

In this section you should record in full any matter which may lead to legal complications, such as:

1. Wills. The date and substance of your latest will and your husband's will should be recorded here. Also a statement of where the original wills are kept, preferably in a safety deposit box at some bank.
2. Leases—the substance of any lease by which you have agreed to rent property from or to another. Copies of such leases should be kept with you in your lock-box.
3. Time of purchases—notation of the property purchased with full description, date, purchase price, down payment, and monthly payment required.
4. A list of insurance policies carried by you or your husband— for each policy, its nature, company, face value, amount of any outstanding loan, if any, etc.
5. Notation of data prepared for claim for pension for widow, and where such papers are filed.
6. Notation of any tickets received for violation of traffic rules and, if any, the fine imposed.
7. Notation of inventory of furniture and equipment of any furnished house or apartment rented by you, and of the checking and release when leaving. Such inventory should be kept in your lock-box.
8. The date and hour of employing or discharging a servant, in states where an employer's compensation law is in effect.
9. Data in regard to federal and state income tax for preceding year, and date of payment.
10. Your power of attorney from your husband. The paper should be kept in your lock-box, with you.

Automobile Record

Your automobile record should contain:

1. A complete identification of your car, including, besides all

the data contained in the registration card, its color, equipment such as radio, heater, etc., the make and identification numbers of tires.

2. License data, state or territory, date of expiration, cost, number. Any special tag or additional license.
3. From whom purchased, date, financing.
4. Location of ownership certificate; from what state or territory present ownership certificate was obtained and when.
5. Auto insurance carried—kind, amount, what company, and date of expiration.
6. Amount of monthly payment on car, if any; date due, paid to whom.

Record of Dates

In this section, arranged by months, you should record the calendar dates of birthdays, anniversaries, or other dates you desire to have recalled to your memory. Being away from her parents, relatives, and friends of her premarriage days, a young wife easily forgets dates. By recording them in this section of your records by months, they may be quickly and easily reviewed.

Card Index

Only your card index remains to be discussed. This is a general depository of information and data. The alphabet guide cards help you to file your data, and in addition you can buy cards of various colors to further subdivide.

Perhaps the most important data are the addresses of your relatives, friends, and acquaintances. Choose a color for address cards, typewrite the name and address, and file under the first letter of the family name, i.e., Miller, Mrs. J. T., 2204 Roland Park Drive, Baltimore, Maryland, Telephone, Roland 8762, and file under "M." It is very desirable, however, to file such addresses also under the name of the city; then in case you are about to visit a city you can, from your card index, review a list of your friends and acquaintances who live there. So choose another color card, say red, for cities, head it Baltimore, place upon it the same data, and file under "B."

You may, of course, use cards of other colors for recording other desirable information, green, perhaps, for salad recipes, yellow for soups, etc. The possibilities are numerous, and by a little concentration you can make your card index a magic box of information and pleasure. You will be surprised to learn to what extent this system of records will add to your enjoyment of Navy life.

To Be Kept in Lock-Box

1. Canceled checks for current year.
2. Power of attorney.
3. Automobile ownership certificate.
4. Auto insurance policy.
5. Copies of leases.
6. Copy of inventory of furniture and equipment of a leased furnished house or apartment.
7. Receipt for donations or for money expended for any purpose which is authorized as a deduction from income in tax returns.
8. Receipts for payment of bill paid by cash.

High Finance in Ensign Circles

A graduate of the Naval Academy is not permitted to marry until he has been an Ensign for two years. Whether or not he is financially able to marry then depends largely upon his careful handling of his finances during his Midshipman days and his first two years at sea.

During the four-year course at the Naval Academy a portion of the Midshipman's pay is withheld in order to provide him upon graduation with a sum adequate to cover the cost of his officer's uniforms and equipment. If he is reasonably economical, this sum, together with the pay due him, should provide, in addition to uniforms and equipment, a moderate replenishment of his civilian outfit. It should also cover, at least in part, his expenses on graduation leave.

At the end of such leave, usually two to four weeks, he reports to his first ship. After reporting for duty, he will be paid mileage at the rate of eight cents a mile from Annapolis to the port in the United States at which he joins his ship, or if proceeding overseas, to the port at which he embarks upon a transport or commercial steamer. Thus it may be assumed that he arrives on board ship fully supplied with naval uniforms and a moderate civilian outfit and, after collection of his mileage, free of debt.

THE ENSIGN'S NECESSARY AND DESIRABLE MONTHLY EXPENSES

An officer, whether married or not, has certain definite expenses, such as his mess bill, which cannot be avoided. There are, in addition, other expenses demanded by normal preparation for the future, a disregard of which frequently leads to later unhappiness and self-incrimination at one's past lack of prudence and foresight. Such inescapable expenses are insurance, savings, and provision for the purchase and operation of a car.

Below, there is presented in parallel columns a carefully considered allocation of the pay and allowances received monthly by an unmarried Ensign, a married Ensign, and a married Lieutenant (junior grade). This is in no sense a suggested budget; it is merely an analysis of necessary and desirable monthly expenditures, with a view to indicating to the prospective Navy wife what may be expected in the field of finance.

This tabulation will give her an idea of the extent of her share of the family income, which if more than $50 for the wife of an Ensign, or about $125 for the wife of a Lieutenant, junior grade, must be obtained by the use of principal saved by the officer before marriage, from outside sources of income, or by the sacrifice of the car or reduction in the advocated financial preparation for the future.

NORMAL EXPENDITURES

| | ENSIGN | | LIEUT. (J. G.) |
	Unmarried	Married	Married
Mess bill	$20.00	$20.00	$20.00
Life insurance	12.80	12.80	12.80
Savings	18.75	18.75	18.75
Car	30.00	45.00	45.00
Clothes	5.00	5.00	5.00
Laundry	2.50	2.50	2.50
Entertainment	25.00	20.00	30.00
Incidentals	5.00	5.00	5.00
	119.05	129.05	139.05
Income tax	6.00	4.00	5.00
	125.05	133.05	144.05
Pay and allow-ances	143.25	183.25	271.50
Excess over ex-penditures	18.20	50.20	127.45

The tabulation indicates in general that in the two-year period after graduation, during which the Ensign is not permitted to marry, a discreet young officer may reasonably be expected to accumulate about $450 in savings, preferably in government baby bonds. He may possibly have an additional $450 as a nest egg, and either own a car or have an additional sum on hand for the purchase of one.

To a prospective bride we offer this advice: Unless your prospective husband's financial situation is as satisfactory as that indicated above, or one of you has outside income, you had better consider postponing your wedding until your fiancé is promoted to Lieutenant, junior grade. We know just how much influence this advice will have, but we've given it and the responsibility is yours. Be frank with each other about financial matters, and make your decisions only after careful consideration of the sacrifices that may be required by marrying without adequate financial preparation.

THE FAMILY INCOME

Unless you, Nancy Lee, or Bill has some income from an outside source, you each will find it necessary to manage your portion of the family income with the utmost care. You should at once prepare a financial plan indicating all fixed charges, such as Bill's mess bill, insurance, and savings, and divide between you the remainder of the family income.

Allotment

One of Bill's first acts after the honeymoon should be to register an allotment to you for such sum as you have agreed upon as your proportion of his monthly pay and allowances. This is the surest method of securing you against financial difficulties in case he is far away on pay day. An allotment is a portion of the officer's pay for the preceding month, a check paid direct to the designated person from the Navy Department in Washington, and mailed on the first day of each month. If you so desire, the check can be mailed direct to you, but on account of frequent changes in your address, it is better to have the allotment made out to the bank in which you expect your funds to be handled. Instruct the bank to place the monthly check to credit in your checking account immediately upon receipt.

BANKING

Every bank account should be registered as a joint account in the name of your husband and yourself; but you should have a mutual agreement that only one of you shall draw on any specific account without previous notice to the other. The advantages of a joint account are that if one of you should be incapacitated the other can draw on the account, and also, in the event of death of either, the money in such an account becomes the sole property of the other without litigation.

INSURANCE

Life insurance is essential for a married officer, and most desirable for every officer. As the insurance rate depends upon age at the time the policy is taken out, insurance should be obtained immediately upon graduation. Because of its cheaper rate, *ordinary life insurance* is preferable to types known as endowment or fixed-term payment, i.e., "twenty payment life," which means one stops paying premiums after twenty years. About one-tenth of one's monthly income should be devoted to insurance of various kinds.

Government life insurance, now known as United States Services Insurance, is available to all personnel in the naval service, but to obtain such insurance a person must make application for it within 120 days from the date of entering the service—considered for Ensigns as the date of graduation. It is the cheapest form of life insurance and because of the limited time during which it is available should be the first taken out.

An Ensign upon graduation immediately should apply for a $10,000 policy, the maximum amount of such insurance permitted. If he is twenty-two years old, the premium if paid monthly is $12.80. This is the amount previously shown as the cost of insurance in the tabulation of an officer's expenses. Steps should be taken immediately after marriage to record the bride as the beneficiary of any current life insurance policies.

As soon as your financial situation warrants, not later than the date of your husband's promotion to Lieutenant, senior grade, his life insurance should be increased. At this time careful consideration should be given to taking out a policy with the Navy Mutual Aid Association. It has but one type of policy, paying $7500. You will find the rate lower than in most insurance companies.

As soon as practicable after the birth of each child an educational insurance policy should be obtained to insure funds for its education.

Insurance on household and personal effects against fire and robbery is not unduly expensive and may safeguard you against serious financial loss.

Automobile insurance, at least against public liability and property damage, is imperative. The United Services Automobile Association of Fort Sam Houston, Texas, is a mutual company of long standing, organized and managed by Army officer personnel. Its premiums to service personnel are lower than those of most automobile insurance companies, and its service is of the highest.

Marine insurance to cover oversea transportation of household effects, or of an automobile, is comparatively expensive, but may save a large financial loss.

As a general precaution, you should read each clause of any insurance policy and be sure that you understand its full meaning. Some such policies are so worded that it takes practically a legal mind to understand them, but stick with it. Any reputable insurance firm will be glad to interpret its policy for you, gratis.

SAVINGS AND INVESTMENTS

Foresight demands the immediate initiation of some form of savings plan. In these days of low interest on savings accounts, the Ensign will be wise to purchase government baby bonds. Each bond costs $18.75 and is redeemable for $25.00 ten years from date, thus yielding nearly three per cent per year at compound interest. Such bonds are redeemable at any date, in case of necessity, but at a reduced interest rate. The cost of purchase of one such bond per month is not too much to put into savings.

INCOME TAX

It is a common and erroneous belief in civilian circles that government employees are exempt from taxes. Under the present federal personal income tax law a husband and wife may file a joint income tax return. If the wife has an income from any outside source, she must keep an accurate record of sums received, with the date of receipt and source of such income.

Borrowing

It is a poor policy to borrow money from friends or relatives. A bank or finance company is the proper place to borrow money. Avoid all unknown loan associations or "loan sharks." Apply first if possible to your own bank or to the Federal Services Finance Corporation. This is a reliable organization and is accustomed to handling Service loans. It has branches in nearly all places where a large number of Service people are situated.

Power of Attorney

In order to permit the wife to obtain automobile licenses, etc. and to dispose of joint property in an emergency, she should be furnished with a duly certified "power of attorney" to act for her husband. Legal blanks for this purpose are available at all Navy yards.

Buying a Car

Although an automobile is not absolutely essential in all stations, it is a great convenience. Modern life seems to center around a car, and the Navy family usually owns a fairly good one even if the home is a one-room apartment. Very often it is bought on the installment plan. Often a second-hand car will serve the purpose of a short stay.

A definite sum of as much as $30 per month should be set aside by a young officer with a view to the purchase and operation of a car.

If the wife is given power of attorney it is desirable that the car be registered in both husband's and wife's names as joint owners.

Look Before You Lease

Just as it is highly important to read over every clause of an insurance policy, so it is equally important to read over every sentence of a rental lease. In view of the temporary plans, both civilian and naval, most landlords rent apartments on the basis of at least one month's occupancy, after which at least ten days' notice is required to terminate the contract. The present shortage of houses and apartments in defense centers is making it increasingly difficult to rent without a lease.

In leases extending for more than a month you should insist on a Navy clause which reads about like this:

In case the said ———— ————, Lieutenant, U.S.N., is detached from his present station, or the ship in which he is serving is permanently detached from the Naval force based in this area, this lease may be vacated upon ten days' notice.

Avoid breaking a lease, for such a procedure is legally and ethically wrong. In addition, it may bring upon you a lawsuit which will have a serious effect on your husband's record and bring discredit upon the Navy. Frequently it is possible to sublet or obtain a new client for your landlord who is willing to take your lease.

WILLS

Both husband and wife should make wills. These should make disposition of all property either jointly or separately owned, and should cover the contingency that both might be killed in the same accident. Even the mention of a "last will and testament" in some families is something to be feared and put off, yet failure to make adequate wills is one of the most frequent causes of strain and confusion in bereaved families. In addition, every well-advised officer should talk over with his wife just what disposition should be made of insurance and any properties that they may own. The sensible wife will want her husband's advice as to investments, annuities, and the safeguarding of her future and that of any children they may have. In the event of his death she will be grateful for his careful planning and interest, and it may save her many financial worries.

A wife should make a will even if she possesses only small

keepsakes and little of this world's goods. She may have trinkets, jewelry and linens, pieces of furniture that she would like given to certain members of her own family or to particular friends. At the time of death, and in the stress and strain of readjustment, valuable possessions which should rightly go to designated friends and relatives are often hastily sold or given away. A will simplifies problems of this sort.

While we are on the subject of wills, there is another important point that is sometimes unpleasant to discuss. Officers and their wives should talk over and come to some decision about where each wishes to be buried. Written instructions to this effect should be left. Family burial plots should be considered, especially if there are children.

A *will* is nothing more than a legal instrument whereby a person disposes of his property in the manner he wishes.

A *testator* is the person who makes and leaves a will in force at his death. A *codicil* is a postscript or addition to a will that must be executed with the same legal formalities as the will itself. An *executor* or *executrix* is the person designated by the testator to carry out the provisions of the will. A wife may be chosen as the executrix of her husband's will, or vice versa.

The *probating* of a will consists of presenting the will to the office of the Registrar of Wills in the county where the deceased had his legal residence.

A WILL MUST BE IN WRITING. The law in most states requires two witnesses. It is well to consult an attorney in drawing up a will, but if that is not possible, then make out a very simple one. An attorney will acquaint you with statute laws of the state in which the will is to be probated, and of any legal angles on which you should be informed.

When one dies without leaving a will, the law considers him to have died intestate. Then the state steps in and distributes the estate through an appointed county administrator, and according to the then existing state laws of descent and inheritance—a share for the wife, shares for children, shares for parents, etc. This method may or may not suit, but even if it should, it is expensive to resort to such litigation. A publicly appointed administrator is entitled by law to fees and is usually disinterested in economical handling of property.

Short Form of a Simple Will

All my estate I devise and bequeath to my wife, for her own use and benefit forever, and I hereby appoint her my executrix, without bond, with full power to sell, mortgage, lease, or in any other manner dispose of the whole or any part of my estate.

Dated April 10, 1942   WILLIAM SATTERLEE TYLER

Subscribed, sealed, published, and declared by William Satterlee Tyler, testator above named, as and for his last will in the presence of each of us, who at his request and in his presence, in the presence of each other, at the same time, have hereto subscribed our names as witnesses this April 10, 1942, at the city of San Diego, California.

....
Witness   Address
....
Witness   Address

The marriage of a man and the birth of his child, subsequent to the making of a will by him, have the effect of revoking such a will in many states. A new will must be made.

Joint bank accounts have been mentioned before. Remember, if cash is deposited in the bank in the husband's name only, his wife cannot draw it out until the will is probated, even though he left it to her by will.

Another technicality in regard to bank accounts is this: It is possible in most states to carry a joint bank account and most banks have a specially prepared contract form setting out the legal status of the account. Such an account is the property of both parties (husband and wife). The contract should contain the provision John Doe and Mary Doe with right of survivorship and not as tenants in common.

If a bank account is in one name only and that individual dies, then the account is frozen and the deposit put in the hands of the executor or administrator.

It is wise to talk these matters over with an officer of the bank with which you are doing business. Banking laws in different states and possessions vary, but the subject is current with the bank's officials, and they can offer positive and valuable advice.

Safety Deposit Box

A safety deposit box in your bank is a suitable place to file wills, deeds, stock and bond ownership certificates, certified copy of your wedding certificate, and a certified copy of birth certificates of each member of the family. The Navy Mutual Aid, if your husband is a member, will keep on file all records for obtaining a pension. It is a great convenience to have all such data in one place.

There are three ways in which a title may be taken to a safety deposit box. Each has its respective merits and also its drawbacks. The first is individual ownership, in which case the box is absolutely private to the owner, but in case of his death, it can be entered only in the presence of a representative of the probate court.

The second method is "joint tenancy" for a husband and wife, in which case each may enter the box independently of the other. However, if either party dies, the box is sealed and may be opened only in the presence of a representative of the State Tax Commission, the purpose being to discover any assets which may be held subject to inheritance taxes.

The third method and probably the best for Service personnel who are married is "individual ownership with appointed deputy." This is nothing more than the first method, except that the box owner appoints a deputy who may enter the box. Actually the owner gives a power of attorney to the deputy, but it is limited in scope to entry and use of the box.

Necessary Papers for Personal File

Many government claims are unduly delayed because of not having at hand properly certified copies of birth and marriage certificates and divorce decrees. Usually an officer takes care of each of these items and does not leave the responsibility to beneficiaries. However, it is good business experience for a Navy wife to know exactly how to handle her business affairs in case of the death of her husband.

First of all, she should know exactly where all the necessary papers, including legal documents such as birth and marriage certificates, insurance policies, etc., are filed. If an officer is a member of the Navy Mutual Aid, this organization will take care of all such papers and will also assist the widow in filing her various government claims. It is wise for a husband and wife to read over and check the following points:

1. Last will and testament. I have made a will. Check when accomplished and where it is filed.
2. U.S. government life insurance policy.
3. Commercial insurance. Forms required: Proofs of death, obtainable from company when death occurs. Beneficiary's age must be proved if insurance proceeds are payable as life income.

Information in Regard to Birth and Marriage Certificates

Probably 75 per cent of people over thirty-five years of age are under the impression that they cannot obtain birth certificates. An officer or enlisted man does not need a birth certificate except in cases of obtaining a passport; however, it is always desirable to have it on file. Practically everyone can obtain a birth certificate if he writes to the proper office of record.

No governmental agency will settle a claim without the proper certified copy of the record of birth and marriage, if it is possible to secure same. From this it may be seen that church records, records of family Bibles, affidavits of parents, "the beautifully engraved certificate given you by the minister who performed the marriage ceremony" are all inadequate. What you *must* have is: *a certified copy of birth and marriage record* issued under *seal* by that office.

If a record of birth is absolutely nonexistent, and according to the book, *Custodians of Public Records,* it is shown that state records were not kept previous to certain dates, then other proofs are acceptable. In these cases, where other proof, in the form of affidavits, is accepted, accompanying the affidavit must be a certified statement from a state or county official verifying that no public record of the birth or marriage is obtainable for the period in which the birth or marriage occurred. That being established, it then is permissible to establish proof in the following ways:

1. *A certified copy* of a church record if the child was baptized in a church. Many churches maintain such records and the present registrar of the church will make a sworn statement of the record.
2. *Sworn statement of doctor who officiated at the birth of the child.* In many cases this cannot be obtained, owing to the death of the doctor or removal from community. If obtainable, the doctor must swear to it before a notary.
3. *Sworn statement of two witnesses present* at the time of the child's birth. This affidavit must be made by individuals who knew both parents at the time of and before the birth. They do not actually have to have been present at the birth itself, but must certify that they knew of the birth and of the naming of the child.
4. *Notarized certificates* from entry in family Bibles of the birth. There are many avenues for fraud in making certificates from entries in family Bibles; therefore, such certificates may be refused and other proof required. Or the family Bible may have to be produced.
5. Request Veterans' Administration to obtain from Bureau of Census the record of the family from first record of the Census which was made *after the birth of the child.* This method is used only as a last resort.

There is an unending delay in the settling of claims while waiting for proofs of age, so all of these details should be in order and in the business file of the officer.

PHOTOSTATIC COPIES

Again, there is much bad information and misunderstanding in regard to photostats. They are acceptable only when made from the official record by the bureau of vital statistics or other official agency in charge of public record. Before a photostat is made, a marginal endorsement must certify that it is an official photostat of the public record. It then must be signed under the seal of the issuing office.

Whenever a widow is claiming pension or compensation for the death of a husband, and it is shown that either the deceased or the widow or both had a previous marriage, a certified copy of the divorce proceedings must be obtained and submitted before the right of the claimant can be established. This copy should be obtained from the court which granted the divorce. It is wise to get this record at once, when it is easiest, as many cases are on record of courthouses burning and records being destroyed.

Getting Ahead

Whenever it is possible to get ahead financially because of some condition in a given place, you can be sure that your next move will not have these charming facilities. It is wise to keep this fact in mind. For instance, service on an isolated station such as Guam or Samoa, where clothes and servants are at a minimum, will give you a chance to catch your breath after a year's duty in Washington. The expenses of a "floating naval household" vary so much according to individual locations and specific circumstances that it takes careful planning and wise spending to get ahead and stay there. A married naval officer supports two establishments, and the old saying that two can live as cheaply as one is an exploded theory.

Chapter IX

THE BRIDE IS ENTERTAINED
AND RETURNS HER OBLIGATIONS

Jack dances and sings, and is always content,
    In his vows to his lass he'll ne'er fail her,
His anchor's a-trip when his money's all spent—
    And this is the life of a sailor!
        (From Dibdin's *The Yankee Sailor*)

IN NAVY circles there is a certain informality about extending invitations to small social affairs. However, if the entertainment is of an official nature, such as a reception, a dinner on board ship, or a formal At Home, then the greatest formality is observed, both in extending and in accepting the invitation.

Formal invitations, whether they are engraved or written by hand, are always in the *third* person. Good usage demands that acceptances and regrets be written in the same person.

The telephone is the means of conveying many invitations; and out of this custom has grown another very modern practice, that of sending the reminder card. It is strictly an American institution, and probably a very smart way of recalling to the prospective guest's mind that the invitation was issued by word of mouth, either over the telephone or vis-à-vis. This may prove quite satisfactory for the hostess who has a social secretary and who entertains a great deal; but it seems really more simple to send out written invitations in the first place.

Often the hostess will find that telephoning her invitations is quite a task, if the party is a large one. What with busy signals, leaving messages for those not at home, and long enforced conversations with those at home, this method takes more time than writing notes. So the written invitation is again gaining favor whether it be formal, informal, or written on a visiting card.

Few Navy people are so formal, except those on legation duty or in Washington, that they send out engraved invitations for dinner. An exception to this is a collective invitation such as the following:

> The Wardroom Officers of the U.S.S. California
> request the pleasure of
> General and Mrs. Eugene Stuart's
> company at dinner
> on Saturday, the twelfth of November
> at seven o'clock

Ship's boat will leave from
Pico Landing at six-thirty

A formal invitation is always answered in handwriting, and the hour as well as the day is repeated so that there will be no mistake. For example:

> General and Mrs. Eugene Stuart
> accept with pleasure the kind invitation of
> The Wardroom Officers of the U.S.S. California
> to dinner on Saturday, the twelfth of November
> at seven o'clock

If it is impossible for you to accept, the form used is:

> General and Mrs. Eugene Stuart
> regret that they are unable to accept the kind invitation of
> The Wardroom Officers of the U.S.S. California
> on Saturday, the twelfth of November

A formal invitation by a group of officers will usually read something as follows:

> The Commander-in-Chief and Officers
> of the United States Fleet
> request the pleasure of your company
> at a reception
> to be held on board the U.S.S. Pennsylvania
> on Saturday afternoon, the tenth of September
> from four until six o'clock

Boats leave from
Pier 10   R.S.V.P.

In the lower right- or left-hand corner, instead of R.S.V.P.,
may be written, "Please reply to flag lieutenant."

Your acceptance or refusal, written by hand on a good
grade of plain white notepaper, should read:

Lieutenant and Mrs. John Pelly Bright
accept with pleasure the kind invitation of
The Commander-in-Chief and Officers
of the United States Fleet
to a reception to be held on board the U.S.S. Pennsylvania
on Saturday afternoon, the tenth of September
from four until six o'clock

Form invitations, which are sometimes printed but are
preferably engraved, are often used for formal dinners. Blank
forms may be filled in, as:

_____

request the pleasure of

_____

company at dinner

on_____ the _____

at _____

The acceptance or refusal should be written within twenty-
four hours, and should follow the exact wording of the invitation. Under no circumstances should a dinner invitation be
accepted conditionally, nor should you ask your hostess if you
can give a reply later.

FORMAL AT HOME INVITATION

At Home
On Thursday, November the fifth
from five until seven o'clock
Chief of Naval Operations House
Observatory Circle

The Informal Written Dinner Invitation

Dear Mrs. Tyler:

Will you and Mr. Tyler (or Ensign Tyler) (or Bill) have dinner (or dine) with us on Friday evening, the sixth of June, at seven-thirty o'clock.

Looking forward to the pleasure of having you with us,

Very sincerely,

Anne Sinclair Barrington

If you accept, you write:

My dear Mrs. Barrington:

We shall be very happy to dine with you and Captain Barrington on Friday, the sixth of June, at seven-thirty o'clock. Thank you so much for asking us.

Most sincerely yours,

Nancy Lee Tyler

If you must decline, then it is imperative to state some reason. It is exceedingly ill mannered to decline without offering an excuse.

My dear Mrs. Barrington:

We are so sorry that we cannot dine with you on Friday, the sixth of June, as we are going to White Sulphur for the week end.

Thanking you for your kindness in thinking of us,

Most sincerely,

Nancy Lee Tyler

Calling-card Invitations and "Informals"

It is customary to use the printed "informals" that are growing so in popularity or a calling card for invitations to luncheons, bridge, tea, and informal dances.

Wednesday, May 15
at one o'clock
Mrs. James Spencer Drew

Luncheon   Pierre's

or:

> *Mrs. James Spencer Drew*
>
> Lunch
> One o'clock   Pierre's
> Wednesday, May 15   R.S.V.P.

This invitation requires an answer at once, the same as a dinner invitation.

If an "informal" or foldover card is used, on the front of the card will be engraved the name of the hostess, and on the inside will be written:

Dear Nancy Lee:

Will you give me the pleasure of lunching with me on Wednesday, May 15, at Pierre's at one o'clock?

I do hope that you can come.

Sincerely yours,
KITTY DREW

COCKTAIL PARTIES

> *Captain and Mrs. William Blake*
> Cocktails   Officers' Club
> 5 to 7   Submarine Base
>   Saturday, July 10

This is the informal invitation to which a written answer may or may not be made. The same holds good for a tea. However, it is a courteous gesture to accept or decline every invitation.

When on foreign duty, an invitation should be replied to in the language of the invitation. French still remains the language of etiquette and diplomacy, though what may take its place in the future—*quien sabe?*

THE TELEPHONED INVITATION

In this modern age, invitations are frequently very casual. Usually the Navy wife keeps an engagement book or social calendar near her telephone and makes a note of her engagements when she receives them. This also proves a good check when one is making up a guest list.

Invitations should not be left with servants and children, although it is quite permissible to leave your number and ask to be called. If you have any choice in the matter, do not indulge in long conversations. It is not considerate to use the telephone for social visits. It is very exasperating to try to get a number only to have it busy because some thoughtless person is chattering.

The telephoned invitation may go something like this:

Mrs. Tyler, this is Elaine McComas speaking. Will you and your husband have dinner with us (or with Admiral McComas and me) on Saturday evening at eight o'clock at the Yacht Club?

Telephone Etiquette

When answering the telephone, before you know who is calling it is quite correct to say simply, "Hello," or "Mrs. Tyler speaking," or "Lieutenant Tyler's quarters" or "residence." Guessing games with names went out when you stopped playing with dolls. The British say "Are you there?" In a social conversation, always say, if you are doing the calling: "This is Nancy Lee Tyler calling." Never say, "This is Mrs. Tyler calling" to a friend or social acquaintance. Should you be phoning a business firm, say, "This is Mrs. William Tyler." Be sure to give your full name and your address before placing your order.

In answer to the question, "May I speak to Mrs. Tyler?" avoid such an abrupt and careless answer as, "Speaking." Life isn't so hurried that it takes too much time to say, "This is Nancy Lee Tyler speaking," or "This is Mrs. Tyler speaking."

Entertaining in the Navy

The average Navy bride, when she and her husband first join a new station, is not overwhelmed with invitations and social courtesies. Your social life will probably start out something like this: callers at first (though you and Bill should make the first call on the Captain of his ship or on his immediate Commanding Officer); then dinner on board Bill's ship will follow, where you will likely be the guest of honor; the Captain's wife may have you to luncheon; perhaps the Executive and his wife will invite you and Bill to dinner or to a cocktail party; then there will be other small informal dinners, teas, bridge breakfasts and luncheons, and Dutch-treat parties given by your contemporaries. Some time during the year the Admiral and his wife may give a reception; again, you may be invited to large teas, concerts, or cocktail parties given by prominent civilians who have elaborate homes and are cordial to naval officers and their families. The last two mentioned social affairs are seldom, if ever, returned by officers in the junior grades.

Navy people usually entertain their civilian friends on board ship and their Navy friends in their own modest homes. Each group seems to prefer this method, and the average civilian or Army guest is quite flattered to be invited on board ship for luncheon or dinner. A meal in the ship's mess is a distinct compliment and is quite different from the usual form of entertainment.

Young Navy couples are not expected to give large, expensive, formal parties, though they do have a very definite obligation to return in some way the social courtesies shown them. A formal dinner (should you be invited by a Captain or Commander) may be returned by a simple home dinner, a small dinner party at a club, hotel, or restaurant, or a buffet supper, a luncheon, a picnic, or a cocktail party.

Remember, every Admiral was an Ensign once, and many of the senior officers' wives have been Ensigns' wives. They know your problems, both social and financial, *first hand*. You will find them most understanding, sympathetic, and thoroughly appreciative of your efforts in returning your obligations. Expensive and formal entertainments by junior officers (even those with an outside income) are definitely frowned upon, and not in keeping with the customs of the Service.

Young Navy couples frequently meet in each other's apartments and cook dinner together. A movie, dancing, or bridge, often played "for love" (no stakes involved), usually concludes the evening. Navy people are generally very frank with each other in regard to finances, since everyone knows to the penny exactly what each officer in each grade draws as a salary. There is no competitive spending or dressing, no "keeping up with the Joneses"; and living beyond one's income causes nothing but adverse comment and criticism from one's contemporaries and seniors.

Reserve Officers and their wives sometimes find the required entertaining and repaying of social obligations a bit strenuous. The most important thing to remember is this: Every social obligation should be returned, but it is not necessary to *repay in kind.*

The Navy Bride at Home

"Home at last," sighs Bill, giving you the traditional kiss as he carries you across the threshold of your new home! He has probably asked you to keep your eyes closed for the big surprise. You are willing, because he is so proud and happy over the fact that he has been able to find an apartment in Honolulu when they are so terribly scarce. Jim McKinley, a classmate, got sudden orders to the Navy Yard at Norfolk, and as is customary in Navy circles, he passed the word on to Bill that his apartment would be for rent.

Your first home—you can scarcely contain your happiness. Right off you want to start unpacking and get settled. Upon exploring the studio apartment, you can see that it won't take long to get settled, nor will your housekeeping duties be arduous.

The studio apartment consists of one large room with one end arranged for dining, a small kitchenette, and an attractive bath with a built-in dressing table and plenty of wardrobe and storage space. The most attractive feature is that it is comparatively new. Done in modernistic style, with native stick wicker and bright cherry hangings, it appears very comfortable. There is a large *hiki-ee* slip-covered to harmonize with the hangings. A *hiki-ee* is a Hawaiian name for a double bed, which consists of a set of double springs set on a frame. It is used on a *lanai* or porch as a couch, in bedrooms, and often in combination living and bedrooms as a bed by night and a couch by day. There are two comfortable chairs. There is a drop-leaf table at one end of the living room which does duty as a dining table, as a writing desk, as a bridge table, or when not in use as a merely ornamental piece of furniture! There is a small bookcase, and lamps that you don't like. But cheer up, for you can always buy attractive, inexpensive shades to suit your taste at the dime store. There are four straight chairs scattered about the room, enough for bridge and extra guests.

The kitchen is fully equipped (so your landlord claims), but you may have to fill in with a few extra utensils from the dime store. The same goes for dishes and glassware. Everything looks new, and the kitchen in a neat color scheme of blue and white tile is a dream. How thankful you are that your mother insisted on your taking a cooking course, and what a surprise you have in store for Bill. Of course you realize you have a lot of culinary skill to acquire, but at any rate you are not as helpless as the mid-Victorian bride who boasted that she did not know how to boil water.

You and Bill think it all rather comfy and nice, but just how modern and nice it is you won't realize, my pet, until you have lived around and about in furnished rooms, small crowded hotels, and in accommodations that will make your honeymoon apartment look like a palace. Enjoy it while you may!

Even the drive to Pearl Harbor (this, of course, was before December 7, 1941), through the maze of endless traffic, seems wonderful, and all too soon you arrive at the Navy Commissary. Bill arranges for a commissary card, then with a hurried good-by leaves you in this huge government Piggly-Wiggly with the advice to stock up the pantry because you will soon be having company, he expects.

The following list is submitted only as a guide for the stocking of your pantry:

1 pound coffee
1 box tea
5 pounds sugar
5 pounds flour
5 pounds potatoes
3 pounds onions
1 pound crackers
1 box macaroni
1 box spaghetti
½ pound bacon
1 dozen eggs
1 box salt
1 box black pepper
1 box red
　pepper(?)
1 box white
　pepper(?)
1 bottle Kitchen
　Bouquet
1 vanilla extract
1 almond
　extract(?)
1 paprika
1 curry powder

1 box cinnamon
1 box nutmeg
1 box whole cloves
1 jar bouillon cubes
1 bottle tomato
　catsup
1 bottle tomato
　sauce
1 bottle Worcester-
　shire sauce
1 bottle Tabasco
　sauce
1 bottle cider
　vinegar
1 can salad oil
1 pound loaf sugar
1 pound powdered
　sugar
1 pound brown
　sugar
6 boxes Jello or
　gelatin
　dessert(?)

1 jar honey (?)
1 jar preserves
1 jar silver polish
1 brass polish
1 baking powder
1 baking soda
3 pounds rice
1 can sirup
1 box soap flakes
1 box laundry
　starch
1 bottle bluing
3 cans tomato juice
3 cans tomato paste
3 cans tomatoes
1 box cocktail
　toothpicks
1 can peanuts
1 can popcorn
canned soups
fruit juices
matches

Small-size cans of staples such as tomatoes, soups, and fruit juices are economical when cooking for one or two persons. This is a fairly complete list, but it may be modified to suit your needs.

Your First Guests

Before you really have your bearings, some afternoon Bill will bring Miles Stearley and another classmate home from the ship with him quite without warning. Perhaps he will ask them by for a drink, but don't be fooled. What he really wants is to show them you and his recently acquired home. He knows you are wonderful. They will think so too if you can

disappear into the kitchen for a moment, whip up some tooth-
some canapés and appear bearing the fruits of your morning's
planning. A good trick is to keep a small covered dish of
highly seasoned Philadelphia cream cheese in the refrigerator
to be spread on crackers. With olives you have a feast on hand.
Or you may have only that can of fresh peanuts on your
pantry shelf, but it will be the little extra touch that turns
the drink into a celebration.

There will be much toasting at this little impromptu house-
warming, and Bill will probably lead off with the familiar
Navy toast as he raises his glass to his guests and says, "Glad
to have you aboard." The visitors' response is, "Glad to be
aboard." Or Bill may simply say, "Here's how," the response
being an answering "How."

This type of gathering often turns into a dinner party, and
you will cordially invite Bill's shipmates to share potluck with
you. When you say it, mean it. This is the supreme test of the
seafaring man's wife—her welcoming of her husband's shipmates.

Your emergency shelf will prove a life saver, and even if
it does make you exceed your weekly food allowance now
and then, in the end it is cheaper than taking your guests to
a hotel or restaurant for dinner. The plain dinner can easily
be turned into a company dinner provided the pièce de
résistance can be stretched to include visitors.

Your guests will be impressed with your culinary ability and
ingenuity, your husband will marvel at your cleverness, and
everything will be lovely.

EMERGENCY SHELF

Canned soups
Canned specialties: anchovies, cocktail sausages, sandwich spreads,
    preserves, jellies, plum and fig puddings
Canned meats (whole chicken or chicken à la king, expensive
    but worth it)
Canned ham
Canned tuna

Canned crabmeat
Canned vegetables: peas, mushrooms, sweet potatoes, spinach, celery, asparagus, artichoke hearts
Canned fruits: pineapple, pears, peaches for salads, whole greengage plums, or apricots
Canned corned beef hash

Luncheon, the first few days in your new home, will be a mythical repast, probably consisting of a glass of milk. Finally, you are unpacked and shipshape. Dinner is planned and you have had a short siesta. You decide to go over to the beach and take a swim.

Suddenly you realize that it is three-thirty, and this is the day you must be at the boat landing by four o'clock to meet Bill. After a hectic drive through the afternoon traffic, you see him at the end of a long line of higher-ranking officers step out of the trim officers' boat. His face lights up at sight of you, and he hurries over to the car. Then a shocked expression comes over his face, and the following conversation takes place:

"Nancy Lee, darling, you're not dressed!"

Hastily you adjust the pretty bandanna scarf tied under your chin.

"But of course, Bill, I've been to the beach and just left there in time to get here. I have on a jacket, and after all, in the car I was sure I was all right. No one can see my bathing suit. Is this the Paradise of the Pacific, or isn't it?"

"But sweetheart, in the Navy you must always be dressed to receive callers from four o'clock until six in the afternoon, and for the next few weeks, since you are a bride, all the officers on the ship and their wives will call on us. It is the only way you will get to know anyone here. Afterwards we'll have to return the calls and so we'll have to be dressed for that. That is just the way things are done IN THE NAVY."

In the Navy—hmmm! Seems you have heard that expression quite a number of times since your wedding day. You wonder if he must always say it in capital letters? Also, you suddenly wonder what they're doing back home in Pinecrest right now!

RECEIVING CALLERS

Bill was right as rain. No sooner had you reached home and stepped into the shower than the doorbell rang. He answered the door, invited the visitors to come in, and explained that you were dressing and would be right out. Secretly you made a promise to yourself that this situation would never arise again!

Nothing went right. Where were the gray slippers for your prettiest afternoon dress? Time was passing, and your hair grew more stubborn with each fresh attempt to do it the way Bill liked it. At last you were ready to make your appearance, but the guests, having stayed their twenty minutes, were getting ready to leave as you stepped into the living room. Bill urged them to stay, but the Lieutenant Commander's wife, after a rather stiff "How do you do" to you, insisted that they had several other calls to make and must be going.

You felt crushed and just about ready to burst into tears, but the bell rang again, and more callers arrived. This time you were ready!

The call went much better, since both you and Bill relaxed. The Captain and his wife were very gracious, and the older woman reminded you a lot of your own mother. They stayed a little longer than twenty minutes and you were sorry to have them go. The talk was general and the officers did not talk shop. You noted that they left cards—two of the visiting officer's, one for you and one for your husband, and one of his wife's, for you. This is an easy way to remember about cards. A lady *never* calls socially on a man; so she leaves a card for each adult woman only. An officer leaves a card for each person called on.

On the small silver card tray which was one of your wedding gifts you found the cards of the first callers. Their joint card read Lieutenant Commander and Mrs. James Russel

King, and it was accompanied by one of Commander King's personal cards.

Immediately after the last callers' departure, you should be prompt to list the calls and the date beside the names in a small engagement book. Even when cards are left, sometimes they are misplaced, and you may forget to return an important call. This is a breach of etiquette on the part of junior officers that is not lightly passed over in Navy circles. Formal calls should be returned within ten days or two weeks.

RETURNING CALLS

How very important first impressions are in the Navy! A young officer is the cynosure of all eyes in his ship. His bride is equally so in the social circles of the Navy.

You must be very careful about returning calls promptly because many older officers attach great importance to this. A formal call should not exceed twenty minutes' duration. Never prolong a call until the farewell becomes a relief for both you and your hostess.

Many young Ensigns and their wives do not know when and how to make their departure. Once you have risen to leave, do so, by all means. In the Army, lingering at the door is called "doing a rug dance." In the Navy it ought to be called "dragging your anchor"!

It is not good taste to make a ten-minute call, but it is certainly worse to make one that lasts three hours and forces your hosts to ask you to stay to dinner. If a servant answers the door, present your cards to him. If the door is opened by a member of the family, place your cards in the card tray on a convenient table.

The bride wears a pretty afternoon dress with her most becoming hat; or if tailored clothes are more to her liking, then a very smart spectator sports dress or suit with an appropriate hat and accessories is quite correct. White gloves used to be always worn (possibly to keep the cards spotless), but now light gloves or whatever your costume calls for in the way of gloves are quite correct.

Bill, armed with a city map, a local Navy directory of officers' shore addresses, and an envelope or cardcase containing your calling cards and his, is ready for the return calls. At each home, whether the occupants are in or out, cards are left according to the procedure given above. Should there be a mother visiting the family, you will each leave an extra card. If there is a father visiting the family, Bill will leave one of his own cards in addition to the original two. As each call is completed, a good plan is to mark it off your list, since sometimes you confuse people, and it would be as ridiculous to call on one couple twice within a short time as it would be rude not to return some other call with the mistaken idea that it had already been repaid.

If you call on officers and families in apartments or hotels and they are not at home, it is well to see that the calling cards are placed in an envelope and addressed to them before being placed in the key box or mail box. This prevents some very embarrassing situations in which the clerks have put the cards in the wrong box.

Some senior officers have also requested that those who call please write their address on their cards.

BILL HAS THE DUTY

Now for the first time the realization comes to you that you are a real Navy wife. Bill will not be at home at four o'clock as usual, since he is in the "duty section." He must stay aboard until the following day, but your heart sings as you dress to go out to see him on board. What shall you wear? Why, Bill's favorite, of course! The aquamarine silk jersey afternoon dress with the close-fitting hat of the same material. It matches your eyes and brings out the gold in your hair, and you are happy as you take a last glance at yourself in the mirror.

Bill said to be at the boat landing at four-thirty and the officers' motorboat would be waiting. You are fifteen minutes early, because already you are learning in the Navy that no one is fashionably late! The remembrance of your first callers and your not being ready to receive them is still with you. Strange rumblings issue from the loud-speaker at the landing, and at last your boat is announced.

One of several enlisted men who make up the boat crew, or some officer who may be returning to the ship, will help you into the motorboat. Long ere this, we trust, you have been schooled in the difference between a boat and a ship, it being one of the cardinal sins in the Navy to call a "ship" a "boat." Usually a boat, my dear girl, is something to be hoisted aboard a ship. A ship is never a boat; it hurts the ears of any Navy man to hear his magnificent battleship referred to as a boat. Boats are small craft, carried by ships (lifeboats, sailboats). Now that is straight.

The fifteen-minute ride out to the ship is fun. There are several other wives aboard, apparently going out on the same mission. You will pass many black camouflaged hulls in the harbor. Finally your boat draws up alongside a great dark monster which is Bill's ship. The small boat tosses and pitches diabolically, but you manage to make the transfer to the gangway and there at the top is Bill. Never has he appeared so handsome as he stands there in his immaculate white uniform awaiting you, but when you reach the top, he is very military, cold, and businesslike. He offers to show you about the ship while it is still light.

Then you see this battleship, this monster, for what it really is! As the *Bluejacket's Manual* says, it is designed "to fight any vessel anywhere." Battleships are considered the backbone of the Fleet. This mysterious mobile machine with its hatches, gangways, turrets, bridges, and turbines is what from now on will take up your husband's time. It is a highly geared, scientific instrument of death. For the first time you realize that the Navy is something more than the glamorous, exciting, and easy life that it appears to be on the surface. It comes to you at this moment that your handsome young Bill is engaged in the grim business of war and that perhaps in the not too distant future he may be forced to try his skill against a deadly adversary. Not a happy thought, by any means, but one that you must understand and face.

Enlisted men hurry about their duties, see that the airplanes are made fast for the night, swathe the small guns in canvas, and put everything in order on this miniature floating city. The sun sinks below the horizon, and there you witness the ship's "colors" for the first time. It is a ceremony performed at sunset each day when the flag is hauled down. On military posts this formation is called retreat. All on deck, officers, and enlisted men, salute during colors. Visitors stand at attention while two sailors reverently and slowly take down the flag and fold it, being careful that it does not touch the deck at any time. On ships having a band, the band plays the National Anthem. If there is no band, the stillness is broken only by the Marine bugler.

Before dinner, Bill tells you that there is time to go below, for he wants you to see his cabin. After a short tour of inspection you arrive, and the moment you enter the door he takes you into his arms. The kiss you have been longing for all day is yours, and finally, being a woman, you ask him why he didn't kiss you when you came aboard. Carefully he will explain to you that an officer in uniform must never do anything that will lower the dignity of the uniform. Eventually you will comprehend this. After a long absence at sea, when he comes ashore in civilian clothes, you can expect to have lipstick smeared all over his face and yours regardless of the bystanders. But should he hurry away from the ship in uniform, then your real greeting will necessarily have to be postponed until you reach your home.

This subject being settled, you look over Bill's small quarters. How you long to fix it up with curtains, pictures, cushions, and an attractive bunk cover, but this is impossible during the emergency. Officers are ordered to carry nothing with them that is not absolutely essential. During peacetime you would be at liberty to add these extra comforts and decorations. Pictures of you, snaps and candid-camera shots, take

up every available space in the room, and Bill tells you that
you are enough decoration for him.

Dinner is announced at this point. Then begins a definitely
tortuous trip through long passages, some lit only by a blue
battle light, up vertical ladders of steel which are narrow and
slippery and offer positively no foothold. It is all fun though,
and at last you reach the J.O. Mess—the "Junior Officers'
Mess." There you enter a combination living and dining
room, the heart of the "officers' country" and meet all the
younger officers and the few wives who have come aboard.

Dinner is on the dot. Being a bride, you are given the seat
of honor at the right of the senior officer on your first visit
to the ship. Remember that you are not just the guest of
your husband but of the entire mess, as the expense of guests
is prorated among the entire group. Naturally you will conduct yourself as though you were dining in the home of friends
and under no circumstances must you complain of anything—
food, service, or appointments. The meal will be served by
quiet, well-trained attendants, usually Negroes or Filipinos
who are enlisted men in the Navy. The mess attendants are
a very important part of the organization, for navies as well
as armies travel on their stomachs and like their food.

It is safe to assume that you will never have cause to complain of the food, service, or appointments aboard ship. Before
you will stretch a long, spotless white table covered with linen
damask. The heavy old-fashioned silver will bear the Navy
seal. The dinner will probably be something special in your
honor; perhaps a good introduction for you will be Indian
curry and rice, a Navy favorite all over the globe. It is an
exotic dish consisting of a stew made of chicken or lamb and
flavored with curry and other spices. First you will be served
rice over which you place the curry, then as many as twenty-
three condiments may be served you—shrimp, fried bananas,
grated cocoanut, grilled bits of bacon, ground pili nuts, grated
hard-boiled eggs, chutney, and many other delicacies. The
Navy got the recipe in Java where it is called *rice-tafel*; there
each dish is presented by a different curry boy, and tradition

has it that it must always be an odd number. Don't expect
to see the Captain at dinner. He eats alone, in silent dignity
in his own mess.

After dinner, everyone lingers in the J.O. Mess for a little
chat before going to the movies out on deck. It is a most
comfortable room equipped with radio and victrola, easy
chairs, well-stocked magazine racks, bookcases, and card tables.
In leisure hours the officers gather here to read, to play bridge,
or for a round of that interminable, indefinable, and omni-
present game, "acey-deucey." When they are at sea, the officers play strenuous topside games such as medicine ball,
deck tennis, or "bull in the ring." Soon it will be time for
the movie, and everyone must be prompt.

Don't go below to powder your nose because the movie
will start as soon as the Captain is seated. Be assured the
Captain will be on time, and when he arrives someone bel-
lows, "Attention!" Everyone stands at attention around you
until he is seated. You remain seated, as ladies never stand in
the presence even of the Admiral, unless he is accompanied
by ladies.

The humor of the happy-go-lucky sailors is irrepressible.
As the movie progresses, pungent comments on actors and
plot are heard from the side lines and are sometimes more
entertaining than the play. Later on, cocoa and coffee are
served in the wardroom, after which the motorboat is brought
alongside to take all visitors ashore.

The ride home alone, then your first night in the apartment by yourself, are only forerunners of what a great part
of your life will be, Nancy Lee. At first you may be a bit
frightened; but that will soon pass, and if you learn how to
adjust yourself and to keep occupied, it won't be too bad.
Certainly not all of your time will be filled with parties, and
early in the game it is wise to learn to budget your time.

The Maidless Household

Of course you know, Nancy Lee, that no amount of
stretching an Ensign's pay can provide a maid. In your small

studio apartment she would be in the way anyhow. Your housekeeping duties will be light, but even so you should have some method to your management of the ménage.

Bill, indoctrinated with four years of system at Annapolis, plus the influence of his well-ordered life aboard ship, will be happier in a home that is not at sixes and sevens. Navy men are accustomed to immaculate surroundings, and the contrast between a slovenly home in port and his shipshape home at sea will be noted, whether he ever mentions it or not. The smaller your home, the more necessary it is to keep it immaculate and pleasant. If you are living in a hotel, even with maid service, it will be necessary for you to take good care of your personal belongings.

It has been said that Navy wives make an obvious effort to entertain their husbands; certainly the divorce rate is exceedingly low among Navy couples. As for a Navy husband, he is the most appreciative and the least critical of any man whom you could marry. After spending months on a rolling ship, meeting strangers in foreign ports, and looking at the same faces aboard ship day in and day out, home means everything to him. The sight of a shining little apartment, a vase of flowers on the table, a home-cooked meal, and the smiling face of one who loves him—those are the things he has been thinking of through the long watches. That home becomes a palace, your face a symbol of heaven. His desire to help in any way that he can knows no bounds, he is so glad to be home again. Your job is easy.

SERVANTS

This should be a chapter in itself, but unless you are stationed in the tropics or in the South, it will not be of much interest to you as the wife of an Ensign or Lieutenant. Such luxuries as servants surely are not often possible in the young Navy household, but there are ways of managing.

It is not unusual for a young Navy wife, if she has occasion to entertain at a formal dinner, to cook the dinner herself and then have a caterer send an experienced maid or waiter to serve it. This gives your household quite an air, but it is usually on the expensive side.

PLANNING MENUS

Menu-planning in advance is almost a necessity if your household includes a maid. If you do not have help, and meals are indefinite, then you will likely find it best to have a general plan with a well-stocked emergency shelf. Many officers breakfast on their ships, since they have to pay for it anyway; but brides often like to send their young officer husbands off comfortably fed and deem it a privilege to make coffee and prepare fruit juice and toast for them. Bill will begin bragging about your culinary ability the moment he gets alone with his shipmates, if you've learned your lesson well.

Plan your dinner menu while you are hungry. Consult your social calendar, and should you be going out to a cocktail party or a tea, plan accordingly. Remember, you never want or need much food after you've filled up on canapés, roasted nuts, and shrimp on sticks! Have a grocery pad and pencil conveniently placed in the kitchen and jot down any staples that are running low. Type your dinner menu on a file card and thumbtack it near the stove. It looks very businesslike and will serve as a reminder. Also, make all the preparations for dinner that you can in the morning. While Bill will undoubtedly appreciate a good dinner, even more than that he will appreciate your wanting to be in the living room with him, even if it is only to sit by and watch him read the evening paper.

Suggestion

Never try out a new dish on guests! Something invariably goes wrong. Practice on your husband first; if you want to try the Baked Alaska for two, use only one pint of ice cream and two egg whites, etc.

It is a good plan to keep two cans of Madrilene or jellied consommé in the refrigerator and frozen vegetables at all times for emergency use.

Acquire the habit of noting the foods, service, and table decorations when dining out. Be open to suggestions, and try out new recipes on yourself.

If you are serving in the tropics, take advantage of the native fruits and vegetables. Learn various methods of preparing them. Mangoes, papayas, and passion fruit make delicious ice cream; bananas and breadfruit can be prepared in interesting ways. The avocados are usually delicious. You will find the native markets most reasonable and perfectly safe, from a sanitary point of view, on thick-skinned fruits. Take a course in the cooking of native foods.

Invest in a pair of butter paddles and a small butter mold. Always place the paddles in a bowl of ice water before using them, then experiment with butter balls, log rolls, and curls. Small touches like this will make you the envy of all your friends, and your husband will be ever so proud.

Learn the different grades and cuts of meat. Cheap cuts are delicious if properly cooked. Give yourself a good course in marketing from books. There is no use learning the hard way, which always turns out to be expensive, when experts have tested and worked out an easy way that is yours for the asking at any good library.

Plan two standard company dinners, the preparation of which will be simple, and always have the necessary foods on your emergency shelf. Of course you will not want to stock up with too large a list of supplies, because ten to one you will have to give them away when you leave. Your common sense will direct you in the amounts to purchase. If practicable, carry your spices, etc. with you, but don't sacrifice practicability for economy by carrying a bottle of ink, vanilla, bluing, or anything breakable that may ruin a trunk full of clothes.

Living Alone and Not Liking It

The young wives of today lead a simple life and are largely together when their husbands are at sea. The Navy has many expressions for the husbands' absences from home. If the ship's movements and orders are secret, a wife simply says her husband has gone "fishing." Recreation periods back to the mainland are spoken of as "love cruises," "play waves," or "strength through joy trips."

Navy wives share with each other. There is a camaraderie that is different from that of any other Service. Your problem becomes that of your Navy friends, and fine friendships are often the outgrowth of your mutual sharing of responsibilities, loneliness, worry, anxiety, and strain. There is no spoken discontent, and Navy wives have little use for the whiner or the complainer.

The wife of a young Reserve Officer called to active duty sometimes finds it difficult to adjust herself to Navy life. She is uprooted from a comfortable and often luxurious home to which she has grown accustomed, and from the town or city where her circle of friends was formed. From her dream of being the wife of a successful business man, perhaps, she clambers painfully down the financial ladder and finds it hard going on Navy pay. Her solace at first is in the comforting thought that her husband is in "only for the duration"; but frequently she likes Service life so well that she begins to look forward to her husband's receiving a permanent commission in the Navy.

As was mentioned before, Navy wives live most informally when their husbands are at sea.

Cocktail Parties

The cocktail party is one of the easiest and most popular forms of entertainment, though often rather expensive. It is a pleasant informal means of entertaining a large number of guests, if given at an Officers' Club. Smaller parties of this type may be given at home.

A caterer may handle the food, but if you prepare the hors d'oeuvres, it is wise to keep them simple. Men like good, filling appetizers—shrimp, with an accompanying bowl of piquant sauce, celery, small knobs of cauliflower, sliced raw carrots or potato chips to be dipped in roquefort or Thousand Island dressing. Large pineapple and Edam cheeses with assorted cocktail crackers are popular. Some hostesses include a platter of assorted cold cuts or a baked ham or turkey with buttered slices of rye and white bread near by. The day of fancy canapés, those "dainty little tidbits over which a hostess and all of her friends used to spend the day laboring" have gone with the well-known wind. The hostess of today likes to enjoy her own party, and leaves the elaborate party sandwiches and canapés to experienced professional caterers.

Highballs of Scotch, Bourbon, and Rye take the lead in drinks, while Martinis, Manhattans, and Old-Fashioneds head the cocktail list. Sherry is often served. Coca-Cola, fruit juices, and tomato juice should be provided for nondrinkers. Never feel obliged to take a drink if you do not want it or if it is against your principles. Stick to your convictions and remember this: You will be better off if you never drink. This applies both to officers and to their wives. People will respect you for the stand you take, provided you are not rude or critical in regard to the drinking of others, or unfriendly and disapproving in your manner.

Luncheons are popular among Navy wives, either small foursomes at home followed by bridge or larger ones at hotels and clubs.

Dutch-treat parties at the Officers' Club in the form of dinners or dinner-dances are greatly enjoyed by the junior officers. Beach parties of the same sort are also popular. Often two Navy couples will give a large joint dinner party or cocktail party in order to repay their obligations. This is quite a proper custom, and often produces a much more successful party than either couple could manage alone.

The Informal Invitation on Board Ship

It is always wise to ask your husband several days beforehand if it will be convenient to invite guests on board ship for dinner on a certain evening. Be sure that it is convenient before you issue an invitation.

Remember that the invitation *comes from your husband*, and not from you. It is *his ship, and his invitation!* Naturally, in a large mess, invitations must necessarily be limited, and don't feel that you are at liberty to impose on the officers' mess in order to fulfill your social obligations. For instance, it is not the proper thing to take your whole family, should they come to visit you. The Junior Officers' Mess and the wardrooms are combination dining and living rooms, as has been previously explained, and are for the use of the officers of the ship. Officers enjoy company occasionally and are always courteous and hospitable to guests, but they do not enjoy having visitors for dinner every evening. When this privilege is abused, the officers among themselves decide to have each officer pay for his own guests, rather than to follow the usual practice and prorate the expense among the members of the mess.

In extending a dinner invitation of this kind, be sure that it is worded properly because Naval officers are very fussy about this point:

Dear Major and Mrs. Chase:

Bill would like to have you out to dinner on the *Enterprise* Thursday evening, May the second. We will meet at the Officers' Club for cocktails at five fifteen, and shall look forward to seeing you.

Sincerely yours,

NANCY LEE TYLER

If you telephone, be most careful to extend the invitation in your husband's name. Say, "Bill asked me to phone you.

He would like to have you and Major Chase come to dinner on the *Enterprise*."

THAT FEMININE TOUCH
OR
MAKING SILK PURSES OUT OF SOWS' EARS

You won't always have a lovely modernistic apartment or the beach at Waikiki, Nancy Lee. Early in her training, a successful Navy wife must learn how to make drab and dreary quarters attractive and agreeable. Fortunate is she, indeed, if she has had a course in interior decorating or is particularly clever with a paintbrush or needle. It is amazing how even changing the position of the furniture in a furnished apartment will sometimes help.

Flowers always lend a festive air. They need not be expensive cut flowers from a florist; anything growing in the way of inexpensive potted plants or even the homely sweet-potato vine gives a pretty, decorative effect. One Junior Lieutenant's wife who lived in a makeshift apartment over a garage in Vallejo disguised the ugly living room heating stove by surrounding its fat middle with a low decorative screen and removing the top cap and filling it with the fluffy yellow blooms of acacia.

Some Navy wives carry a couple of Chinese scrolls, tapestries, or a panel of colorful chintz along in their trunks to give a pretty touch to the faded, impossible wallpaper that one often encounters in furnished flats that masquerade under the title of apartments. Personal photographs scattered about the rooms give a note of individuality at times, although no visitor loves to feel as though he has stepped into the middle of a Victorian family album!

If the furnished curtains or hangings are too, too awful, and you feel that you will be permanent long enough to warrant the buying of inexpensive material, then, in your spare time, put up something to your liking. It will pay you and relieve the strain of ugliness that jars on your aesthetic soul. Try to sell them to your landlady when you leave, be-

Navy officers, and this rule is so strictly observed that young officers upon occasion have been silenced by their brother officers for speaking ill of a lady's reputation.

7. Avoid gossiping, promoting rumors, or listening to gossip.

8. Always wait for the guest of honor to leave before saying good-by to your hostess. The ranking lady always leaves first.

9. Don't make the mistake of speaking of "our ship," "our orders," etc., or say, "When we were Lieutenants . . ." It is your husband's ship, the orders are his, and he is the only one who holds a commission.

10. While there is no rank among women in the Navy, a junior officer's wife should always show courteous deference to older women and especially to the wife of the officer under whose direct command her husband is serving, though in no way that smacks of "bootlicking" or currying favor.

11. Should your husband confide in you (which he probably won't, with all official business and ships' movements so necessarily secret), use tact and common sense in keeping it to yourself. In your conversation in public places, among civilian friends, and before servants be most discreet. In this regard, "Silence is golden."

12. It is considered unmilitary for an officer in uniform to carry an umbrella or packages.

13. It is customary for officers and enlisted men, whether with or without side arms, to remove the cap when greeting ladies. This custom is rapidly becoming obsolete. It is now becoming the custom to salute instead of removing the cap.

14. Chaplains are always addressed as Chaplain.

15. All petty officers and men are addressed by their surnames.

16. It is customary for a committee of officers to make the round of calls on New Year's Day on all ships in the same port. In Washington it is customary to call on the Secretary of the Navy and other high officials on New Year's Day, full-dress uniform being worn. (This custom does not apply during the emergency.)

Chapter X

FOLLOWING THE SHIP

Oh! there'll be high elation
On the far China Station
From Crabtown to ships at Timbuctoo;
And we'll drink a merry toast
To the boys who love to boast
They're the wearers of the good old Navy Blue.

FOLLOWING the ship, in addition to making it possible to be with your husband more often, has many interesting features, among the most enjoyable of which are seeing new places and meeting new people.

However, being able to follow the ship usually hinges on the same old story—Navy pay! Youth has a tendency to be unduly optimistic, especially in financial matters, but it should never forget that there is more unhappiness in the Navy from lack of financial foresight than because of temporary separations.

There is no group of young married people who must maintain appearances and meet high social demands on such a small sum of money as Navy couples. The old inexpensive boardinghouses have vanished, and today the thrifty Navy wife lives in a small apartment and is her own maid. Modern conditions make an automobile a necessity, and much of her commuting from port to port is done in her car.

Frequently a group of young wives whose husbands are on the same ship band together in one or more cars and follow the ship up and down the west coast from San Diego to Seattle. When there are several cars they call it a "driving caravan." They proceed on a predetermined route and make several stops during the day at fixed points, and before proceeding make certain that all cars are accounted for.

These girls are experienced chauffeurs who can change a spark plug or a tire in a 1-2-3, and they make a joy trip out of the whole expedition. Later in this chapter there is given detailed advice concerning motor trips to which wives inexperienced in touring should give careful attention.

At the end of the journey, their husbands will be waiting for them with open arms. As one lucky young officer, married to an heiress from Texas who could afford to be at every port, expressed it, "Life in the Navy is just one series of honeymoons."

SILENCE IS GOLDEN

Today, Nancy Lee, because of the war, our nation is engaged in the movement of Navy ships, and their places of operations are secret. Frequently, even the Captain does not know the destination of his ship until he receives orders after clearing the port. Should Bill, by chance, know the plans for his ship, he is not permitted to divulge this information, even to you, his wife. There have been specific cases in which, because of infractions of this secrecy order, officers have been court-martialed. Wives of officers, too, have been required to leave the vicinity of a naval base because of "talking too much" or "relaying official information."

Moral: Don't ask your husband questions concerning the movement or operations of his ship; and above all, don't advance your personal opinions in regard to such movements or operations. You might just happen to be correct in your supposition and should your remarks come to the attention of higher authority, your unbridled tongue might prove to be dynamite to your husband's career and to you.

Information concerning ship movements or operations, whether true or false, coming from an officer's wife, impresses the average civilian and is apt to be quoted. Remember, too, that alien operatives disguised as servants, taxi drivers, clerks, and even casual acquaintances may be very much interested in getting you to tell what you know about ship movements.

No Navy wife would willfully jeopardize the lives of officers and men of the Navy, possibly her own husband's life, yet that is exactly what she may be guilty of should she divulge any information concerning ship movements and operations.

Here is an example for you to follow. On a recent trip to Long Beach, a cruiser was moored to a buoy in plain sight of persons at the Navy landing. A Bluejacket waiting for a boat was approached by a civilian who asked: "Do you know the name of that ship moored to the buoy?"

"No, sir," replied the Bluejacket.

"What ship are you on?" inquired the civilian.

"That ship moored to the buoy," said the Bluejacket with a grin.

If the civilian did not know of the secrecy order he probably had a poor opinion of the mentality of naval personnel, but it is much better to *appear* dumb than to *be* sorry.

ON THE ALERT

When ships are to go to a port for leave and liberty, officers and men are usually given the information with permission to inform their families of the place and approximate date of arrival; in other cases, where a ship arrives unexpectedly at a port for some days' stay, permission to inform their families may be given after the arrival of the ship.

In these hectic days even more than in normal times the modern Navy wife keeps herself mobile! She can be ready to take a train, a Clipper, or to drive her own car upon a few hours' notice, to meet her husband for a few days' happy reunion. For this reason it is important that she have suitable luggage and a definite idea of the clothing and necessary equipment which can be carried by plane, by railroad, or in her car. As a general principle, she carries a minimum of clothes and baggage. Usually she travels at her own expense, as the government pays for her transportation only when her husband receives orders for a permanent change of station.

The Immobile Wife

Of course, circumstances are often such that it is impossible for a Navy wife to follow the ship. Owing to illness, to certain abnormal responsibilities such as the care of an aged parent, or to unusual conditions in regard to the health and education of the children, it is sometimes best for a Navy wife to settle down in some suitable place, preferably on or near the coast on which her husband is stationed, and make a home while her husband is at sea. In the Navy of long ago this was the normal procedure for families; but now, with the government paying for transportation for dependents upon permanent change of station, and with transportation and educational facilities so well developed, there are very few Navy wives who do not move as far as the home port of the husband's ship. Those who refuse to move at all may save money, but their lives usually are lonely and drab.

The typical Navy wife enjoys this nomadic life which gives her intermittent relief from housekeeping responsibilities, the opportunity of living in many United States and foreign ports, a chance to see the world and to make many interesting contacts. The life of a Navy wife is stimulating; at times it is tragic, but the advantages usually far outweigh the disadvantages, and most Navy wives find it attractive, satisfying, and thrilling.

Waiting

Early in their careers they must get used to waiting. What is more, they must learn to wait patiently. In these nerve-racking days, Nancy Lee, weeks may go by without a letter, and when one finally arrives it may require a complete change of your plans, or may leave you stranded in a strange port until you get further orders from Bill "to proceed."

In such situations it's bad enough to feel tense and jittery, but it is worse to show it.

More trivial but frequently trying to the novice are upset plans and periods of waiting due to minor occurrences which prevent a husband from coming ashore at the appointed time. When you drive down to the boat landing to meet Bill, always be prepared for a delay. Such periods of waiting seem like eternity unless you have some way to pass the time. Knitting is one constructive means, and many Navy wives carry copies of their favorite magazines and keep up with current events by reading while they wait.

LETTERS OF TWO NAVY WIVES

If you are a Navy wife, or just a fiancée, perhaps it will be possible for you to make connections once in a while when "his" ship is in port, but if this is not practicable, the next best thing is to have a letter or letters awaiting him at his destination. To write a good letter is an art, and don't think of it as a lost art—or something that went out with the quill pen.

The type of letter we all love to receive is the one that carries so much of the writer's personality that she, or he, seems to be sitting beside us. Picture the joy and happiness of a Navy man who having been at sea for a long time finds upon his return to port a package of mail awaiting him. Suddenly his face lights up and he finds the letter from his loved one. He tears it open eagerly, his mouth upcurving at the corners as he lingers on every word. One knows by the smile on his face that the sweetheart or wife he left behind puts all the best she can devise or save for him into his life as well as onto the paper.

Emily Post's advice to engaged girls is equally valuable for brides. She says, "If you are engaged, of course, you should write love letters, the most beautiful that you can, but don't write baby talk and other silliness that would make you feel idiotic if the letter were to fall into strange hands." You should remember that censorship is possible at any moment.

If there are children you will see the Navy father chuckle as he reads his wife's description of little Joe's latest escapade. His chest will expand with pride when he reads how his ugly duckling Susie passed to the third grade with honors and won the junior swimming meet. His face will beam with happiness if there is a candid camera shot of his wife and the children.

Now let us watch, while he is going through his mail, the Navy man who has a complaining, irritable wife to whom life is a pain, and the life of a Navy wife particularly so. Reluctantly he will pick up his wife's letter, look at it, hesitate, then possibly push it aside. His expression says plainly, "I can't face that just now." Then by and by, because he is a Navy man and knows his duty, with his lips set in a hard line he will doggedly open the letter to see what the trouble is now.

If for once there is no trouble or grief, he sighs with relief, relaxes, and goes about his work. More often, though, he frowns, looks worried, and groans as he reads of his wife's chronic and often imaginary state of ill health, that Jimmy is failing in his school work, that Joan has to have braces for her teeth, and that the roof of the rented house leaks terribly and the landlord refuses to do anything about it! More than likely all of this is a forerunner to the announcement that her allotment won't cover the current bills and that he must send her more money.

In a letter to your fiancé or husband be careful not to unburden your soul or to write needlessly of unhappiness and misfortune. "Anger in a letter carries with it the effect of solidified fury"; written words are there forever. The letter you write, whether you realize it or not, is always a mirror which reflects your personality, your interests, appearance, taste, and character. After all, a letter is a gift, a gift of yourself, and if it is worth writing, it should be done well.

THE ART OF MAKING FRIENDS

By cultivating an ability to make friends quickly and with varied types of people, a Navy couple can soon establish many worth-while friendships among civilians as well as Navy personnel—friendships that may open up avenues of happiness not alone for the present but for the future years.

A naval officer's commission gives him and his family entree into the best circles of society.

Remember that no civilian enjoys hearing his home town run down. Cultivate any worth-while civilian contacts; above all do not be so provincial that you fail to appreciate the fine qualities of foreigners, and such attentions as they may show you. Recognize customs and where practicable comply with them. Pay polite and customary deference to the native aristocracy. Show an interest, even if partly assumed, in the customs, culture, and religions of different people whom you may have the good fortune to meet. These contacts will serve to broaden your viewpoint and make your life more interesting.

Dale Carnegie has said, "Most people, when introductions are being made, are inattentive or do not take the time and energy to concentrate and fix names indelibly in their minds." It is quite proper to ask to have a name repeated in an introduction if you have not understood it. If the name is unusual, and circumstances permit, ask the person to spell it. Of course a formal receiving line would not be exactly the place to start such mental gymnastics.

Ability to remember people by their names is a valuable accomplishment which will stand you in good stead, for everyone is flattered to be remembered, especially if you can call him by name.

AVOCATIONS

An avocation for a Navy wife is greatly to be encouraged. One way to meet people having a common interest is to be what is termed "a joiner." If your avocation is a practical one, such as writing, painting, etc., which you may be able to turn into greenbacks, so much the better for you and your husband. However, you may prefer to cultivate some talent simply for the pleasure and enjoyment that you get out of it.

If you are taking up something new, be sure to consider your choice from a practical standpoint. Music is splendid, but to learn to play a harp would not be very practical in your itinerant life, as the cost of moving your golden instrument would be prohibitive. A piano can nearly always be rented for about $5.00 a month, unless you are a temperamental genius and happy only with your own concert grand.

If you are in a strange city and lonely, consult the local newspaper, see what is offered in your field, then go in pursuit of it. The Navy Relief and the Red Cross rank highest these days on the list of activities. In addition to doing your patriotic bit, you will meet interesting people who will give you a warm welcome if you meet them halfway.

To play a good game of bridge is a social asset. Contract bridge is a favorite form of amusement of many Navy wives, and the girls get together when the boys are at sea. It helps to pass many hours that might otherwise be lonely. If you have never played, you should take lessons and gain a little experience before joining in competition. Most young couples play for "love" (nothing) or perhaps twenty-five cents a corner. If you are playing for money with a new group of people, always ask about the stakes and be sure you understand exactly.

If you enjoy reading, join a circulating library where you will have access to the newest books, both fiction and non-fiction, and apply for a card at the free Public Library. It is an excellent plan to read up on local history whenever you visit a new city.

If you have histrionic ability or are interested in the theater, by all means make an effort to join up with the Little Theater or Community Players. The dramatic groups are always composed of interesting people, and they have lots of fun. They need decorators for sets, make-up artists, prompters, and actors, and you will be very welcome.

SPORTS

Golf is a very popular sport and increasingly so among women. Again some lessons are desirable. There are other costs which make golf a fairly expensive pastime, though a very beneficial one. If your husband loves golf, you had better learn to play.

Tennis and swimming are likewise excellent sports and probably less expensive than golf. Most clubs charge moderate dues, but if such dues constitute a problem, investigate the local Y.W.C.A. or municipal park facilities.

ATTITUDE OF A NAVY WIFE

A Navy wife should be proud of the Navy and her connection with it, and never by word or deed should she cast any discredit upon it. Times will be hard and separations may be long, but she should present to the world a cheerful agreeableness rather than a resigned stoicism. The Navy doesn't particularly care for a wife who is *too obviously* carrying her load. Take life as it comes in your stride, my dear, and you'll be loved all the more for it!

HERE WE GO

There still remain to be discussed perhaps the most important activities pertaining to following the ship, namely, transportation and matters connected therewith. There are four general types of situations that may arise:

1. A short visit of from three to four days, usually involving a trip of several hundred miles, from the home port to another port on the same coast, to which your husband's ship is going to participate in a celebration such as Memorial Day, Independence Day, or Armistice Day, or for the purpose of granting leave and liberty.
2. A trip overseas, such as to Honolulu or Panama, during winter cruises of the fleet, or to Puget Sound during a summer cruise usually made by a portion of the fleet.
3. A visit to the home yard where the ship goes for regular overhaul, usually extending from two to three months.
4. A permanent change of station.

THE SHORT VISIT

Your first inclination, no matter how short the visit, will be to hop into your car and drive the three or four hundred miles to meet Bill. Granted it will be a grand and blissful reunion; but unless you are as fortunate as that wealthy Texas bride who was on hand in every port—can you afford it, my darling? Remember that in all probability Bill will have the "duty" one of those four days, that the rent on your apartment at the home port will be going on just the same in addition to the cost of your trip, and that one always spends more than usual when visiting a new city! Oh, I know just how hard it is to be practical when you're in love, but upon second thought you may agree that it is unwise to make any great sacrifice for such a short visit. Of course, if you and Bill have been separated for some time, as is quite possible in these days, the sacrifice may be justified. Let your conscience be your guide.

Before you decide to make the trip, be honest with yourself. Make a careful estimate of the additional cost involved. Knowing this, make a frank decision, talking it over with Bill if possible, as to whether or not the pleasure of the trip will be worth the required sacrifice. Then if you go, later when the sacrifice is demanded, be a good sport and don't regret your previous decision. No person has a right to expect to be correct in his decisions much more than half the time, so be philosophical and learn early not to regret past faulty decisions; just try to improve your percentage in the future.

Again, the ship may expect to remain in port for from ten days to two weeks for a leave and liberty period. The temptation grows stronger, doesn't it? If you have just received a check from home, or have the moral stamina to forego the evening dress you had your heart set on, then pack up and go by all means. It will be fun, there may be invitations to parties on shore; however, you know how it is—these invitations are more frequently extended to bachelor officers who are always in demand, or to those of higher rank.

But just seeing Bill may be worth it all! Probably there will be places of interest to see, good theaters in the larger cities, dining and dancing. What fun it must be to have an outside income, you think. Well, watch out—that idea may be the serpent slithering into your and Bill's Eden. It takes character to face financial facts and figures, but if such a visit as this has been properly prepared for and you can swing it, you will enjoy it all the more.

TRAVELING BY AUTOMOBILE

Most of the traveling for short visits is done by automobile, so Navy wives should be expert chauffeurs. At first thought it may seem an extra expense to join the A.A.A. (American Automobile Association), but it is considered advisable to do so if you contemplate frequent trips. The towing service that the Association provides in emergencies may be very welcome some time, and its tag on a car affords a certain degree of protection against vandalism.

Frequently, longer trips, such as to the home yard or even a permanent change of station, will be made by automobile. In any case there should be definite preparation for the trip. Navy officers in preparing guns or torpedoes have what they call a check-off list comprising all steps in the preparation for firing. Each item is checked when completed. For the novice, and as a reminder to the more experienced, there is presented here a check-off list for desirable preparations for a trip by automobile. The longer the trip, the more important is attention to these items.

1. Try to get some other wife to go with you; most wives who have cars will want to drive their own cars but someone who has no car may be glad to go with you and share expenses of fuel and oil. If you are unable to find a driving companion try to find several wives who are driving cars on the same trip and form a "driving caravan." Such a caravan, if well planned as to route, speed, and stops, permits a check of each car's progress and a possible reduction in expenses by sharing accommodations.

2. Plan your trip carefully. The following suggestions may help you:
    a. Decide upon your route. Obtain an automobile route book such as is published by the A.A.A., or a tour aide for the

state or states through which you will travel such as are provided free upon request by some tourist bureaus and by oil companies. Consider routes with a view to the time of year, distance, and points of interest. If traveling in the West, you may arrange a visit to Yosemite Park, the Redwood Forest, etc.

b. Decide upon your schedule. In scheduling a trip plan to get an early start each day, seldom base your schedule on an average speed in excess of thirty miles per hour, and avoid driving after dark, too long at a stretch, or too far in a day.

c. Decide where you will spend each night and the hostelry you desire to use, and write or telegraph for a reservation. It is most undesirable for a wife traveling alone to find herself in a strange place without a reservation at a suitable hostelry. Be sure to inform your husband of your contemplated address at your destination. The information concerning lodgings and eating places is quite complete in many tour aides. In selecting places to eat and sleep many people have found very satisfactory advice in two books by Duncan Hines entitled *Adventures in Good Eating* and *Lodging for a Night.*

d. If you are driving in a caravan, decide upon the stops and the exact place at which all cars are to check in. Cars should always be checked in at the end of the day's drive, and preferably twice a day. It may be desirable for a caravan to consider stopping at some one of the better tourist courts or motels. Many such now have accommodations on a par with moderate-priced hotels, are cheaper, afford a solution to the parking problem, and are more convenient for making an early start in the morning.

e. Decide upon the luggage you are to carry in your car. Try out, empty, the suitcases, hatboxes, etc. in the trunk compartment and determine the most satisfactory stowage. For long trips when your car is to be crowded this procedure will save much time and patience.

f. Be sure that you have the following items with you:
1. Registration card and valid automobile operator's license.
2. Insurance policy or card.
3. Your husband's card with name of his ship, in con-

tainer with registration card; also your own last address and future address if known.

4. Tools and spare parts, including a jack, wrench for wheel nuts, large screw driver, small chemical fire extinguisher, flashlight, and a spare spark plug. If traveling north or if anticipating mountain driving, consider the possibility that your car may require chains and your radiator an anti-freeze mixture. If your car is of ancient vintage include a spare fan belt.

5. A vacuum bottle filled with cold water.

6. Route maps and schedule for your trip.

7. At least one warm blanket per person and if traveling north a warm coat.

8. In your purse a duplicate insurance card or a card containing data in regard to your insurance policy, and complete identification data for your car, including license number, engine number, and the manufacturer's numbers of your tires, including the spare.

This identification data is essential in case your car is stolen or a dishonest garage shifts tires on it while put up for the night. It has been adequately demonstrated that dishonest garages take advantage of women traveling alone.

You should have in cash, preferably in small bills, a sum sufficient to cover one day's expenses, adequate traveler's checks to more than cover your trip expenses, and your checkbook. It is desirable that your traveler's checks be carried on a string around your neck rather than in your purse, so that a lost or stolen purse will not deprive you of money.

This check-off list may appear long and too detailed, but there is included not one item which, if neglected by you, may not result in delay, inconvenience, or possible embarrassment to you and your husband; for a wife's errors are usually charged to her husband's ignorance or inefficiency in instructing her in motoring.

The Trip

For you, Nancy Lee, as for many others, this may be the first motor trip you have made in which you have had the sole responsibility. May we give you just a few more items of advice as to your trip:

1. The early morning is the best part of the day for motoring unless you have retired late. There is less traffic and this early-morning period can be used for no other purpose than sleep, of which, if you turned in early, you should have had plenty.
2. Keep within the speed limit and watch carefully for road signs indicating curves, detours, and desirable shift of gears, i.e., as to shift to second in descending a steep hill.
3. Buy only nationally known brands of gas and oil and only from respectable-looking service stations, or you may get watered or otherwise faulty gas or oil. Never let the gas in your tank get below one-quarter full and have your crankcase oil checked each time you buy gas.
4. Check water in radiator frequently in hot weather and in mountain driving.
5. Check tires frequently in hot weather, especially in desert driving. Remember that heat expands the pressure and is the cause of many a blowout.
6. Take time to eat proper meals.
7. Carry no liquor in your car and never indulge in even one intoxicating drink, if at all, until your driving for the day is finished. Alcohol is responsible for many automobile accidents, and alcoholic liquor in your car or the smell of alcohol on your breath, in case of a collision or other accident, prejudices your case at the start.

IF TRAVELING BY TRAIN

Any trip that can be made by automobile can be made by train. But when traveling at your own expense, you will find train fare too expensive to permit many trips.

THE OVERSEAS TRIP

During winter cruises of the fleet to Hawaii or Panama the period actually spent in port seldom exceeds two weeks. Only wives with outside financial resources can afford to make such trips. They are wonderful if you can afford them, but in most cases during winter cruises Navy wives make a visit home, visit other relatives, or join together to share the expenses of an apartment while their husbands are away.

Sometimes when a Navy wife comes home for several months during a winter cruise her presence there is not understood by civilians. Her long separation from her husband may be cause for rumor of unhappiness and possibly of divorce. The wise Navy wife just smiles and suffers; she knows that upon Bill's return she will join him and all gossip will be silenced.

Visit to the Home Yard

When the ship that is tired returneth
   With the signs of the sea showing plain,
Men place her in dock for a season
   And her speed she reneweth again.
                   Captain Hopwood's "Laws of the Navy"

Each ship has a specifically designated home port and home yard. The home port is the port of operating base from which the ship normally operates from six to nine months of the year. The home yard is the Navy yard designated to perform the regular overhaul of the ship, which requires from two to three months at periods of eighteen to twenty months. Also, should it become necessary to make any emergency repairs at another time, they are usually made at the ship's home yard.

Regular overhauls are scheduled many months in advance. As such periods normally exceed any other continuous stay of the ship in any port, most wives, even when there are children, move then from the home port to the home yard.

Such a trip must be made at your own expense. It involves giving up your apartment or home in the home port and obtaining a new place to live in the vicinity of the home yard. With the present crowded conditions in the vicinity of Navy yards, to find any place to live is most difficult.

Usually one Navy ship is leaving the yard, completing its overhaul, as another ship of the same type arrives to begin her period. As the number of officers on each ship of the same type is approximately the same, there are usually about as many wives about to leave as there are arriving, hence prior to leaving they try to pass on their apartments to the new arrivals.

For those wives who have no experience in the details of closing a home or apartment, here is a check-off list for your convenience.

1. Never pick up stakes and start for a Navy yard city without being certain of a place to stay when you arrive. If you have been unable to obtain an apartment or a house you may be able to obtain hotel accommodations until other arrangements can be made, or you can wait at the home port until your husband arrives and obtains a place for you.
2. Notify your present landlord of your departure by as much advance notice as is required in your lease. You must avoid breaking a lease. Frequently a landlord will permit you to sublet or will terminate your lease if you can find a new tenant.
3. In case you have been occupying a furnished house or apartment, you should arrange with the landlord to check with you before your departure the inventory of furniture and equipment. You must arrange to have the house or apartment thoroughly cleaned, soiled linens washed, and blankets dry-cleaned. It will save you trouble if the landlord in lieu of such cleaning will permit you to pay a cleaning charge.
4. Notify the gas and electric light companies of your expected departure; also the telephone company if you have had a private telephone; and the municipal agent controlling the water supply if you have been paying for your water supply.

At least forty-eight hours before your departure you should make arrangements for the final reading of the gas and electric meters on the day of your departure, and for paying the respective bills by making a deposit or by furnishing to the companies if agreeable to them the address to which they are to forward your bill. You will have made a deposit with each of these companies when its service was started; be sure you receive credit for such deposit.

The telephone company normally requires payment for its monthly service in advance. You should therefore have a credit unless you have had excessive charges for long-distance calls.

Unless you have been living in a house you probably have not been paying for the water; but if you have been, be sure to arrange for payment of any outstanding bill.

5. When moving to a home yard for several months' stay, your packing problem is complicated; you should:

    a. Put in storage any furniture or bulky articles not required during your stay at the home yard. Number each box put in storage and list the nature of contents of each in your log and legal record, stating date, place, and name of storage company.

    b. Pack your trip essentials in suitcases and hatbox. If you are traveling by car, try to make a place in the trunk compartment for a box containing such canned goods, condiments, spices, etc. as you may have on hand. A cardboard box containing such items will assist in setting up the new apartment and will save more money than one would suspect. Other articles you will require which cannot be carried in the car should be packed in boxes and sent by freight, or fast freight, to your destination. Fast freight is nearly as rapid as express.

6. Stop all regular deliveries of milk, eggs, newspapers, etc.

7. Stop all charge accounts you may have opened; notify stores of date of your departure and pay all outstanding bills before leaving.

8. Cancel any engagements you will be unable to keep.

9. Obtain card from post office on which you notify the postmaster of your change of address; if your new address is not known, have your mail sent to the ship in care of your husband. As an additional safeguard, it is desirable to ask a friend, neighbor, or accommodating landlord to forward any mail that may be left for you. Under any conditions you should leave a forwarding address with your landlord.

10. If you have a checking account in a local bank, it generally will be desirable to close it out.

11. If you have subscribed to any magazines, notify the publishers of your new address. Magazines will not be forwarded without prepayment of additional postage.

The Arrival

Before you and your husband say good-by, you should agree on the procedure to be followed upon either's arrival at the home yard. Normally it is better for the wife to arrive a day or two after her husband. This will permit him to make the preliminary arrangements for gas, electricity, and water, and possibly save a day for you in having the telephone connected. If you are going to a hotel, these preliminary arrangements will be unnecessary.

If you have decided ideas on what you want in the way of a place to live, it may be more satisfactory to go to a hotel at first until you can select your own place. Your husband will not mind being relieved of the responsibility for the selection.

During the war no car is allowed to enter a Navy yard without an official permit. To obtain such a permit from the Office of the Captain of the Yard should be one of your first objectives after your arrival. If you have not had time to get a permit you can await your husband at the gate, but be sure you know which gate, as every Navy yard has several.

The Permanent Change of Station

For line officers a permanent change of station usually means a change from shore duty to sea duty or vice versa. It may mean the same to officers of the Staff Corps or of the Marine Corps, but for officers of these corps transfer from one shore station to another shore station is much more common than it is for line officers. It may be a change of from one ship to another, in which case, if the two ships have different home ports, the officers' families will have to move. In any case a permanent change of station usually involves a complete uprooting and transplanting for the family.

For the wife and family the term "station" means, in the case of an officer on sea duty, the home port or the home yard of the ship to which the husband is assigned. Transportation for dependents is furnished by the government when the permanent station is changed. The dependents may choose the home port or the home yard as their destination. This alternative should always be kept in mind when making a change from shore duty to sea duty; for although the home port is normally the better destination for the family, a current or approaching overhaul period may make the home yard the better choice.

There are two great differences between travel performed in making a permanent change of station and travel to a port for a short visit or to the home yard for an overhaul period. The first is: The government furnishes dependents with necessary rail and steamer tickets; or within the continental United States, if dependents travel by automobile at their own expense, the government will reimburse the officer after his dependents have completed the trip. The second is: In many cases the officer in making a permanent change of station is able to travel with his dependents.

In normal times, provided an officer's services are not urgently needed, the Bureau of Navigation in its orders directing a permanent change of station grants a number of days' delay in reporting to the new station. In changes from sea duty to shore duty the Bureau endeavors to grant up to thirty days' delay.

Reimbursement for Automobile Travel

Officers' dependents may travel within the continental United States by private automobile if they so desire. Upon completion of such travel, the officer is entitled to reimbursement of the amount such travel would have cost the government if performed by train. It usually requires a month or six weeks before the submitted claim for reimbursement is settled. As the cost of shipping an automobile is high, many families prefer to proceed to the new station by auto.

One other important advantage of traveling by automobile is that an officer not only saves the cost of his trip by rail but also is allowed as a deduction from income on federal and state income tax returns the cost of actual travel by car, provided this does not exceed cost of travel by rail. This includes gas, oil, a reasonable amount for car and tire depreciation, and cost of lodging and meals for the distance and time consumed in normal automobile driving between new and old stations.

In this case, it is imperative that expense deductible from income be meticulously recorded. If the family, without the officer, proceeds by car, no deductions are allowed, and the entire sum received as reimbursement for dependents' travel must be recorded as income.

RAILROAD TRAVEL AT GOVERNMENT EXPENSE

When the officer is ordered to a new station, his dependents are entitled to transportation by rail for the necessary travel within the continental limits of the United States. If such transportation is desired, it must be requested by the officer. Upon approval of the request the dependents will be furnished railroad tickets and first-class Pullman car accommodations on any regular-fare train on any regularly traveled route. An extra-fare train or any desired unusual route may be used by paying the difference in cost. Dependents must pay for meals except in commercial steamer travel where meals are included in the fare.

TRAVEL BY GOVERNMENT TRANSPORT

If overseas travel is involved, dependents are often required to make the sea trip in a transport, either Army or Navy. Because of the infrequent transport trips, your husband may be required to precede you by other naval or by commercial transportation. In case you are to travel by transport, you will be informed by the Bureau of Navigation as to the name of the ship on which you will embark and the day and approximate hour of sailing.

Now, Nancy Lee, you, like the sailor, "joined the Navy to see the World," didn't you? Well, you are going to see it from one of the most interesting angles you can imagine. There is nothing that quite compares with travel in an Army or Navy transport. To begin with, government transports have a habit of sailing if and when they choose; about the only thing you can depend upon is that they almost always sail at high noon. You are advised to arrive at the port of embarkation twenty-four hours ahead of scheduled sailing time, and it is wise to do so in order to check on the latest information. You may be delayed for days, or again you may sail ahead of schedule. Very aptly, in the Army, transports are spoken of as "phantom" ships.

Anyway, they get you there, and in pretty fine style, though you shouldn't expect anything fancy like afternoon tea, cocktails, or morning bouillon. The food is splendid, and meals are served right on the dot. Being fifteen minutes late for a meal on transports means that you automatically skip that meal.

Your accommodations as to staterooms, seating in dining salon, priority for use of baths will be in accordance with the relative rank of your husband compared to that of the husbands of other wives on board. You will be required to pay for your meals at the rate of about $1.75 a day, and you will be able to buy cigarettes, stationery, candy, soft drinks, and numerous toilet articles.

The passengers and the ports of call, though, are what make the trip most interesting. Should you have the experience of traveling on an Army transport, you will learn a lot about that branch of the Service that you never knew before. Army wives will be equally interested in you and your life. You will find comparisons—each side thinks the other Service gets all the gravy; Army wives think that Navy wives do nothing but travel, live in good hotels, and have a fine time; while Navy wives look covetously upon the comfortable quarters provided on Army posts—don't lose any sleep over it. Neither group would exchange its life for the other; they are both smugly satisfied.

Travel by Commercial Steamer

If you are sailing in a commercial steamer your reservation will have been made for you, and you will be informed where to call to obtain your ticket. On commercial steamers meals are included in the fare, but you will be required to pay for any extras such as drinks and steamer chairs.

TRANSPORTATION FOR HOUSEHOLD EFFECTS

When an officer receives orders changing his permanent station, he is entitled to shipment of a definite weight (according to rank) of household effects at government expense. "Professional books and papers owned by Naval Personnel may be shipped without charge against the weight allowance." (Manual Bu S & A.)

The weight allowances of effects, packed and crated, are:

Ensign	6,000 lbs.
Lieutenant (J. G.)	7,500 lbs.
Lieutenant	8,500 lbs.
Lieutenant Commander	9,000 lbs.
Commander	10,000 lbs.
Captain	11,000 lbs.
Rear Admiral (lower half)	12,000 lbs.
Rear Admiral (upper half)	14,500 lbs.
Vice Admiral	18,000 lbs.
Admiral	24,000 lbs.

Household effects may be packed, crated, and shipped as soon as orders have been received and proper application made, even previous to the detachment of the officer; or, if preferred, they may be delayed a reasonable length of time after the officer's detachment. Shipment of household effects includes packing, crating, drayage at point of shipment and at destination, unless otherwise stated.

It is not essential to send all household effects in one shipment. They may be divided into several shipments, each or any of which may be sent to any one of the authorized destinations. The latitude allowed in the points to which shipments may be made, and in the number and times of shipments, is of great assistance to families.

Drawing a "Dead Horse"

A transfer in station involving a long automobile trip and possibly a month's leave often presents a serious financial problem. Neither the officer's mileage nor reimbursement for the dependent's travel is collectible until the new station is reached, nor normally is the officer able to draw pay during the period between his detachment from his old station and his reporting at the new.

In order to cover such cases, at least in part, an officer transferred to a new station, provided he applies before his detachment, is authorized to draw a limited amount of advance pay. The amount that may be drawn depends in general upon the distance and probable period of time required to travel from the old to the new station. Such an advance in pay in the Navy is called "dead horse," a term which has come down to us from the British Merchant Marine.

Although it is most undesirable to draw a "dead horse" except in an emergency, the possibility of such advance when making a permanent change in station should be known, and in case there is a real need, an officer should not hesitate to take advantage of the permission. Money so advanced must be repaid to the government by deduction from future pay, at a rate not less than one-sixth of such advance per month.

The origin of the custom of drawing a "dead horse" is very interestingly told by Captain Leland P. Lovette in his book *Naval Customs, Traditions and Usage*:

Much to many a naval officer's regret, this old custom survives. A real ceremony was connected with the days when the crew "stopped working for nothing." In the days of sail, both in the Navy and particularly in the British Merchant Service, it was approximately a month's advance pay when the sailor shipped. After five weeks at sea or at whatever time the advance money has been worked off, the men made a horse out of canvas stuffed with old cordage and waste material or out of a cask, with oakum tail and mane, and permission was requested to light it and hoist it out to the end of a boom or yard. This was done amid cheers, and marked the time that the crew started to "accumulate wages on the books." The advance was usually spent in high living in the port just left. Plans could now be made for the next port.

Both watches used to sing in chorus the following chantey:

"Now, old horse your time has come
And we say so, for we know so!
Although many a race you've won,
Oh! poor old man,
You're going now to say good-bye,
And we say so, for we know so;
Poor old horse, you're going to die."

The Magic Trunk

Living out of suitcases, or perhaps one trunk, if one is never lucky enough to have been given time to pack it before being evacuated from war-torn zones, is a feat today. You brides who have time to plan, by all means take your backgrounds with you and make a home out of the barest hotel room. *Live* and enjoy every moment that HE can be with you. When he is ordered to duty you will be thankful for your happy memories!

In *my* trunk I brought two bedspreads with three pairs of chintz curtains to match. Mine were from our guest room and are in a luscious shade of Gauguin pink. (If I were a bride and *buying* them, I would prefer two maroon corduroy spreads or some favorite shade of blue or gold that might be more appropriate in the average hotel bedroom.) I managed two small Chinese rugs, but a fur rug would be nice to have. Naturally I included personal photographs and a few colorful flower prints. My trunk also contains a lovely Dresden powder box (which never fails to remind me of the time I missed the train in Dresden to buy it), some favorite small vases, a silver cigarette box, a silver tea set, my flat silver, an electric clock, a heating pad, my best linen, an iron, and a folding ironing board.

Other articles that occur to me which might have been included are two small lamps and shades, a bedside radio, toaster, and percolator.

Chapter XI

NAVY JUNIORS

In 1867, the old U.S.S. *Franklin* was making a Mediterranean cruise, and had anchored for a brief visit in the harbor of Naples. During the stay of the vessel in port, the King and Queen of Italy paid a visit to the ship.

The Queen was chatting with the Captain, and as she had a raft of children of her own and was greatly interested in youngsters, she paused for a moment to ask, "Captain, have you any children?"

"Yes, Your Majesty," answered the Captain, "I have three; one five years old, one ten years old, and one fifteen years old."

Whereupon the Queen with a twinkle in her eye replied, "Why, Captain, what long cruises you American officers make."

(From *The Navy's Best Stories*, Lieutenant Commander Hockey)

CHILDREN of naval officers are always spoken of in the Service as "Navy juniors," and children of Army officers are affectionately called "Army brats." The latter seem to have acquired their title from the West Point cadet's description of a Kaydet whose father is in the Regular Army. The *Howitzer* further notes that "one can always tell these Army children. They ride well, know all the Army answers . . . and outside of being 'high-ranking' and wanting Blue Uniforms, they are pretty regular kids." At Annapolis, Navy juniors also become "Navy brats." Whether or not these cherubs merit the opprobrious title is not for me to say. Anyway, theirs is a hard row!

They cut their teeth on brass buttons, and many a Navy junior motors all day and likes it! In the old days, small infants learned to use a bureau drawer for a crib, and probably they do today. They are accustomed to frequent moves. It is not unusual to hear a five-year-old roll off such jaw-breaking names as Tsingtao, Chefoo, Shanghai, Nagasaki, Chinwang-tao, Zamboanga, and Guantanamo. Their geography is first hand, and in their speech they often scatter in a little Chinese along with bits of Tagalog acquired from a Filipino house-boy. They know all about typhoons, earthquakes, pythons, and air raids, and in characteristic childish fashion they like to tell wild hair-raising stories, some of which they have pieced together from those told by their elders. Little boys like to make collections of shrapnel and shell splinters from air raids they have experienced in Shanghai in '37, and any souvenir from Pearl Harbor to them is priceless. These children have not only seen history made before their eyes; they have lived it.

To a Navy junior his dad is a hero and his ship is the largest and finest on the seas. There is something very touching in hearing a group of Navy youngsters boast about their fathers and their ships. And when Father comes home—what a welcome he gets! No New England sea captain of the old days could have received a finer reception than that accorded by ten-year-old Tommy, who is about to burst with pride as he waits at the landing for Daddy! Five-year-old Susie is beside herself with joy as she squeezes her mother's hand and displays a toothless grin in greeting. Already she is demanding a treasured dime for each missing tooth, even before Daddy has had a chance to kiss Mother or Susie's radiant fifteen-year-old sister who is also on deck for the homecoming.

You see, dear reader, the ages of the children in this Navy family correspond with the little story at the head of the chapter—perhaps there is something to be said for five-year intervals when it comes to having a wide-awake, interesting family. There is nothing like youngsters to keep one young in spirit, though on the Navy wife and mother falls the greater part of the responsibility in raising the family. She, in most cases, must make the important decisions in regard to their rearing, their schooling, the building of their characters; and it is she who plays the role of strict disciplinarian. The children rather learn to take her for granted, but Father is that rare and honored individual whose infrequent visits are red-letter days in the lives of his family.

Although travel offers a liberal education, frequent moves are somewhat of a hardship for the Navy family both economically and socially. Acquiring the ability to make adjustments readily to changing conditions is perhaps the thing that really molds the characters of Navy juniors. They are a tough, resilient, and self-reliant group of youngsters. Early in life they learn to solve their own problems, to get along with all classes and kinds of people, and to make necessary social adjustments. It is no small thing for an adolescent boy or girl, well established in a good school with pleasant connections and surrounded with congenial friends, to be suddenly transferred to a foreign country where the entire setup is different. Yet this happens every day to Navy families.

CHRISTENINGS

Before we get the adolescent too far along, perhaps it might be wise to get the poor child christened. Let us go back to his infant days.

In the Navy many young couples who have been married in the Chapel at Annapolis wait until they can return there to have Junior christened in the same church. There is a certain sentiment connected with these events.

Birth announcements should be very simple affairs. The proper form is a "Mr. and Mrs." card, or "the Mrs. card," to which is attached with a narrow white ribbon a smaller card with the baby's name on it and the date of birth. Printed forms of birth announcements bought at stationers are never in good taste.

The first step in the christening of a baby is the selection of a name. The parents and relatives decide upon it as best they may. This is something about which no outsider would be foolish enough to make suggestions; yet parents should avoid odd and fancy names that may be a source of embarrassment to the child when he or she grows up. Often a particular name will have a wave of popularity. We can all recall the days when every other little girl was named Gloria; then came the numerous little Bettys, and finally Marina, after the lovely Duchess of Kent. This is a matter of choice, naturally, but later your little girl may resent being dated. Of course there are always the doting parents who for sentimental reasons prefer to call their offspring after themselves. It is truly a matter of personal taste.

Most christenings are very simple affairs, attended only by relatives and close friends who may be invited by telephone or by informal note.

Godparents are chosen from among one's intimate friends. The Episcopal Church expects two godfathers and one godmother for a little boy and two godmothers and one godfather for a little girl. The Catholic Church asks only two, but both must be of the Catholic faith. In the Catholic Church the christening takes place usually before the baby is two weeks old, and if possible it is performed in church. In the Protestant churches the average christening takes place between the ages of two and six months, and may be performed at home or at church.

Arrangements should be made with the Navy Chaplain who is to perform the ceremony. He will probably suggest Sunday afternoon as an appropriate time. If the ceremony is held at the Chapel, the nurse takes charge of the infant until time to hand it over to the godmother, who holds it during the baptism. As soon as the ceremony is over, the godmother gives the baby back to its nurse, who carries it immediately to the waiting car, and she and the baby return home.

The baby is dressed all in white. If there is a christening robe in the family, it is a nice custom for the baby to wear it. The mother wears a street dress or a suit to the church.

When the christening is at the church, the friends and family go there at the appointed time and seat themselves in the pews nearest the font. The parents and godparents stand close to the font.

If the baby is christened at home, the procedure is about the same. It is usually easier and prettier to have the ceremony at home. At the last moment the baby can be brought downstairs by the nurse, and there is no danger of its taking cold. The house can be decorated appropriately, with the tea table daintily arranged with white roses and baby's-breath.

Everything should be placed in readiness for the Chaplain. The table, preferably a small high pedestal type, should be covered with a dainty cloth. A bowl of silver or crystal is used as a font.

After the ceremony there is usually some kind of christening feast at which the guests drink the baby's health. If the christening takes place at high noon after the Sunday services, a buffet luncheon may be in order.

If gifts are brought they may include a silver mug, porringer, or knife, fork, and spoon. Blue is the color of wearing apparel assigned to little boys, and pink for little girls, or vice versa. It really makes little difference to the modern mother. Flowers and notes of congratulations are usually sent to the mother.

Educational Insurance

This type of insurance, taken out as soon as practicable after Junior's arrival, is a popular means of saving. It is a boon to young parents and assures Junior of a college education when he reaches the age of 17 or 18. The premiums are small, and later, when expenses are heavier, the educational insurance matures. It is a convenient way of meeting the expenses of a college education.

Nursery Schools

In most of the large cities you will find nursery schools; yet there are some young parents who fail to recognize their value and what an important part they may play in Junior's future. In the first five years of life the little child learns faster than he can ever hope to do at any later period of his education. He will never in any other five years make such progress in the mastery of the mother tongue; he will never advance at an equal rate in gaining control over his body; the senses have received and the brain recorded countless impressions of form, color, size, sound, texture, and the basis has been laid for judgments of quantity, direction, and relationship. Many children have learned social behavior of a high order; habits (physical, mental, and moral) are being formed. Therefore, do you not agree that the best type of instruction possible is the heritage of your child in these formative years?

Little children love order. They like routine and they enjoy the well-rounded programs of a good nursery school. The nursery school had its beginning in England during the last World War. Mothers who had to work left their children for the day or part of the day under the supervision and care of trained teachers. The schools became increasingly popular after the war, and later were started in this country.

Eighteen months of age is not too early for a child to enter nursery school. The young child is learning constantly things which may be desirable or undesirable. Habits are being formed, character is in the making, attitudes and skills are being developed for better or for worse.

The average mother is busy with her household and her many duties while the nursery school teacher is a specialist who becomes mother-teacher, a companion, a playfellow, a story teller. To her is given the privilege of molding character and of shaping the lives of the most wonderful of all creatures, little children.

In a modern well-staffed nursery school the child is taught good health habits. There will be rest periods when he will learn to relax, proper eating habits at the table with a modicum of table etiquette thrown in, toilet habits and personal cleanliness. The companionship of children near the same age is one advantage, especially for the only child. In this group, he learns to share his possessions such as toys, books, and materials with other children. Most valuable of all, he learns to live and play in a group. The development of proper attitudes is an important aim of the nursery school, and learning to follow directions and take orders are processes of education which the preschool child should have.

After two years in a good nursery school where the important habit and attitude foundations of his future are laid, the child can skip a year before going into the kindergarten. This will prove one of the most important years in his life and yours too, as he goes through the question-asking stage. He is a veritable interrogation point. His imagination knows no bounds. He will want to investigate everything and everybody, so the schoolroom is too narrow for full growth—he needs the great outdoors and the surrounding world for his workshop.

When he is five years old he will be ready for kindergarten or preschool. The modern up-to-date kindergarten offers units of work that are related to the child's experience. Special emphasis and freedom will be given the child's initiative in the various activities offered. For instance, a kindergarten on a naval station would undoubtedly have a unit on transportation. Ships of various kinds and classifications ranging from battleships to submarines would be constructed from blocks, boxes, and orange crates, visits made to the dock where different types of ships would be inspected. The interest in this type of project is dynamic, and the children learn first hand through an activity of this sort.

It is all right to postpone reading and writing till the child is seven or older, but the numberless habits and qualities that go to make up character should be started with the start of life. The first seven years are the most important of all years.

On isolated stations where there are no preschool facilities, often some enterprising young mother will subscribe to an extension course, such as the Calvert system. It is best if she can teach a group of children between the ages of four and six, since training in a group is necessary for the best all-round development. Many mothers have tutored their children through the elementary grades with excellent results, though some training in pedagogy is usually necessary.

The kindergarten lays the foundation for reading by giving the children first-hand experiences which in turn make the printed page mean something to them. A rich play life is provided, frequent excursions are taken, pets are cared for, flowers and plants are grown. All of these activities are developed with the idea of enriching the life of the child. The delightful introduction to good literature, the direct exposure to good music, the best in art and art appreciation all point to a well-rounded curriculum.

Through grammar school, Navy children have to take the breaks and changes as they come, but fortunately the courses of study throughout the United States are standardized to some extent. Often summer school must be attended to make up certain credits and requirements; but on the whole they seem to make out and come through with flying colors.

PREPARATORY SCHOOLS

Many Navy parents place their children in boarding schools when they are old enough, so as to avoid the frequent moves, school transfers, loss of time and credits, and above all the emotional upsets that are bound to occur when young lives are uprooted so often. To me this is one of the sad features and disadvantages of Service life; children should somehow take root like plants. They should have stability, a stable home, childhood friends, an organized home and community life.

On the other hand, the average Navy junior is at home any place; he never meets a stranger. If they don't play handball by the same rules he learned in Hong Kong, then he learns the rules by which they play in San Diego. He has many little shipmates like himself, and when a chance meeting occurs with a former little friend of years ago, it is like old home week.

SCHOLARSHIPS

By the way, the Bureau of Navigation, Navy Department, Washington, D.C., publishes a list, Schools and Colleges Granting Concessions to Sons and Daughters of Officer and

Enlisted Personnel—U.S. Navy. Concessions and scholarships are offered by schools, colleges, universities, and summer camps. "Determination of the classes of persons who are
included as 'naval personnel' rests with the authorities of
the individual schools." Not included, however, are children
of Navy or Marine Corps Reserve and children of ex-officers
or ex-enlisted men of the Navy or Marine Corps whose connection with the Service has been severed.

Certain schools, namely, Ogontz School, Randles School,
and the Rensselaer Polytechnic Institute, have requested the
Bureau of Navigation to nominate the recipients of the
scholarships. Available scholarships or concessions should be
confirmed when making arrangements for attendance at the
school concerned. It is suggested that a letter similar to the
following be addressed to the authorities of the school:

Dear Sir:
I understand that St. Edmond's School offers a concession of
$200 in its fixed charges for tuition, room, and board for the bene-
fit of sons of naval personnel.

I am anxious to have my son, William Thornton, attend school
at St. Edmond's beginning with the school year 1942-1943. Will
you therefore send me a form for applying for entrance, an outline of the school charges, including any reduction which you
offer me by virtue of my connection with the Navy, and any other
instructions necessary for entering my son.

I am a chief petty officer of the Navy and am on active duty
on board the U.S.S. *Tennessee*. These facts may be verified by an
inquiry addressed to the Commanding Officer, U.S.S. *Tennessee*
or to the Bureau of Navigation, Navy Department, Washington,
D.C.

Very truly yours,
JOHN THORNTON

Registrar
St. Edmond's School
Bardstown, Ky.

In addition, there are scholarships given under the authority of state law for World War orphans, though it seems

that those for the last World War should be about completed. The La Verne Noyes Scholarships are awarded in a creditable list of universities and colleges. They provide for the payment of tuition in part or in full of deserving students *needing* this assistance to enable them to procure university or college training. This is to be done without regard to sex, race, religion, or political party, but the scholarships are only for those who shall be citizens of the United States and either shall "themselves have served in the Army or Navy of the U.S. of America in the war into which our country entered on the 6th day of April 1917, and were honorably discharged from service or shall be descended by blood from some one who has served in the Army or Navy of the U.S. in said war who either is still in said service or whose said service in the Army or Navy was terminated by death or an honorable discharge."

Then there are scholarships for girls offered by the Daughters of the *Cincinnati*.

The John Chester Scholarship is a postgraduate scholarship established at Teachers College, Columbia University, New York. This is a particularly generous one of $300 per annum, and in addition the society gives the incumbent an allowance toward maintenance of $500 per year.

The General Robert Anderson Scholarship is also a postgraduate one established at Teachers College, which gives $250 per annum. In addition the society gives the incumbent an allowance toward maintenance of $300 per year.

The Army and Navy Scholarship is founded by the Daughters of the *Cincinnati* by contribution of its members. The income amounts to $300 annually, besides an allowance toward maintenance for the year. This scholarship is unattached and can be used at any recognized college selected by the applicant. The income is paid direct to the college and the maintenance grant direct to the student herself.

Julia Chester Wells Maintenance Scholarship was established in 1938. It amounts to $300 a year for a period of four years. This scholarship is unattached.

Application for the last four scholarships mentioned should be made to Mrs. Thomas Cooke, 71 Macculloch Avenue, Morristown, N.J.

The George Washington Scholarship and the Thomas Jefferson Scholarship are established at the College of William and Mary, Williamsburg, Va. Each covers a full college course. Application should be made to Mrs. Henry Lyne, c/o First National Bank, Baltimore, Md.

APPOINTMENTS TO THE NAVAL ACADEMY

While scholarships may be one thing to win, an appoint· ment to the Naval Academy is another. It is becoming increasingly hard for sons of naval officers to obtain appointments. There are six kinds of appointments:

1. "Appointment by Senators, Representatives and Delegates in Congress and by the Vice President."

   Applications for Congressional appointments should be addressed personally to the two Senators from the State in which the applicant lives, or to the Representatives from the applicant's Congressional District, or to all three. Even Representatives-at-large should be approached. They all have appointments.

2. Appointments at large and appointments from the District of Columbia by the President.

   Applications for such appointments should be addressed to the Secretary of the Navy, Washington, D.C., and should give the full name of the candidate, his address, the date of his birth, and the name, rank, or rating of his father. There are 25 Presidential appointments.

3. Appointments by competitive examination from the enlisted men of the Regular Navy and Marine Corps.

   There are 100 appointments open to enlisted men of the Navy and the Marine Corps who have served one year, nine months of which has been at sea.

4. Appointments by competitive examination from the enlisted men of the Naval Reserve and the Marine Corps Reserve.

   There are 50 appointments open to the Naval Reserve and Marine Corps Reserve each year.

5. Appointments by the President from among the sons of deceased officers, soldiers, sailors and marines of the World War.

There are 40 of these appointments made each year. Applications for appointments should be addressed to the Bureau of Navigation, Navy Department, Washington, D.C.

6. Appointments from the honor graduates of educational institutions designated as "Honor Schools" by the War Department, and from the members of the Naval Reserve Officers' Training Corps.

There are 20 of these appointments each year.

(These figures as to the numbers of appointments during the war period will undoubtedly be stepped up to meet the needs of the emergency, but at present the increase in numbers of appointments has not been made public.)

There are some very stiff requirements that a prospective applicant for an appointment should know. He must be a citizen of the United States and have good moral character. He must be not younger than 17 on April 1 of the calendar year in which he expects to enter the Naval Academy, and not older than 21.

He must be unmarried; he must never have been married. Also, he must agree not to marry within two years after his graduation from the Naval Academy. (War may change this last requirement.)

The physical requirements are more than exacting. Eyes seem to come in for the most critical examination. Each must have a normal vision of 20/20.

The Navy Department publishes annually a government pamphlet with the full details concerning entrance requirements to the Naval Academy. Free copies will be sent upon application to the Bureau of Navigation, Navy Department, Washington, D.C.

If you have chosen the Navy for your profession and desire to follow in the footsteps of your father, let us wish you luck. May you be one of those Midshipmen to whom "Navy

Blue and Gold" is not only a hymn but a tradition, a song
of the Service charged with sentiment and tenderest memories.

> Now, College men from sea to sea
>   May sing of colors true;
> But who has better right than we
>   To hoist a symbol hue?
> For sailor men in battle fair,
>   Since fighting days of old,
> Have proved the sailor's right to wear
>   The Navy Blue and Gold.
>
> For years together by the bay
>   Where Severn joins the tide
> Then by the Service called away,
>   We're scattered far and wide;
> But still when two or three shall meet
>   And old tales be retold,
> From low to highest in the fleet
>   We'll pledge the Blue and Gold.

Blue and Gold

"The blue is to represent the dark waters of the Ocean,
and is essentially the Navy's color. The gold represents the
ornaments of an officer's uniform." (From *The School of the
Sea*, Leland P. Lovette, Captain, U.S.N.)

Chapter XII

NAVY LIFE IN THE NATION'S CAPITAL

I N NAVY circles Washington, being the seat of naval administration, is considered the hub of the universe. To many Navy families it spells "home." The site for the nation's capital was selected by President Washington, and the city was planned by a young French engineer, Major Pierre Charles L'Enfant. With the Capitol building, the White House, the new department buildings, art galleries, and memorials, broad avenues and extensive parkways, it is one of the most beautiful cities in the world. It is called the city of magnificent distances, and because of these distances and its formal atmosphere, it is sometimes said that "here one loses his friends but makes many acquaintances."

Service in Washington for the Navy carries with it definite rules and regulations in regard to social and official life. Duty there is a shore assignment that most naval officers and their wives welcome despite the high rents, frequently servantless apartment life, and costly living conditions. Generally the Navy wife considers these disadvantages outweighed by the cultural advantages that are offered in the form of wonderful concerts and musicales, interesting lecture courses, the theater, and the thrill of being an integral part of the social and official life of the capital.

Etiquette in Washington is exacting, and the dominating influence is the official side with its problems of rank and precedence. In other words the *first shall be first.* Whatever may be the precedence in heaven, in official Washington the first precede and the last must be content to bring up the rear.

In normal times "calling" is a very definite part of the

social and official life of Washington; but during the war even the customary practice of leaving cards at the White House has been abolished. Also, by order of the Secretary of the Navy, official calls on the Secretary of the Navy, the Under Secretary, the Assistant Secretary, the Assistant Secretary for Air, the Chief of Naval Operations, and the Chiefs of bureaus and offices in the Navy Department shall be considered as made and returned. So obviously afternoon calling in busy Washington is practically a thing of the past, at least for the duration. In the hope that the emergency may soon be over, and that we will return to the golden days of yesterday's peacetime, the normal procedure of calling will be outlined:

There are certain definite calls to be made by the newcomer, but except for the call at the White House and other specified official calls general calling follows the normal routine. The calling hours are from four to six in the afternoon, and evening calls are seldom made except upon intimate friends.

Calling at the White House is merely a form of respect, as neither the President nor his wife receives callers except by special appointment. Calls are made by driving to the Pennsylvania Avenue entrance and leaving cards with the doorman, who usually comes to the car to receive them. Such calls are not returned, but later those who have left cards may be invited to a tea or a musicale at the Executive Mansion.

Two of the officer's visiting cards are left and one of your own. A card index of callers is kept as an invitation list for teas and social affairs, so you should write your address plainly on each card. If you have relatives living with you, their cards should also be left. On each card should be written the address, and under the name should be stated the relationship, as: "Mother of Lieutenant William Satterlee Tyler, U.S. Navy." If Reserve Officers on active duty call, they should indicate their status by writing "Active Duty" on their cards.

Should a personal interview be desired, one calls first at the

White House and leaves cards. Then it is customary to write to the private secretary asking that a date be set when one may be received.

It has been the custom in recent years for the Secretary of the Navy and his wife to give one or more large receptions for all naval officers on duty in Washington and their wives at the Mayflower Hotel, the Army and Navy Club, or some other suitable place. Attendance at such a function, where one leaves cards, takes the place of calls made and returned.

The Chief of Naval Operations and his wife usually give three receptions of a similar nature in their home near the Naval Observatory. At times a Chief of a bureau may hold a reception for the officers on duty in his bureau. At such receptions cards should be left on which your address is plainly written.

In recent years calling has been greatly reduced. Even before the emergency, only officers of the rank of Captain and above were expected to call on "the powers that be." Officers below the rank of Captain should, upon reporting, inquire of the Aide or Assistant of their own bureau as to policy of calling in effect. At your earliest convenience, it is customary to call on the Assistant Chief of bureau or office, and on the head of the division or section to which your husband has been assigned. No other calls are required.

Calling at the various embassies is optional, but to make a tour of the embassies is definitely not in good taste. Should you have some tie, a mutual interest or connection, however, it is quite proper to call. Wherever you decide to call in official Washington, inquire if there is a specified day "at home." Friday is the official day chosen by diplomats, and during the season (January until Lent) they receive between four-thirty and seven o'clock.

It is a tactful and gracious gesture for a naval officer and his wife to call upon the Congressmen and Senators from his home state. Appreciation for past or future appointments to the Naval Academy may be the basis for this little attention.

INVITATIONS

The President of the United States usually holds four special receptions during the social season. The first to the Diplomatic Corps; the second to the Judiciary; the third to Congress; and the fourth to the Army and Navy. These have been curtailed during the war.

In normal times, the diplomatic reception ranks first in splendor and resembles scenes of court life at the European capitals of yesterday. The foreign diplomats in their full-dress uniforms resplendent with decorations and medals and the ladies in the smartest of Paris creations give an air of brilliance to the occasion.

The Army and Navy reception ranks next in magnificence. Officers of the Service are in full-dress uniform. Gold lace, literally miles of it, gold belts, fore-and-aft hats, sabers and swords, serve as a colorful background for the formal evening dress of the Army and Navy wives.

Those attending the annual Army and Navy reception enter the White House by the East Door, which is on the street level opposite the Treasury Building. If you are wise you will take a taxi to the White House. It is simpler than trying to find a parking space. Evening wraps, officer's capes and chapeaux are deposited in the cloak room. The guests pass through a long corridor in which are exhibited paintings of many of the past First Ladies, then go upstairs into the East Room, where the line is formed in order of precedence. At an official reception, the officer precedes his lady in being presented.

The President and his wife greet the Secretary of War and the Secretary of the Navy with their wives before making an appearance. Promptly at nine o'clock the wide doors of the Red Room giving on to the lobby open, and the bugler sounds "Attention." This is followed by four ruffles and flourishes of the bugle and drums—the signal that the President is about to make his appearance. The next moment the President and his wife appear and the scarlet-coated Marine Band plays "Hail to the Chief," the anthem with which the President is always greeted when appearing in public. Upon completion of the march, the President, accompanied by his wife and preceded by four military and naval aides (facetiously called by their comrades "the four horsemen"), crosses the lobby via the Red Room to the Blue Room. The Secretaries of War and Navy with their wives follow to the entrance to the Red Room, then leave and enter the Green Room.

In the Green Room the guests there assembled line up in the following order of precedence: the Secretary of War accompanied by his wife and by the Chief of Staff of the Army and his wife (the Secretary of War precedes the Secretary of the Navy because the War Department was established first); the Secretary of the Navy accompanied by his wife and the Chief of Naval Operations and his wife; the Under Secretary and Assistant Secretaries of War and their wives; the Under Secretary and Assistant Secretaries of the Navy and their wives; the Chairmen of the Senate and House Military and Naval Affairs Committees and their wives. After these dignitaries come the officers and their wives in a line formed in the East Room.

The President and his wife receive in the Blue Room. An aide presents the guests. The President is addressed as "Mr. President"; the First Lady as "Mrs. ——." It is not correct to more than greet the President unless addressed by him.

From the receiving line, the guests pass through the Red Room into the State Dining Room where they join groups of friends. It is a great occasion for renewing old friendships. Light refreshments are served, and sometimes, after all guests have been received, the First Lady comes in and mingles with the guests. The President usually retires to his apartments, and the reception is officially over with his withdrawal. The guests often linger for a while and enjoy dancing in the East Room.

Any formal invitation to dinner or to a reception, if an answer is requested, should be answered within twenty-four hours. Good form requires that replies to White House invitations should not be mailed, but should be delivered in person or by messenger. Invitations to the White House take precedence over any other invitation, since they are regarded more or less as a command. Should illness or absence from the city require one to decline, then the refusal containing the explanation should be sent immediately. When one has dined at the White House, cards should be left as a courtesy call within one week.

PRECEDENCE

Even experienced Washington hostesses who know most of the answers in social and official realms are often hard put to it when it comes to "precedence" and "who ranks whom."

In entertaining Service people the *Army Register* and *Navy Register* may be consulted to obtain the dates of commissions of officers of corresponding rank. In the United States the Secretary of War takes precedence over the Secretary of the Navy. The Chief of Staff of the Army is senior to all other Army officers. The Chief of Naval Operations is senior to all other naval officers. Among all other officers of the Army, Navy, Marine Corps, and Coast Guard, precedence goes with rank, and if of the same rank, then by date of their respective commissions. An exception to this is the Staff Corps whose precedence is given in a so-called "list of running-mates" in the *Navy Register*. Retired officers take precedence over active officers in accordance with date of commission in the rank they hold on the retired list.

Officers of the Navy and Coast Guard above the rank of Captain are called Flag Officers, while officers of the Army and Marine Corps above the rank of Colonel are called General Officers.

One happy thought is this: As a junior officer's wife, you won't be concerned much with precedence and seating arrangements for formal dinners, although it is nice to know. By the time Bill gets to the rank of Captain (if you are observant) it will come very naturally to you to know how to seat people. If not, you know where to get the information.

You can depend upon the *Register*, that good old Blue Bible for Navy hostesses. If only Navy personnel are concerned, the Aide to the Bureau of Navigation may give you assistance.

If, by chance, you are entertaining diplomatic representatives, we suggest that you consult the Chief of Protocol at the State Department; he may untangle the knotty problem for you. Foreign naval attachés are usually given precedence over officers of our own services when of equal rank purely as a courtesy.

SEATING ARRANGEMENTS

It is customary to seat the guest of honor at the right of the host, but at large official parties when toasts are to be given or speeches made, the guest of honor is seated opposite the host. On such occasions, if the table is long and narrow, the host and guest of honor are seated in the center of the length of the table, not at the two ends.

The second and third ranking guests, counting the guest of honor first, are seated on the right of the host and of the guest of honor respectively, the fourth and fifth ranking guests on the left of the host and guest of honor respectively. Should there be a guest (not the guest of honor), an officer of the same Service as the host and much senior to him, he is frequently given the seat otherwise occupied by the host and the host takes the seat opposite the guest of honor.

Where civilians are concerned, account must be taken of prominence and public office held. Among those having no public office, age and local prominence are the best guides, but Navy guests irrespective of age should be interspersed among civilians, especially if the dinner is on board ship.

How many times throughout this book we have stressed that there is no rank among women; yet when officers are accompanied by their wives at a formal, official dinner they are seated according to their husbands' rank.

At a ladies' luncheon, opinions may differ on this point! However, the senior officer's wife present is usually placed at the right of the hostess if there is no guest of honor. The seat at the right of the hostess, the seat on her left, and the seat at the opposite end of the table are all places of special honor.

Equivalent Ranks of Officers of the Navy, Army, and Marine Corps

Admiral	General	
Vice-Admiral	Lieutenant General	
Rear Admiral	Major General	Major General Commandant
Commodore	Brigadier General	Brigadier General
Captain	Colonel	Colonel
Commander	Lieutenant Colonel	Lieutenant Colonel
Lieut. Commander	Major	Major
Lieutenant	Captain	Captain
Lieutenant (J.G.)	First Lieutenant	First Lieutenant
Ensign	Second Lieutenant	Second Lieutenant

How to Distinguish the Rank of Army and Navy Officers

The rank of an officer is primarily indicated by the number and kind of stripes on his sleeves. It is also indicated on epaulets and shoulder marks, and in part by the markings on the cocked hat, cap and full-dress trousers and belt. Gold-lace, as it is called, is the principal distinguishing mark or rank for commissioned officers, worn upon the sleeves of the blue uniforms and on the shoulder marks of the white service coats, mess jackets and overcoats.[1]

In other words, the more gold lace, the more rank! Aviation officers and submarine officers wear sleeve stripes of black braid on their working uniforms.

Admiral	one 2-inch stripe with three ½-inch stripes above it (gold shoulder mark with four silver stars)
Vice-Admiral	one 2-inch stripe with two ½-inch stripes above it (gold shoulder mark with three silver stars)
Rear Admiral	one 2-inch stripe with one ½-inch stripe

[1] J. Bunkley, *Military and Naval Recognition Book.* D. Van Nostrand Company, Inc., New York, 1941.

	above it (gold shoulder mark with two silver stars)
Commodore	discontinued except for existing appointments
Captain	four ½-inch stripes
Commander	three ½-inch stripes
Lieut. Commander	two ½-inch stripes with one ¼-inch stripe above it
Lieutenant	two ½-inch stripes
Lieutenant (J.G.)	one ½-inch stripe with one ¼-inch stripe above it
Ensign	one ½-inch stripe
General	four stars
Lieutenant General	three stars
Major General	two stars
Brigadier General	one star
Colonel	silver eagle
Lieutenant Colonel	silver leaf
Major	gold leaf
Captain	two silver bars
First Lieutenant	one silver bar
Second Lieutenant	one gold bar

The Marine Corps is an integral part of the Navy, but the rank is the same as that of the Army.

Each arm and service has distinctive insignia. The line officers comprise the command group and the specialist group. Besides the line there are five corps called the Staff Corps. In lieu of the five-pointed star, which line officers of the Navy wear above the stripes on their sleeves and as shoulder marks, Staff Corps officers wear a Corps insignia:

Medical officers	a silver acorn embroidered upon a gold spread oak leaf
Dental officers	a gold spread oak leaf with a silver acorn on either side of stem
Supply officers	a gold sprig of three oak leaves and three acorns
Civil engineers	two crossed sprigs, each of two gold live-oak leaves and a silver acorn
Chaplain	a gold Latin cross

Officers of the Naval Reserve wear the same sleeve markings as prescribed for officers of the Regular Navy of the same rank and corps.

Service Medals and Badges

The custom of decorating those who have distinguished themselves by deeds of valor goes back a number of centuries, but until recent years it was customary to bestow decorations only upon those of high rank. In our own country during the Revolutionary and Civil Wars, medals were awarded for victories on land and sea by the government but they were usually of great size and not intended to be worn. The Commanding Officers received gold ones and they were kept on display; the subordinate officers received replicas in silver. On December 21, 1861, by an act of Congress, the United States government established its first decoration. Since that time, various medals and decorations have been awarded in recognition of an outstanding act of heroism or some especially noteworthy service rendered by individuals.

Prominent among United States decorations, medals, and ribbons are:

The Navy Medal of Honor
The Navy Distinguished Service Medal
Navy Cross
Gold Star (awarded when a second citation is given)
Distinguished Flying Cross
Gold and Silver Life Saving Medal
Good Conduct Medal
Medal Commemorating Battle of Manila Bay
Medal Commemorating Naval Engagements in West Indies
NC-4 Medal (First Trans-Atlantic Flight, U.S.N.)
Medal Commemorating Byrd Antarctic Expedition
Victory Medal
Navy Expeditionary Medal
China Relief Expedition
Philippine Campaign
Yangtze Service Medal

As the various medals are too cumbersome to wear all the time, the ribbons of the medals are authorized to be worn in their stead. It is an honor to be authorized to wear decorations and medals. Under no circumstances should they be worn by anyone except the person who has earned the right to them.

"Medals and decorations are, for the most part, worn on the left breast. This custom may be traced from the practice of the Crusaders in wearing the badge of honor of their order near the heart. Also, the left side was the shield side of the Crusader for the large shield, carried by the left arm, protected both the heart and badge of honor." (Pamphlet prepared by Twelfth Naval District.)

LIFE IN WASHINGTON

To the Navy wife a tour of duty in cosmopolitan Washington can be fun. The life is stimulating; somehow you feel that you are in the swim. Suddenly you find yourself very much concerned and interested in the passing of certain laws and bills. The government and its intricate machinery takes on a new meaning for you. The glamour of the embassies and legations thrills you, and all in all you feel that you are a very definite part of capital life.

Regardless of how the climate is berated, either for its beastly hot summers or below-zero winters, you will enjoy the springtime with its cherry blossoms and the gorgeous autumns that are all too short but beautiful beyond description.

Navy people rent or buy homes anywhere from Alexandria, Virginia, to Spring Valley or Chevy Chase in Maryland. Others join the cliff-dwellers and live in compact or sizable apartments, while a third group prefers hotel life. The Wardman Park Hotel is popular as a residential hotel; also the Martinique, the Fairfax, and the Brighton give Service rates both to permanent and to transient guests. Whatever your needs, it is wise to secure the help of a real-estate agent. Commander Frankinburger, U.S.N. (retired), with the Sandoz Real Estate Agency at No. 2 Dupont Circle, will help you out if you have trouble in finding just what you want.

In order to take advantage of all the opportunities offered you, in the way of the theater (many of the Broadway hits have their try-outs before critical Washington audiences), interesting free lectures and concerts, courses of all kinds, it will be necessary to simplify your style of living. This will be easy, with usually only breakfast and dinner to prepare, since practically all of the officers lunch near their offices. Many of the apartment houses have a dining room in connection, and a great majority of Navy families dine out in preference to having a servant.

Washington is full of good restaurants and hotels that are popular for dining and dancing. At the moment, the Shoreham is probably the most popular with Navy personnel. In the summer there is dancing on the terrace. The Mayflower Hotel has an attractive cocktail lounge. Tea dances there are a meeting place for pretty debutantes and handsome diplomats. The Carlton also has an inviting cocktail lounge.

Pierre's and L'Escargot are the two best French restaurants. Pierre's is very popular for luncheons and there one sees the best-dressed women in Washington. It is also a favorite place for dinner, but there is no music.

It is interesting to go down on the wharf for some of the best sea food you ever tasted. Among the famous restaurants are Herzog's, Hogate's, and O'Donnell's. The Occidental, one of the oldest in Washington, is well known for its sea food and steaks. Its specialty is "rum buns." Normandy Farms, Md., about ten miles from Washington, serves special parties. Allies' Inn, opposite the State, War, and Navy building, has a splendid cafeteria.

CLUBS

Washington has many private clubs at which a great many Service people do their entertaining. Some of these are:

The Army and Navy Club: Initiation fee, $55.50; dues, $6.60 per month. Officers find it convenient to lunch there. The cocktail lounge is attractive and ladies are welcome to dine at the Club, but the lobby writing rooms, library, and lounge are restricted to the use of officers. There is a special ladies' lounge.

The Army and Navy Country Club: Initiation fee, $100.00; monthly dues, $6.60. Located 3 miles from Washington. It affords golf, swimming, weekly dances, and many social advantages.

Chevy Chase Country Club: It has a long waiting list and is expensive.

Washington Golf and Country Club.

The Columbia Club: Splendid golf course.

Kenwood Country Club: Good golf course.

OTHER CITIES THAT ALSO SPELL HOME TO THE NAVY

Long Beach, California, has long been called "the West Coast Capital of the Navy" because for twenty-one years it has been the base from which the Pacific Fleet operated. In the spring of 1940 the Fleet moved to Honolulu. To Navy families in general, but to the enlisted personnel especially, Long Beach spells home—it spells *heaven*.

Numerous Navy families live in San Diego, Coronado, Los Angeles, Vallejo, San Francisco, and Seattle. Honolulu was also a mecca for Navy families, but few dependents venture far into the Pacific at present.

On the Atlantic coast, Annapolis is spoken of as "the Cradle of the Navy"; while at Newport, Rhode Island, is located the Naval War College, the Torpedo School, the Naval Training School, and a Naval Hospital. Newport is a fascinating old town famous as a summer resort in the gay nineties. It is very proud of its history. Many of its few remaining older residents like to drive cars of ancient vintage, wear old-fashioned hats of the Queen Mary type, and keep up the appearance of living in the past.

New London, Connecticut, as the site of the Coast Guard Academy and the Submarine School, is home to many families. Norfolk, Virginia, an important operating base and Navy yard; Charleston, South Carolina; Pensacola, Florida; and New Orleans, Louisiana—each has its own contingent of Navy personnel who always in the back of their minds hope to retire to or at least go back to revisit the place that to them offered friendship and hospitality during their service.

With all of the new bases and cities that will become Navy centers in the future, other ties will be formed. But the cities mentioned will always remain dear and will spell home to the old Navy.

Chapter XIII

ILLNESS AND HOSPITALIZATION

Old sailors never die, never die, never die,
Old sailors never die, they just sail away!

Medical officers on duty at navy yards and naval stations are, in addition to their official duties, required to attend the families of officers and enlisted men.

At the Naval Dispensary, Navy Department, medical attendance will be accorded the families of officers and enlisted men on duty in Washington, D.C., not otherwise provided for, and retired officers and enlisted men and their families within the residential area prescribed by the Navy Department.

The family of an officer or enlisted man shall include only those relatives who are dependent upon him for support, and not persons employed by him. The widows of deceased naval personnel, active or retired, are also entitled to medical care.

Officers and enlisted men will exact of their families consideration in their relations with medical officers, requiring those who are physically able to visit the dispensary, to do so.

Article 1185, *Navy Regulations*

FOR enlisted men and officers hospitalization, medical supplies, and medical and dental attention are given; but in general, only the service as stated above is allowed the family of an officer or enlisted man. Dependents must necessarily be cared for only after the needs of the officers and enlisted personnel have been met. During an emergency it may be impossible for the dispensaries to administer to other than the active Service personnel except in cases urgently demanding immediate attention.

It is often necessary for Service families to live where naval medical care is not available. In such cases, upon arriving in a strange place it is wise to inquire and get the name of a good civilian doctor and write his number on your telephone pad for a possible emergency. An obstetrician's services, naval or civilian, should be engaged in advance and arrangements made for hospitalization reservations, should such service be needed.

The Navy, fully appreciating the fact that adequate medical care for dependents of Service personnel is a great aid to morale, has expanded this service to a size considerably greater than originally contemplated. An extensive dispensary service staffed with medical officers specially trained in the diseases of women and children is available at all of the larger naval stations and at many of the smaller. At the larger stations these specially designated doctors devote practically their entire time to the medical care of Service personnel. In general the dispensaries are equipped and operated practically the same as are offices of civilian medical practitioners. Regular office hours are provided for outpatients. Eye, ear, nose, and throat specialists are in attendance at the larger dispensaries and are available at all naval hospitals. The important prenatal care for expectant mothers and after-care for both mothers and babies is provided, and parents are urged to take advantage of them. Mothers are requested to bring in their babies at regular intervals during the important first year in order that diets, weights, etc. may be checked and corrective measures promptly instituted if necessary. Accurate records are kept of all patients.

Medical attention thus provided is equal to the best provided by civilian communities. In these days of financial stringency many officers and men cannot afford to pay for first-class civilian medical care without going seriously into debt. It is therefore a great comfort to all, and especially to officers and men at sea, to know that their loved ones have fully competent specialist naval medical care available. This includes specialists in surgery, internal medicine, obstetrics, pediatrics, etc. Except in emergency, dental care is not provided Service dependents.

Varying in detail at different stations, especially as regards distances covered, medical attendance for dependents sick at home is provided at all naval stations. The naval family practitioner is available at all hours for sickness and does not keep office hours. Patients requiring hospitalization are taken to civilian or naval hospitals, as the case may be, and cared for there by the naval doctor in attendance. As in civil practice, the same doctor usually attends patients sick at home or in hospital until the case is completed, though others may be called in consultation. While all naval medical officers have to take their tours of sea duty, the naval family practitioners are rotated in such duty ashore so far as practicable.

NAVAL HOSPITALS

Formerly few Naval hospitals, except those on isolated stations such as Guam and Samoa, were equipped to care for dependents. These hospitals have wards with private, two-, and four-bed rooms available for dependents. All facilities obtainable in the better civilian hospitals are provided, including the delivery rooms for obstetrical patients and nurseries for newborn babies. At stations where such hospitals are located the outpatient dispensaries for dependents are situated near these wards, the whole forming a family practice department. This greatly facilitates the work of the doctors detailed to this duty.

Dependents are charged a flat rate of $3.75 a day for hospitalization. Of this sum, $0.75 per diem is credited to the naval hospital fund, a trust fund for the maintenance of naval hospitals which derives its revenues from within the naval service and is administered by the Secretary of the Navy, the trustee of the fund, subject to the control of Congress. Each officer, seaman, and marine has the sum of $0.20 per month deducted from his pay and credited to this fund. The remaining amount of $3.00 per diem is deposited to the credit of the ship's service store of the hospital, accounted for separately from all other monies, and is expended by direction of the Commanding Officer to defray those costs of hospitalization not provided by the law.

The naval hospital fund provides subsistence, the more usual medicines, X-ray films, surgical dressings, laboratory services, and incidentals. The hospitalization costs of dependents borne from sums deposited with the ship's service officer include the wages and subsistence for additional employees required for the care of dependents, such as civilian nurses, maids, and culinary employees; the service of civilian specialists when required; blood transfusions; and the cost of special medicines and drugs not regularly stocked by the naval medical department.

Naval hospitals have definite visiting hours, usually from one to four in the afternoon. Needless to add, quiet behavior in passing through the corridors and in private rooms is expected and required. It is customary to request permission at the information office to visit a patient. If permission is granted, you will either be directed or escorted to the patient's room. Be careful to make your visit brief. Doctors usually prefer that the visitor carry on most of the conversation, which should be kept in a cheerful vein. However, if the patient wishes to tell you all of the gory details of her operation, your only recourse is to be a sympathetic listener. Avoid comparing an operation you once had with the patient's more recent one. "Comparisons are odious," and especially so to a sick person who at this time fancies herself a heroine or a martyr and is interested only in her own case history. The kind thing is to let her enjoy her big moment!

FLOWERS AND GIFTS

Flowers are always a welcome gift. Since government hospitals have a very limited supply of vases and flower receptacles, it is well, if you take flowers, to have the florist arrange them in inexpensive containers. Small blooming potted plants are quite practical, since they last longer and do not require much care from the busy nurse.

An amusing book, a best seller, or several of the small, inexpensive, paper-bound pocket editions make welcome gifts.

Book stores make up charming packets of six or more current magazines directed toward the interests of the patient. These arrive in bright cellophane wrappings and add a cheery note to the sickroom. A box of mints or candies or a basket of tempting fruit resembling a small "bon voyage" basket, in which are placed small jars of jam, marmalade, or jelly, often appeal to a convalescent. But always think twice before your selection is made. Don't send books to a person recovering from an eye operation, and don't send fruit—especially sour fruit—to a friend who is still gagging and groaning from a tonsillectomy.

For children, any little novelty or a "surprise basket" will help pass the long, tedious days of recovery. Gift departments in the larger stores make a specialty of these novelty baskets and boxes. They can be made as individual as you like. For instance, there may be a surprise planned for each day in the "week basket." A note explaining the system and clever little verses accompanying each gift make it "sort of a treasure hunt idea," so that the child will enjoy today and look forward to tomorrow. The basket may contain inexpensive books, games, puzzles, and a limited amount of sweets (if they are permitted). What children, especially little boys between the ages of six and twelve, really adore is a large bundle of those horribly stupid books of comics. Why is not for me to question. The tastes of little boys have always been a puzzle to me. They like comics, and if you want to please them, you'll take them comics.

NAVY DOCTORS

While all medical and dental officers of the Navy have the official title of the corresponding line rank, those below the grade of Captain are commonly addressed as "Doctor." Admirals and Captains of the Medical Corps are usually called by their line title. "After all, many men can be officers in the Navy," as someone explained, "but not all naval officers can be Doctors, and for that reason many prefer to be called 'Doctor.'"

Navy Nurses

The Navy Nurse Corps (female) is under the jurisdiction of the Bureau of Medicine and Surgery, which in turn is under the direction of the Secretary of the Navy. Established May 13, 1908, the Nurse Corps consists of a superintendent and an assistant superintendent, appointed by the Secretary of the Navy, whose terms of office may be terminated at his discretion, and of as many chief nurses, nurses, and reserve nurses as may be needed in time of emergency.

Navy nurses are eligible for duty at naval hospitals and on board hospital and ambulance ships. All nurses in the Corps are appointed or removed by the Surgeon General, with the approval of the Secretary of the Navy. They must be graduate nurses of an accredited school and registered three-year course, and their promotion is subject to an examination as to their professional, moral, mental, and physical fitness.

Nurses are *not* allowed to receive gifts from patients or from relatives or friends of patients for services rendered when on duty. Also, according to Navy Regulations (Article 1649), the authority of a nurse, necessary for the performance of duty to which she may be assigned, shall be duly recognized and enforced.

Navy nurses have the same pay, allowances, subsistence, and quarters as are allowed Army nurses, the only difference being that the latter are given rank and insignia comparable to commissioned officers of the Army to the grade of Major. A bill is before Congress at present designed to secure similar rank and insignia for Navy nurses.

Members of the families of officers and enlisted men are not entitled to the services of Navy nurses. When in the opinion of the commanding officer of the hospital or the medical officer at the station, such services are required for great emergencies and in the manifest interest of humanity, he may require that they be performed, and he shall report the circumstances to the Surgeon General. If this emergency is other than of a temporary character, or should the situation render the services of civilian nurses impossible, a Navy nurse, if she so desires and if her services can be spared, may, with the approval of the commanding officer of the hospital or the medical officer of the station, be granted special leave without pay and allowances in order to take the case, such leave not to exceed 30 days in the calendar year for an individual nurse. (*Manual of the Medical Department of the U.S. Navy*, Article 362.)

The Navy Relief Society

In any life, no matter how well organized and conducted, emergencies often arise. In any such emergency, in the absence of her husband, the wife should immediately report her situation to the nearest representative of the Navy Relief Society. This society was organized and is supported primarily by Navy personnel. Its objective is to furnish assistance, financial or otherwise, to Navy personnel in time of emergency. There are representatives in all cities in which is located any large naval activity.

In the event that there is in the city no representative of the Navy Relief, the wife should apply to the Red Cross or Y.M.C.A., both of which organizations gladly and effectively render assistance to Navy personnel.

The Navy Relief Society is kept informed by the Bureau of Navigation and Commandant of the Marine Corps of all deaths occurring in the Navy and Marine Corps. The Bureau of Navigation furnishes in each case the name, address, and relationship of the nearest of kin as given on the man's enlistment record. If the relationship is that of mother, wife, or child, the Society immediately investigates the circumstances of the dependent survivor. The investigation is systematic, expeditious, and confidential. Assistance is rendered wherever an urgent need exists and is in the form of lump sums or of monthly allotments.

Death

The Navy is like one large devoted family. In times of illness or death no intimate circle of friends of long standing can be closer or more deeply stirred. There is no limit to their true understanding and genuine sympathy because many of them have experienced sudden tragedy in their own lives, and all of them know that on any day they may suffer a similar loss.

Navy wives share everything with each other, even sorrow. Their lives in the Service become intertwined, they watch each others' children grow up, they know well the family ties that exist, and when death strikes, their hearts beat in sympathy and understanding. No one can overestimate the value of the sustaining help and comfort they extend to each other in times of grief. The loving handclasp of a friend, a simple note or message of sympathy to the bereaved person, or a bouquet of flowers are always forthcoming when they are needed. Intimate friends render any personal assistance they can and in every way possible try to relieve the grief-stricken family of the burden of trying details. Funeral arrangements in the case of an officer's death are taken care of by the Navy, subject to the approval of the family and depending of course upon the circumstances and place of death.

Mourning

An intimate friend or a servant should be at the door of the home to receive callers, to take messages, and to receive cards. No one should ask to see the bereaved person unless either the person receiving or some member of the family suggests it. Navy wives are schooled in being practical. Often they purposely busy themselves with their personal affairs as soon as possible. There are certain immediate adjustments to be made, and they are wise in not wishing to be alone with their thoughts. Unless prostration or illness from the shock prevents, to keep as busy as possible is the best course. A morbid preoccupation with one's own tragedy is as distressing to others as callous flippancy. Dignified, honest sorrow is no discredit to any person, man or woman, and is never out of place.

Mourning apparel does not receive the formality and regard

it did in former years. A Navy widow looks through her wardrobe and usually finds appropriate black dress, coat, or suit. Stores and all dressmaking establishments give precedence to mourning orders, and will often open shop after hours and on holidays to accommodate a customer. Often friends or acquaintances offer to lend veils and wraps.

Military Funerals

Military funerals for naval officers are divided into six classes as follows:

1. With chapel service
2. Without chapel service
3. With graveside service only
4. With ceremony prior to shipment of remains
5. Burial at sea
6. Memorial services

The selection of honorary pallbearers, if they are desired, is made by the family of the deceased or its representatives.

The pallbearers march at the side of the hearse, the junior to the left and leading, the next junior to the right and leading, and so on. Depending upon their age and the distance to the place of interment, they may ride in advance of the hearse. Eight men are selected as body bearers, and march immediately behind the body.

If the deceased was a flag officer, a unit commander or captain of a ship, his flag or pennant or the commission pennant is draped in mourning and displayed at halfmast in the bow of the boat carrying the body. The flag or pennant is also carried immediately in advance of the body in the funeral cortege to the grave, but not upon the return from the grave.

Funeral Procession on Shore

A funeral procession on shore shall be formed as follows (Article 342, *Navy Regulations*):

Escort commander and staff
Band

Escort
Clergy
Pallbearers (when riding)
Bearer of personal flag or pennant, or the commission pennant
    of the deceased
Body and pallbearers (when marching)
Family of deceased
Mourners in inverse of rank:
a. enlisted men
b. officers from ship of deceased
c. other officers
d. foreign officers
e. distinguished persons
f. delegations
g. societies
h. citizens

It is said that at the funeral of George Washington the
troops came first, then the clergy, and next the General's
horse with the two colored grooms. After the body came the
mourners with Lord Fairfax as the last mourner. Captain
Leland P. Lovette describes the recent funeral of a distinguished and greatly beloved Admiral in which two old colored retainers preceded the honorary pallbearers, all of whom
were high-ranking officers of the Navy. Death is a great
leveler, and as Captain Lovette explains, "the reversal of
rank at funerals is an acknowledgment that at death all men
are equal. Seniors take their proper precedence in the procession after burial. This form of the 'last shall be first and first
shall be last' is carried out in the recessional and processional
of churches."

On the march to the place of interment the procession
moves in slow time, the music being an appropriate funeral
march; the ensign and the ship's battalion colors, the latter
draped in mourning, are carried in the center of the escort;
the drums are draped in mourning and muffled.

Upon returning from the place of interment, the column
moves in quick time, and the mourners march in order of
rank. When clear of the cemetery, the mourning and muffling

is removed from the battalion colors, and the drums and music play a march.

An officer or pallbearer wears a mourning badge on the left arm and sword hilt. Regardless of the grade or rate, the coffin is covered with the national flag. According to Navy Regulations 1882:

1. The naval appropriation act approved June 30, 1914, provides, "That the Secretary of the Navy be authorized at his discretion to issue free of cost the national flag (U.S. national ensign No. 7) used for draping the coffin of any officer or enlisted man of the Navy or Marine Corps whose death occurs while in the service of the U.S. Navy or Marine Corps, upon request, to the relatives of the deceased officer or enlisted man, or upon request to a school, patriotic order or society to which the deceased officer or enlisted man belonged."

FUNERAL ESCORT

Navy Regulations, 1313, par. 5, provides that an escort not to exceed one person may be provided to accompany to place of burial the bodies of officers, enlisted men, or nurses who have lost their lives in the naval service. The escort furnished under this authority may be a relative or friend (not in the Service) of the deceased.

With an unmarried officer, a brother officer is usually asked to escort the remains to the home of the deceased, but in the case of a married officer, it is customary for the widow and children to act as escort to the place of burial.

BURIAL AT SEA

In this day it will seldom be necessary to commit a body to the deep; nevertheless the ceremony of time-honored tradition should be known by all. If for any reason the deceased is buried at sea, the body is placed in canvas or coffin with weights to insure its sinking. An American flag is placed over the body and gently pulled off as the body is released over the side.

It has ever been customary for all officers and men not on duty to attend the services of a late shipmate. The chaplain, or in his absence, the captain or an officer detailed by the captain.

reads the burial service at sea. In most cases the Episcopal prayer-book service is used. The ritual ends with the very beautiful and time-honored words, "we therefore commit this body to the deep, to be turned into corruption, looking for the resurrection of the body, when the sea shall give up her dead, and the life of the world to come . . ."

At this point of the service, "we commit the body to the deep," a seaman tilts the grating or wooden platform, slips off the flag and the body is projected into the ocean.[1]

Origin of Certain Customs at Military Funerals

Firing three volleys at military funerals dates back to old Roman days, when these ancient people cast earth upon the coffin *three times*. It was also customary for the Romans to call the dead *three times* by name, which ended the funeral ceremony, after which the relatives and friends of the deceased pronounced the word *"vale"* (farewell) *three times* as they departed from the tomb. Another, less pretty version, is that three volleys are fired into the air at imaginary devils which might get into men's hearts at such a moment as the burial of a comrade-at-arms (pure superstition).

The more comforting thought is that when the firing squad discharges three volleys over a grave, they are, in accordance with the old Roman custom, bidding their dead comrade "farewell, three times!"

Taps or Nunc Dimittis

"This practice involves a deep-felt sentiment—Rest in peace." It is the last bugle call, but it gives promise of reveille in the life to come. There is no other call so beautiful; it is the call of comfort and peace.

Memorial Services

In case of death and burial on foreign shores, or loss of life at sea or in any disaster when no military burial services

[1] Leland P. Lovette, *Naval Customs, Traditions and Usage.* United States Naval Institute, Annapolis, 1939.

have been held, it is customary to hold memorial services in honor of the deceased. The services are conducted according to the denomination that has been requested. The Navy Department generally announces the wishes of the widow if a memorial service is to be held; and while it is a painful ordeal for the bereaved to undergo, it often brings consolation and helps to assuage their grief to a small extent by honoring the memory of a dear one.

The following account of a memorial service was taken from *The Army and Navy Register* (names, dates, and places have been changed):

The Navy Department announced on March 20, that in compliance with the wishes of his widow, the ashes of the late Lieutenant Commander Scott Kenner, U.S. Navy, killed March 5, in the crash of an R.A.F. Ferry Command plane, are to be scattered from a naval plane on Pensacola Bay, Florida.

Simple non-military memorial services, conducted by Chaplain James Raphael, U.S.N., will be held in the Chapel-by-the-Sea, near the Air Station.

The ashes were sent from England on March 15, after funeral services in Edinburgh, Scotland, on March 8, and memorial services at St. Martin-in-the-Fields Church, Trafalgar Square, March 10.

FLOWERS

If the family prefers to avoid the added complication of flowers, the following notice is added to the funeral notice which appears in the daily papers: "Friends are requested not to send flowers," rather than the phrase "Please omit flowers," which is often seen but is rather abrupt.

In the last year or so the Army and Navy Memorial Aid, the secretary and treasurer of which is General Charles D. Roberts, 6510 Maple Ave., Chevy Chase, Md., has become popular with Service personnel. It is an organization which helps officers and enlisted men's families which the Army Relief and the Navy Relief cannot help because of restricted activity.[1] The Memorial Aid helps Service families all over the United States and is supported by memorials in the form of checks which are sent in place of flowers to a funeral. A card is sent to the bereaved family stating "a Memorial has been placed in the Aid Society by Commander and Mrs. Charles Grant Brown." It is a very nice way to show sympathy and to do some material good at the same time.

If flowers are sent, the officer in charge or someone designated by him should remove the cards and record a brief description of each offering. The list is turned over to the family of the deceased after the funeral.

Expenses of Burial—Monument or Marker

The necessary and proper funeral expenses of officers and enlisted men of the Navy and Marine Corps are allowed only when death occurs while in active service and shall in no instance exceed $200.

If the widow or family does not provide a monument in a national cemetery, the Government erects a white marker headstone of regulation pattern inscribed with the rank, name and branch of service of the deceased. The widow or family should not contract for a private monument until both the design, material and inscription have been submitted to and approved by the Quartermaster General.[1]

Navy Mutual Aid

If an officer is a member of the Navy Mutual Aid Association, his widow or dependents will need no outside legal advice or help in the filing of necessary government claims. Practically all widows have to ask help in filing claims and securing their benefits, and if a lawyer is employed, of course it costs money. If the Navy Mutual Aid attends to these important transactions there is no charge. Upon official notifica-

[1] Formerly, the officer or man must have passed away before either the Army or Navy Relief Societies could give assistance. But this has been modified. An officer or enlisted man may now receive loans to cover hospital costs or funeral expenses, and the repayment is made by monthly allotment.

tion of a member's death, the Association telegraphs the beneficiary $1000 immediately, and the remainder of the policy upon request.

If the necessary official documents are filed with the Navy Mutual Aid, the Association will upon request file the following claims upon proper signatures:

BENEFITS FOR WIDOWS AND DEPENDENTS

Six Months Gratuity: This payment is a lump sum equal to 6 months base pay, including longevity, flying pay, submarine pay, and pay for qualification in the use of arms. Payable to widows, and children under 21 years of age and unmarried or otherwise, to designated dependent relatives, as determined by the Secretary of the Navy.

This is paid ONLY when the officer is on active duty and is not payable to the Naval Reserve.

Write: Bureau of Supplies and Accounts, Navy Department, Washington, D.C.

(Application must be in duplicate Standard Form 1057.)

Arrears in Pay: Write Bureau of Supplies and Accounts, Navy Department, Washington, D.C.

(Fill out application, Standard Form 1055, and forward by registered mail.)

The disbursing officer carrying the account forwards the application to the beneficiary. Letters testament should be sent if the claim is filed by executor of the estate. Receipted, itemized undertaker's bill must be enclosed if one is claiming reimbursement for funeral expenses.

Government Insurance: Not over $10,000—must have policy and affidavits in support of insurance claim (in duplicate).

Write: The Director of Insurance, Veterans' Administration, Washington, D.C.

Pension: Director, Dependents' Claims Service, Veterans' Administration, Washington, D.C.

Application on Form 534 from widow, or guardian or custodian of child or children under 18 years of age, and application on Form 535 from dependent Mother or Father.

(Explanations too lengthy and too involved to list here.)

The executive order prescribes the following rates:

Widow under 50 years of age receives, monthly, $22.00
Widow 50 to 65 years of age receives $26.00
Widow over 65 years of age receives $30.00
Dependent mother or father receives $13.00
Or both, each $11.00

The rates vary for children according to age and number. To be entitled to a pension for death of veteran due to peacetime service, the widow must have been married to the veteran prior to the expiration of ten years subsequent to his discharge or retirement.

INFORMATION IN REGARD TO PENSIONS

1. Write in for information in regard to pension claim as soon as possible after an officer's death. Payments do not begin until after all necessary papers to substantiate claim are filed and approved.
2. Death certificate unnecessary if filed with claim for other benefits payable by Veterans' Administration.
3. *Certified copy* of public or church record of *marriage*. In event of prior marriage, certificate of custodian of public record or other acceptable proof of death of, or certified copy of decree of divorce from, the former husband or wife.
4. *Birth* or *baptismal certificate* of widow and each child under 18 years of age.

There are several other benefits and compensations to which widows and dependents of Navy officers may be entitled, such as aid from American Legion, aid from Veterans of Foreign Wars, United Spanish War Veterans, and Regular Veterans Association.

Dependents when making a claim are always badly unnerved, and an officer is wise who relieves his wife and dependents of this unnecessary strain in time of grief. Also, it should be emphasized that a widow should write in for information in regard to pension claim as soon as possible after an officer's death. Payments do *not* begin until after all necessary papers to substantiate claim are filed and approved.

LETTERS OF CONDOLENCE

Many find a letter of condolence difficult to write, yet a truly sincere note at a time of sorrow is always appreciated. The letter should not be long, nor should it be filled with biblical quotations, platitudes, or affected sentiment. A person in grief, whose eyes are dimmed with tears and whose heart is aching, does not feel up to reading a long philosophical dissertation.

The letter of condolence should show admiration of character or fine traits of the deceased, and express genuine affection. If you cannot honestly say anything of this nature, don't give false praise to the dead, but write a sincere word of sympathy to the bereaved ones. Avoid harrowing the feelings by too-familiar allusions to the deceased.

A simple letter of friendship or a telegram expressing genuine sentiment, showing admiration for the one who has passed to the great beyond, is about the greatest solace that we can offer. A sincere handclasp without a spoken word, a note conveying three lines of sincere sympathy, or often just the presence of a quiet friend will speak volumes to a broken heart.

Abraham Lincoln's famous letter of condolence to Mrs. Bixby, the mother of five sons who died for their country, is a classic. It is simple, sincere, and dignified.

The type of letter of sympathy to a close friend whose husband was killed in a submarine disaster or airplane crash:

Dearest Mary,

I know the shock of this has been very great. It's useless to try to say all the things I want to say. If there is anything I can do, let me know immediately. In any case, I will be over to see you. May I come soon?

Yours devotedly,

Letter of condolence to a young mother who has lost a beloved child:

My dear, dear Margaret,

Even a devoted friend feels helpless at such a time, knowing that so little can be said or done that really brings comfort, but your friends are with you in understanding and love. Perhaps later on the memory of this may bring some of the consolation that I so long to give you now.

Devotedly,

Type of letter or note to a friend whose husband was a shipmate of your husband:

Dear Betty,

If there is anything that Bill and I can do, I really hope that you will let me know. We, like everyone else, are terribly shocked, and our thoughts and love are with you.

Most sincerely,

Answers to Letters of Condolence

There is no necessity for haste in answering letters of condolence, telegrams, or floral tributes; however, they should always be answered with a personal note of appreciation unless the grief-stricken person is prostrated or for some reason is unable to write. In that case, some member of the family should perform this service.

One may simply write, "Thank you so much for your kind sympathy" on a visiting card. Engraved cards of thanks for letters of condolence are not regarded as good form except in the case of some very prominent person, when hundreds of such expressions of sympathy would have to be answered by some simple method. Most persons are so touched by the love and tenderness shown them by their friends in a recent sorrow that they really want to write a sincere and genuine note of thanks.

Chapter XIV

ETIQUETTE FOR CIVILIANS VISITING A NAVY YARD

> FIRE those Navy salvos;
> CRASH they rip and roar!
> BOOM! those Navy broadsides
> On to VICTORY!

THERE is no such thing as "crashing the gate" any more when it comes to visiting Uncle Sam's Navy yards. Formerly, visitors were welcomed, and on certain days, such as Navy Day, the Fourth of July and Washington's Birthday, receptions were held and the public was cordially invited. Ship visiting during the present war, except for Navy personnel, civilians engaged in business, and officers' guests, has been abolished.

What is more, it takes practically an Act of Congress even to get into a Navy yard without a permit. The tense international situation makes an explanation superfluous. The term "Navy yard" will hereafter be used as a generic term including all types of naval shore establishments. Naval personnel, families of officers, civilians authorized to enter the yard in order to conduct business, and civilian employees are required to carry permits or passes. Such a pass contains a photograph of the bearer and identifying data. For naval personnel attached to ships, passes are issued by the ship; for all other personnel, they are issued after application and proper identification by the Office of the Captain of the Yard.

If you are a visitor without a pass and you wish to enter a Navy yard or station on business or for calling, you must stop at the gate and inform the sentry on duty of the name of the person you desire to visit. If you can be identified over the

telephone by an officer or a member of an officer's family, then
you will be allowed to enter. When an officer is expecting
many guests he sends a list of his guests to the gate, or he may
send an officer with a guest list to identify them. Guests should
bring their written invitations as a means of identification.

All Navy yards and smaller naval establishments except
those fronting upon water are enclosed by walls or wire fenc-
ing, and all gates therein are guarded by sentries, usually
Marines. By no means should you take exception to the guard
or sentry questioning you; he is only complying with orders
and doing his duty. Except by special permission after identification of the owner, no automobile or motorcycle is allowed
to enter unless it carries special license plates issued by the
Office of the Captain of the Yard. Also, no privately owned
motor vehicle is permitted to operate within the yard except
by special permission unless it is covered by special liability
insurance to the extent of $5000 for injury to one person and
$10,000 for injury to two or more persons.

Traffic Regulations

Assuming that you have been identified, there are one or
two points that may save you some embarrassment and grief.
Motor vehicles upon approaching a Navy yard gate must
reduce speed, dim lights at night, and stop abreast of the
sentry for identification.

The sentries are a part of the police organization of the
yard. Their orders require them to control traffic in the vicinity
of the gate, to inspect and identify all motor vehicles entering
and leaving the yard to insure that no unauthorized property
enters or leaves the yard, to suppress reckless driving and
boisterous conduct, and to prevent defacement of government
property. Sentries are authorized to arrest suspicious persons,
or any person who is intoxicated or guilty of improper or dis-
orderly conduct.

Sentries in the performance of their duties are representatives of the government. They are required to be military in
bearing, courteous, and civil, to be vigilant in executing their

orders and to insist that all persons show them the proper respect. When they give an order, they must see that it is obeyed. They are armed and are authorized to use arms to enforce obedience. (Should you encounter a sentry who has recently returned from Manila or Pearl Harbor, mind your *p*'s and *q*'s because those boys are said to have trigger fingers.)

Speed limits, usually twenty miles an hour in the residence zones, are strictly enforced. Parking regulations are numerous and dot the countryside; also they are not placed without a definite purpose. Cars parked in improper areas are simply removed and taken to the Office of the Captain of the Yard. It may sound like "the pound" to you, but just try to get your favorite jalopy pound-free and see! More than two speed charges or minor infractions in parkings for permanent personnel often result in an officer's not being allowed to use his car for thirty or sixty days, depending upon the seriousness of the charge.

Too, nothing may be said to you as a guest, but your host may receive a letter later stating that certain parking regulations were disregarded by his guest on a certain date, and it may cause him some embarrassment in answering by endorsement.

Colors

All cars driving in the yard during morning or evening are required to stop during the playing of the National Anthem or the sounding of "Colors" on the bugle. All persons walking should stop and stand at attention. Officers and men of the Navy salute during the playing of the National Anthem or Colors. Men (civilians) uncover and hold their hats over their hearts. Women stand with their hands at their sides and face the colors.

Recently, a bride was driving her car through a Navy yard at sunset. She heard a bugle blowing but paid no attention to it and kept merrily on her way. She was quite surprised several moments later to hear a shrill whistle. Looking back, she saw a Marine bicycle patrol waving her to the curb.

As the patrol overtook her and came to a stop, courteously he said to her, "Madame, you were violating yard regulations."

Immediately the bride hastened to explain that she had not parked in the wrong place and that the speed of her car was within the speed limit.

"I did not refer to parking or speed regulations," replied the patrol, "but to the regulation which requires all cars in the Navy yard to stop during Colors."

"Why doesn't somebody tell me these things?" lamented the bride.

Well, we are telling *you*, Nancy Lee, along with all the other civilians who do not know much about Navy regulations or what makes this fine organization click! In these times no detail, no smallest regulation, must be overlooked; there must be no loopholes for the enemy, for saboteurs, or for anyone to get near our defenses unless he has real reason to be there. And his reason must be 100 per cent American!

Restricted Areas

In most Navy yards certain sections are restricted and certain roads may be used only by officers or by visitors to officers' quarters.

Smoking is permitted except in definite restricted areas plainly indicated by signs, but in any part of the yard care must be exercised in the disposition of lighted matches or burning cigars or cigarettes.

No cameras are permitted to be carried into any Navy yard without special permission. Neither firearms nor dogs may be introduced into the yard. Intoxicating liquor may be carried only in unopened packages between the gate and an officer's home in the yard or the Officers' Club.

How to Tell an Admiral from a Bluejacket

In Chapter XII, "Navy Life in the Nation's Capital," no doubt you heard enough about gold braid to make you think everyone in the Navy is an Admiral, but such is not the case "once you leave the charmed circle of Washington." However, the lowliest sailorman has some pretty decorations too. But it takes a rather sophisticated eye to tell just exactly what each bit of tape, embroidery, and braid means. Rest assured each decoration does mean *something*, and to the experienced eye each man's record is an open book. By his uniform one can tell how long he has been in the Navy, his branch of Service and if he has any ratings, also his pay practically to the penny. No, not quite that close, because the Navy has a unique system on pay day of paying off nearest the dollar in even money! The only time an old-timer can be mistaken is when no insignia is worn and the men are in work garb of blue denim dungarees.

Kendall Banning in *The Fleet Today*[1] tells the following dungaree story:

"Working for the Admiral?" a passing seaman asked a grimy individual working on a motor car near the Admiral's residence.
"Yes."
"Been working for him long?"
"Ever since he's been an Admiral."
"Got your stripes yet?"
"No."
"Does the Admiral pay you anything?"
"No."
"Been in the Navy long?"
"Oh, about 30 years."
The sailorman snorted. "Huh," he sneered as he turned to go. "Ain't very bright, are you?"
The grimy individual in dungarees was *the Admiral*.

All of which goes to prove you can't tell your man or his rank in dungarees! The average civilian seldom sees Uncle Sam's sailors except in their navy-blue uniforms or their immaculate white "too-tight" uniforms.

Up to the rating of a Chief Petty Officer, all enlisted men wear the blue or white jumper with corresponding bell-shaped trousers, a blue cloth cap, a black neckerchief, and black

[1] Funk & Wagnalls Company, 1940.

shoes. With the white uniform, small circular monkey caps are worn that have wide, upturned brims. White tape trimming is used on the blue uniform, and blue tape on the white uniform.

Three stripes outline the wide sailor collar of both uniforms. They were adopted by the British Navy in memory of Lord Nelson's three great victories: Aboukir, in Egypt; Copenhagen, in Denmark; and Trafalgar, off the coast of Spain. The black neckerchief was originally a "sweat rag." As Mr. Banning says, "black was chosen because it does not show dirt —much." In foreign ports enlisted men are required to wear uniform at all times. They are not even allowed to have civilian clothes on board ship.

In very cold weather sailors wear a short jacket called a peacoat but they have no overcoats, poor dears! The blue flat cap is also a jaunty bit of headgear. In peacetime the cap ribbon indicates a sailor's ship or station—the gold lettering on the black band may read U.S.S. *Tennessee* or U.S. Naval Training Station. In wartime there may be no identification at all, or if there is, it may be a blind and misrepresent the name of the ship or station.

Here are a few distinguishing marks:

1 braid around the cuff is worn by an apprentice seaman 3rd class.
2 braids around the cuff are worn by a seaman 2nd class.
3 braids around the cuff are worn by a seaman 1st class.
White braid around the right shoulder sleeve on the blue uniform or blue braid around the right shoulder sleeve on the white uniform indicates that the enlisted man belongs to the seaman branch.
If the braid runs around the left shoulder, it is red and shows that the enlisted man belongs to the engineer force or artificer branch.

Service Stripes or "hash marks":

1 diagonal strip of red or blue braid worn on the left sleeve denotes 4 years' service.
Gold stripes mean that he has served in the Navy for at least 12

years and has won the maximum number of 3 good-conduct awards, 1 for each 4 years.

Chief Petty Officers, or C.P.O.'s, are often called the backbone of the Navy. They have worked up to the highest rank below the grade of Warrant Officer and they have their own mess. The C.P.O. is the direct tie between the officers and the enlisted men. They are efficient in their line, having had from twelve to sixteen years' experience in the Navy. Among them are chief radiomen, chief torpedo men, gunners' mates, electricians, quartermasters, water tenders, and boatswain's mates. After their long association with the ships to which they are attached, they have become experts in their particular field.

They wear brass-buttoned coats and slacks cut on standard lines. Petty Officers of the seaman branch wear chevrons on the right sleeve. One single stripe in the chevron (like the single letter V) is worn by the lowest or third-class Petty Officer. A double stripe in the chevron shows the wearer to be a second-class Petty Officer. A triple stripe indicates a first-class Petty Officer.

Rating badges are worn directly above the chevrons; the whole is topped by an eagle (and in the case of a Chief Petty Officer by an arch as well). The sailors call the eagle "a bird."

The specialty marks are too numerous to go into thoroughly, but should you note a bugle, it is easy enough to surmise that the individual has a rating as a bugler. A printer wears an open book, a musician or band master a golden harp. Chief commissary steward is appropriately distinguished by a pair of keys. Cooks and bakers wear a half-moon or maybe it is supposed to represent a cookie—I wouldn't know, but someone with a sense of humor must have thought up the designs for these emblems of ratings. Literally, there are dozens of them, and Mr. Banning, when he says that the sleeve "of a sailorman who has had a long and successful naval career assumes the aspect of a totem pole," isn't far wrong in my opinion.

WARRANT OFFICERS

Warrant Officers rank just above C.P.O.'s and just below
the commissioned officers. They wear a stripe of gold braid
a quarter of an inch wide, broken at two-inch intervals by a
quarter-inch of blue. On the blue uniform this braid is worn
just above the cuffs, on the white uniform and overcoat it is
placed on the shoulder mark.

Chief Warrant Officers wear braid one-half inch wide.

Yeomen? For a long time this rating confused me—I think
I must have been thinking of that well-known operetta by
Gilbert and Sullivan, *The Yeomen of the Guard.* Well, in
the Navy a yeoman is an enlisted man who does clerical work.
He doesn't sing arias!

Remember this: There is a very definite line of demarcation
drawn between officers and enlisted men, both in official and
in social circles. The first is a military necessity and needs no
explaining; the second may impress the average civilian as
unnecessary and a bit high-hat. However, the enlisted personnel understand the system perfectly and would not have it
otherwise. So unless you belong to the Navy, don't worry
about it. No one else does.

The Bluejacket of today—and by the way he doesn't like to
be called by the slang term "gob," which sailors were given
during the last World War; he likes to be called "sailor";
"Hi-ya, sailor" is one good seaman's greeting to another—is
a typical American. These young men come from all parts of
the United States and from lots of other places too, and most
of them are fairly well educated. They are perfect specimens
of manhood from a physical standpoint and they enlist to serve
their country. They are the finest type of American youth.

The Bluejacket today differs greatly from the sailor of our
early Navy who as Hanson Baldwin says

was a rollicking customer . . . hard-swearing, hard-drinking,
hard-living, hard-fighting; his back was scarred with the livid
welts of the "cat"; he lived on salt pork and ship's biscuit;
wounded in a fight, the surgeon and his mates strapped him to

a table and gave him a leather gag to chew on while they sawed off his leg. He slept in a hammock, and when he died he was sewed up in a hammock with a brace of round shot at his feet, the last stitch through his nose for luck, and he was given a proper sea burial with the sough of the wind as his threnody, and with Davy Jones awaitin' to receive him below.[2]

Enlistment in the Navy is for six years. To get into the Navy, an applicant must pass a rigid physical examination, and he may be as young as sixteen or as old as thirty-three. Enlistment in the Naval Reserve is for four years, with an understanding that active duty is for the duration of war. It is the enlisted men who, under the orders of officers, do the actual work of firing guns, running ships, maintaining planes and Navy property. These men realize their importance to the Navy and are the best investment the American citizen can have. They comprise our first line of defense.

The modern sailor likes to refer to his ship as a happy ship. He and his shipmates may criticize it among themselves, but no one else dares make comparisons. *His* ship is always the best in the Fleet! To prove it, he will fight at the drop of the proverbial hat. He will work hard to keep it shining and clean; work hard for accuracy at the guns and give his all in any competition, whether in maneuvers, torpedo practice, in the ring, on the baseball diamond, or in real war, that his ship may win.

Now, if you are still confused about rank among officers, I suggest that you turn back to Chapter XII. One socially inclined young civilian that I know has bothered only to learn the Admiral's stripes. Every other officer, even Ensigns, she addresses as Captain—and they all love it.

Ship Visiting

Civilians desiring to visit a ship must request by letter permission to come on board, or request the issue of a pass if

[2] *What the Citizen Should Know About the Navy.* W. W. Norton & Company, New York, 1941.

business will require frequent trips. Written permission or a
pass must be presented to the Coxswain in charge of the boat
if the civilian is on business. A guest must be identified by
an officer or, if the Coxswain has been informed by the Officer
of the Deck of the names of the expected guests, by the
guests presenting a written invitation, or if no written invitations have been issued, then by the presentation of his personal calling card.

In case there are many guests, it is customary for the host
or an officer representing him to meet them at the landing in
order to identify them. Wives of officers attached to a ship
are given passes authorizing them to take passage in the ship's
boats, except during working hours.

In hopes that the present war will soon be over and the
Navy will be able to return to normal procedure, there is
included the following additional data relating to peacetime
procedure. The Navy maintains Navy landings at . . . various ports. At other ports, private or municipal lands are used.
(In accordance with security regulations the location and
names of the landings in various cities have been deleted.)

At each landing there are one or numbers of Shore Patrol,
comprising both officers and enlisted men, to regulate the boat
traffic, to preserve order, to announce the name of the ship
whose boat is ready to embark passengers, and to furnish
information to civilians regarding the ships which are present
and their respective boat schedules.

Shore Patrol personnel are in uniform and wear on the left
arm a brassard of blue cloth on which are superimposed the
letters S P in yellow cloth. In normal time the Shore Patrol
will have the following data:

Names of Navy ships in port
Rosters of officers of ships in port
Landing places and boat schedules of ships present

At present, although he may have the information, you will
find the Shore Patrol noncommunicative in so far as civilians

are concerned, but if a Navy wife has the proper identification, he will be glad to assist her in so far as permitted with regard to information on boat schedules of the ship to which her husband is attached. He will also be pleased to deliver to the Coxswain of a ship's boat any written message she may desire to send to her husband.

In addition to the numbers of Shore Patrol at the dock there are others, usually with headquarters at the local police station, to care for naval personnel who are victims of accidents or who get into any kind of trouble. A Navy wife, should she have an accident or require assistance for any reason, should telephone the Senior Patrol Officer, inform him of the case, and ask him to get word to her husband.

BOAT ETIQUETTE—EMBARKING

A lack of understanding of boat etiquette frequently results in confusion when a group of people are about to embark in a ship's boat. There are two general rules: (1) Passengers embark in inverse order of precedence; except that (2) Ladies embark ahead of gentlemen. In this as in all other cases where precedence will be mentioned, the precedence of a Navy wife corresponds to that of her husband; civilians holding diplomatic rank or political office are given the precedence to which such office entitles them, and their wives are given similar precedence; civilians holding no office are given precedence in accordance with age or, when known, in accordance with national or local prominence. The procedure of seniors embarking last being at variance with the usual custom of seniors going first does cause confusion. Young Navy wives can assist in reducing such confusion by hurrying into the boat. Naturally one does not stop to inquire dates of commissions before getting into the boat, but knowledge of the general rule will lessen the confusion.

Upon embarking, juniors take the seats nearest the bow of the boat. Ladies in taking seats should leave room between them for a gentleman embarking later to be seated.

Disembarking

In disembarking the passengers leave the boat in order of precedence, ladies disembarking first. An exception may be made to this extent: When at a landing or alongside a ship ladies require assistance in disembarking and there is no officer on deck or gangway ladder platform to offer it, then one or two officers may precede the senior lady on to the landing or gangway platform in order to provide such assistance.

There may be times when because of wind or sea conditions a lady should be assisted all the way up or down the gangway ladder. In such case a gentleman should precede a lady and help her on the ladder.

Etiquette on Deck

Your host may be on board ship expecting you; he may accompany you to the ship in the same boat; or (in normal times) this may be a surprise visit. In any case, you will first see the Officer of the Deck. You may distinguish him from other officers by the telescope he carries as an insignia of his position, and by his wearing gloves.

Should your host be on board and anticipating your visit at a definite hour, he will be on deck to greet you. In such case, you should give the Officer of the Deck a smile and a "How do you do?" Then speak to your host, who will make such introductions as may be appropriate. If the number of guests is large, introductions are usually limited. If your host is in the boat with you, lady guests will arrive on deck ahead of him. In this case, a lady speaks to the Officer of the Deck as previously mentioned, then steps to one side clear of the gangway and awaits her host's arrival on deck. He will then make the introductions. If your host is the Captain of a ship, or a Flag Officer whose flagship this is, there will be on deck, in addition to the Officer of the Deck, one or two officers to receive the Admiral or Captain. They should likewise be greeted, but it is probable that unless they have met you before, they will wait to be presented by the host.

Gentlemen guests, upon reaching the upper gangway platform, should salute the quarter-deck. If the position of such civilian entitles him to any honors, he should remove his hat while the honors are being rendered.

DEPARTING

In leaving a party on board ship, seniors depart first if more than one boat is to be used, but of those leaving in the same boat, juniors embark first. The breaking up of the party will usually be indicated by the "calling away" of the boat. Juniors should be prompt to say good-by to the host and to assemble near the gangway. As adieus are usually made by couples, the senior lady will be late in getting to the boat. In this case it is proper for junior men to accompany their wives in embarking even though this is contrary to the general rule that ladies embark first.

The governing principles are these: First, seniors should be in the boat the shortest period of time; second, in embarking at a landing ladies embark first to make certain that all have seats.

OFFICERS LEAVING A SHIP

An officer or enlisted man always salutes the colors at the top of the ladder or gangway and then the Officer of the Deck, as he comes aboard. This is reversed in leaving the ship, when he salutes the Officer of the Deck with some such remark as "I have permission to leave the ship, sir," and then at the top of the ladder faces aft and salutes the colors.

In battleships the colors and quarter-deck are saluted by officers and men on coming up from below decks. Some of this ceremony dates from the time when religious images were carried in this part of the ship. Later the flags of kings were hoisted, and all of the naval Service took off their hats as a salute. The quarter-deck has been a dignified and sacred area from the earliest days.

The starboard side of a ship is always used as the honor side and kept clear for senior officers. It is used by all commissioned officers as their side for leaving and returning to the ship. The port side is used by enlisted men in order that there will never be a time when the ladder is so clogged up that the Admiral or Captain couldn't easily get away from the ship. There is a common-sense reason for practically every Navy custom.

GENERAL INFORMATION FOR THE CIVILIAN

(Taken from *What the Citizen Should Know About the Navy*, by Hanson Baldwin.)

The Fleet is said to be the first pillar of American security.

The Fleet is composed of many different elements and of various types.

The five principal combat types in any first-class Navy are:
1. Battleships
2. Carriers (aircraft) may be large or small
3. Cruisers may be light or heavy
4. Destroyers may be of many classes
5. Submarines may be of many classes

Battleships are called "battle wagons" . . . floating cities with floating forts. They are designed to give terrific punishment and also to take it. Many people argue that the battleship is outmoded, yet the proud battle wagons still rule the waves.

The longsweeping top deck is covered with teak, which the sailors scrub white. About 12,000 plans and countless blueprints are worked out before the actual building of a battleship, which normally takes four years . . . but this will not be true during the emergency. Production will be stepped up, and factories, shipyards and workmen will produce ships in the shortest period possible. Our shipyards are running full time, turning out new battleships, destroyers, submarines and other demons of destruction.

Carriers are the Navy's mobile airfields . . . a carrier's job is to give punishment but not to take it. The main weapon and the only reason for a carrier is its brood of planes.

Cruisers are the scouts of the Fleet. They are in one sense the jack-of-all-trades of the ocean highways.

Destroyers are the "trouble boats of the sea" . . . they are thin, fragile, steel splinters, packed with power. Destroyers are torpedo carriers and gun carriers, as well as depth-charge carriers; they are equipped to hunt submarines, or to launch a torpedo attack against an enemy battle line, to escort a convoy, patrol the seas, or to harass commerce.

Submarines are sometimes called "pig boats." The sub is an excellent long distance scout . . . its functions are too well known to comment upon.

"Mosquito boats" are small, fast torpedo boats. They are a constant threat to enemy craft.

The Mine Force of "layers" and "sweepers" is sometimes spoken of as "mine host." These ships protect our coasts, harbors, and bases.

Battleships are named for states such as the *North Carolina*, *California*. Heavy cruisers are named after large cities—*Indianapolis*, *Louisville*. Light cruisers are named after smaller cities—*Boise*, *Honolulu*. Aircraft carriers are named after famous ships that figured prominently in the early history of the American Navy, and after names of famous battles. Destroyers are named after naval officers, enlisted men and civilians who have rendered distinguished service to the U.S. Navy— *Hammann*, *Helm*. Submarines are named after fish and aquatic animals—*Salmon*, *Seal*.

In the early days of the sea, men had to find names for the various parts of the ship and her gear. Rather than invent new names they naturally named them after things ashore of which they reminded them. Thus we find: Head, Waist, Stern, Eyes, Apron, Bed, Cradle, Dog, Pudding, Saddle, Tiller (the man behind the plow), and Stays (supporting the mast).

It will be noted that even the ship is named after the human body; for one thing, she is always feminine (the cynical say because she is sometimes difficult to handle). Thus, in the previous list, we find that the *head* is the bow of the ship, the *waist* is the amidships or middle section, and the *stern* is the after part of the ship. The *eyes* of the ship are at the very bow. Those of you who have been to China will have noted eyes painted in the bows of the junks even to this day.

The wooden decks of ships often get very dirty, and it is customary to clean them using water, sand, and holystones. These latter are a form of brick; the grinding action removes the dirt from the deck, as well as part of the deck. In the olden days, it was customary to take up a kneeling attitude to manipulate them. Hence they were called "holy stones" because of the prayer-like attitude of the user.

The term "grog," meaning a mixture of spirits and water, is derived from a nickname applied to a British Admiral. The sailors drank their liquor "neat" for many years—that is, undiluted. Josephus Daniels made the American Navy "dry."

Women used to be allowed to live on board in the days of sailing ships of the British Navy, but only if they were married to some member of the crew. It is to this strange circumstance that we are indebted for the expression "son of a gun." There was a child actually born on board, probably under a gun and only sheltered at birth from the view of the ship's company by a canvas screen. As it was impossible to tell the paternity of the child, it was called a "son of a gun."

Chapter XV

BEYOND THE CONTINENTAL LIMITS
THE ASIATIC STATION

Oh! we'll all go up to China in the spring-time
    Oh! we'll all go up to China in the spring-g-g-g
Oh! we'll hop aboard a liner
    I can think of nothing finer
Oh! we'll all go up to China in the spring.

Book of Navy Songs

AT PRESENT, Guam and Manila are rather painful memories to all of us, but God willing, our American Navy and Army will change these conditions. The world will never forget Pearl Harbor, but we will also make sure that the enemy never forgets. At present there are no Service dependents on the Asiatic Station or even allowed in Hawaii and Alaska, and probably Navy wives with their children will soon be returning from the Caribbean bases.

This seems the best policy, and no matter how hard it is to leave one's husband and home, every Navy wife realizes in her heart that her husband as an officer will be more efficient to his country without the added responsibility of having his family in enemy territory. This chapter was completed early in the writing of this book, after endless communication to receive the latest data concerning the stations mentioned; so it shall stand.

There will always be a China! Henry C. Wolfe says that "it is Japan who is weakened after four years of 'victories' in China." China remains untouched except that the war has united her forces. This unity of her people will give her the strength to absorb the small nation of Japan, and eventually will make her the ruling nation of the Far East.

269

In time, and it won't be accomplished overnight, Manila, Guam, Wake, Midway will see us and know us as Navy wives again. No changes have been made in the data, in the hope that this explanatory note will cover the situation.

In the good old days everyone looked forward to duty on the Asiatic Station. In those golden days it was customary for the Fleet to winter in Manila, and in the spring the squadron usually went north. China and Japan were the favorite sojourning places of those lucky mortals who found time and opportunity to go there; and there were certain ports, cities, and resorts where whole colonies of Navy wives spent the summers. Tsingtao and Chefoo on the China coast were two of these popular summer resorts, while Peking, Tientsin, Shanghai, and Hong Kong were always desirable spots for sightseeing, for marvelous shopping facilities, and for sheer good living.

The exchange was splendid in those days. Most Americans lived in luxury with flocks of servants and wonderful food and drink. What a Navy wife (provided she knew how to shop and bargain) couldn't buy in China on her Ensign husband's pay wasn't worth buying. The pay check always seemed much more than it was, because it was in gold; and it was fun to barter with the Chinese and exchange "big money and little money" for exquisite linens, Chinese rugs, and those gorgeous furs that always looked so alluring in the shops but molted their silky hairs on the landscape from Peking to Greenwich Village. One Navy wife had the experience of buying a bona fide leopard coat, only to have the painted spots wash off in the rain as the transport sailed away toward Manila.

Peking, the Celestial City, was the pièce de résistance of China. Dilapidated though it was, it still held an incredible charm. The faded Pompeian-red walls of the Forbidden City; the pumpkin-gold roofs of the imperial palace; the passing grandeur of the summer palace with its marble boat; the diverting social life made up of members of the legations, representatives of the armies and navies, old residents (some of whom were fictional characters); the polo, played on shaggy little Mongolian ponies; the wonderful shops in Flower Street, Bead Street, Jade Street, and Lantern Street; the ricksha boys; the beggars; the streets of brown and black dust; the steady rains in the summer, and the icy winds from the Gobi Desert which, in winter, made the air almost cruelly stimulating—all of this was Peking.

For shopping it was a woman's paradise. And such polite shopping! While bartering over a rare piece of Tribute Silk or an objet d'art, several cups of Canton tea would be drunk and its maker complimented. To hurry such a transaction was to lose face.

Shanghai was equally popular, though bizarre and fantastic in its contrast to Peking. Only too well it deserved its self-appointed title, "the Paris of the Orient." Located on the Whangpoo River which swarms with vari-colored sampans and dragon-eyed fleets of junks, Shanghai presented an interesting picture of China, the old, the changeless, against China, the changing and new. Today, ravaged by several years of war, that picture has changed, but still the famous Bund teems with rickshas, motor cars, wheelbarrows, sedan chairs, and the ever present blue-clad breathless coolie. What fun it was to ride down Nanking Road past ornately fronted silversmith shops, shops that overflowed with jade, laces, silks, carved ivory, and mandarin coats. Close by the International Settlement lay the old Walled City, with interesting side trips to the Bird Market, the Willow Pattern Tea House, the Lungwha Pagoda, and Bubbling Well Road.

In those halcyon days the Sunday afternoon tea dances at the famous old Majestic Hotel were something to remember. The Majestic was really an old palace, built by a wealthy Scotsman who married a Chinese singsong girl. At his death his heirs sold it to a company who remodeled it into one of the smartest hotels in the Orient. Its ballroom was terraced with a large crystal fountain in the center, around which pretty Eurasian girls in native dress danced with under-secretaries or older men who had been in the Orient too long.

The smart Cathay Hotel on the Bund and Nanking Road took its place in time and, along with the Little Club, the French Club, which boasted of having the longest bar in the world, and the numerous night clubs, provided plenty of gaiety for the restless population of Shanghai. Always, even before the war, there was a restlessness and a tension in the city which "the old China hands" cursed yet adored. The gay night life was intoxicating, and American naval officers on leave and officers in the uniforms of many nations were seen at the international gatherings. Today war has taken its toll, Japanese troops occupy the International Settlement, bombs have rained over Shanghai, many lives have been lost and buildings wrecked beyond repair, but the Chinese are constant. Never will they be beaten or absorbed by their hated enemy; instead, they will in time absorb him. They have faith in China, they know that China is never defeated, never afraid. "There is time for everything," the Chinese say. "If you have not the time, your son will have the time or your son's son; inherent in every task (even war) is completion." They believe that the Dragon and the Eagle fly with the same wings!

True, there were other things that made China unforgettable. Each city had its own traditional charm, but it also had its own peculiar smells, as is indicated by the following verse:

> Oh, we lived ten thousand years in old Chefoo.
> Oh, we lived ten thousand years in old Chefoo.
> And it didn't smell like roses
> So we had to hold our noses
> When we lived ten thousand years in old Chefoo.

In the autumn when the Fleet returned to its winter base in Manila, there was a general exodus of Navy wives from China. Like migrating birds they flocked back to a gay winter in the tropics. Accommodations were rather limited in Manila, and the ramshackle old frame building which bore the title

Army and Navy Annex housed many of the junior officers' wives. The spacious, well-equipped Army and Navy Club with its comfortable "pash parlors" (passion parlors), as the lounges were called, was the meeting place for the Navy and for all branches of the Service.

The American colony in Manila, but particularly the Army personnel, welcomed the return of the Fleet. That was a sign that the hot season was over, and social life would take on a new meaning with new faces and some new blood in their midst. The naval officers were glad to renew civilian and Service friendships while their wives had fun disporting themselves in their latest Paris creations bought in Shanghai. When the Fleet returned, the social life started looking up and everything was gay. There was a pleasant camaraderie and a good-natured rivalry between the Services.

On Saturday nights the club was particularly gay with dinner parties; then late dancing at the Manila Hotel and breakfast at the Polo Club. Sunday afternoons saw everyone at the polo games, dressed in their very best, and afterwards there was always a very elaborate tea dance. Friday and Sunday nights were popular evenings for Navy bachelors to entertain at dinner, and the officers' boats carried many gay parties out to the lighted ships anchored in Manila Bay. The parties usually culminated in a song-fest back at the Army and Navy Club, where some obliging guest relieved the orchestra by commandeering the piano.

For the present, those good times are no more, since all Service wives have been evacuated from the Asiatic Station, but let us hope that service in the Far East (when officers are allowed to have their wives accompany them) is not a thing of the past.

Fortunate are those of us who knew China before the Japanese invasion, and who knew Japan as a peaceful little nation whose people celebrated the Cherry Blossom Festival, loved beauty, and worshiped at their Shinto shrines in Nikko under the shadow of their beloved Fujiyama.

Navy Life in Samoa

Little did you ever dream as you sat through Jeanne Eagels' splendid performance of *Rain* (or if that was before your time perhaps you may have seen the movie version of *Sadie Thompson*) that some day you would be on your way to the South Seas. The very words South Seas are somehow entrancing and insidious. They seem to stand for everything we want—and haven't got! Sun, sand, time—blue oceans, coral reefs, swaying palms and romance——

By this time we trust that you are an experienced Navy wife to whom surprises in the way of orders to strange places are all in the day's work. At any rate, it isn't everyone who is lucky enough to have the opportunity of spending a year or eighteen months in Pago Pago (pronounced Pango Pango. Why? Your guess is as good as mine).

The United States Naval Station is located in Pago Pago harbor in the center of the island of Tutuila, the largest of the group of islands of American Samoa. The beauty of the horseshoe-shaped harbor of Pago Pago is comparable to that of Sydney, Rio de Janeiro, and Hong Kong. The mountains form a background and are covered with bright-colored flowers, with Madagascar flame trees rising in silhouette against a brilliant blue sky.

The United States was first allowed to occupy American Samoa in 1878, and the island of Tutuila was used as a coaling station. Its government today is the same as that of Guam, with the Naval Commandant appointed by the President.

The Samoan chiefs are interesting and affectionate people with a great deal of inherent dignity and solid sense. They look upon the Naval Commandant or governor as a potentate of the greatest power. Sometimes their use of English is a bit confusing and provides merriment for the recipients of their state pronouncements; but their ideas are usually sound.

The following letter, received by the wife of a recent governor of Samoa from a native chief, shows in what high esteem the First Lady, who lived in Government House on top of the hill, was held (by permission of Mrs. Hanson, wife of Captain E. W. Hanson, U.S.N.):

Pago Pago
June 12, 1939

Majesty—Mrs Hanson

With deep regret that I am dropping your Excellency, Mrs Hanson Mother of all most high rank of American Samoa. This is your humble family Mr. and Mrs. Mauga, and Mr. and Mrs. Hanson are true relationship not only in American Samoa, but in the United States Navy too.

The following request is through you Mrs. Hanson. Be kind. Arrange favor for me to go to Fiji next trip please! The Bible said, "Call upon God heavenly Father in days of Trouble."

Therefore Mrs. I know and am full aware that all American Samoa are under your Controll-ment (sole authority) Isaiah: Chapter 55, verse 6. I know I can get a (necklace bear teeth) from my family over there Fiji & other useful things prepared by Mr. and Mrs. Mauga for Mr. and Mrs. Hanson. Will present them to you personal before you leave American Samoa. God we trust.

Yours,

Mauga

Government House is a tremendous set of quarters, well staffed with ten or more native servants and completely furnished. Fortunately the government provides a sufficient number of frame quarters for officers on duty in Samoa. It would be just too bad if Uncle Sam did not look after his own here, since there is no hotel, houses are scarce, and the nearest thing that would resemble an apartment is the "Sadie Thompson," a two-story barnlike frame building managed by an elderly half-caste Samoan woman.

The quarters along the Officers Row (popularly known as Centipede Row) are ideally located, facing the beautiful harbor, and the area in back of them is used as a golf course. The houses have screened porches running two-thirds of the way around them and, while by no means luxurious, are comfortable. Coal-burning stoves and kerosene stoves are used for the cooking, and the native servants do not seem to mind the heat.

But speaking of heat, the climate is slightly warmer than that of Hawaii but it is very enervating. The nights are always cool and the frequent showers make the climate pleasant. People who exercise too much generally suffer physically and mentally. Occasional physical breakdowns or increased irritability and forgetfulness are some of the symptoms; at least, the movies like to make every white man out in Samoa a beachcomber or a "lotus-eater" of the first water. Hurricanes strike on an average of once in three years with varying degrees of intensity. Strong hurricanes result in a food shortage but seldom in loss of life.

Servants are plentiful but good ones are scarce. Cook boys, for it seems that the males are usually the better cooks, are soon known by their ability. Their pay varies from $7 to $25 per month depending upon their merits. The problem of servants taking food out to their relatives, or the phenomenon of relatives moving into the officers' quarters, is a common one. Wives have to keep a sharp lookout to keep their commissary bills within reason. Some dishonesty is to be expected, but it is difficult to convince a Samoan that taking food home to his family is a crime.

Schools

The schools are equipped for kindergarten through the grammar grades; above that it is necessary to resort to tutoring. Instruction in French may usually be obtained.

Transportation

A car is a rarity, not a necessity, and bicycles *are* a necessity. They are used by everyone.

General Information

The Navy Commissary is well stocked although fresh milk is almost unheard of. Once in a while some may be purchased from New Zealand on the day it arrives by boat. Milk substitutes are generally used. The Commissary carries Klim, and children seem to thrive on it. The water supply is ample and of high grade. The food on the whole is good; the meat, butter, and eggs are procured from Australia and New Zealand; the native markets supply tropical foodstuffs and their small pineapples and fresh bantam corn are particularly delicious. Locally grown fresh vegetables are scarce.

As to clothes, see the suggestions given for Guantanamo, Cuba. Add to these cotton umbrellas, overshoes, a light evening wrap, and some heavy clothing in the possibility of a cruise to Australia or New Zealand. Up to six years old, most children wear sun suits and sandals. Older children wear the simplest of summer clothing. Both men and women wear shorts for golf and tennis. Lightweight woolen sweaters are useful.

You are advised to include a dinner service for twelve, or better, eighteen. It need not be expensive, but you should take plenty of dishes and glassware since no replacements are possible in case of breakage. Freight rates are high. Also, stock up on a supply of inexpensive bridge prizes. Calling cards are a necessity, so come prepared. For persons dependent on eye glasses, there should be a reserve supply. The nearest optical company is 2276 miles away, in Honolulu.

There is an Officers' Club on Goat Island where monthly dances are held. The dues are nominal, about $1.25 per person. Golf and tennis are the most popular sports while fishing ranks third. The Samoans are good fishermen. They catch many small fish on lines and in nets, trap eels and lobsters on coral reefs, spear mullet, and maneuver sharks alongside their boats, then noose them and tow them to shore. (Gentle occupation, what?)

The mail situation seems to be the most unpleasant feature of service in Samoa. Even in peacetime the Matson liners called at Pago Pago rather infrequently. Today even those steamers have been taken off the South Seas route. Thankful indeed must be those who are stationed there for the Pago

Pago radio station which links America with New Zealand and Australia.

Hawaii

There's the perfume of a million flowers
Clinging to the heart of old Hawaii.
There's a rainbow following the showers
Bringing me a part of old Hawaii.
There's a silver moon, a symphony of stars
There's a Hula tune and the hum of soft guitars
There's the Trade Wind, sighing in the heavens
Singing me a song of old Hawaii!

(No Navy wives are in Hawaii now, of course, but the following sections indicate what life there has been and will again be.)

Honolulu is decidedly a Navy town, and most of the Navy personnel enjoy duty in and near Honolulu. Service in Hawaii should definitely not be considered foreign duty, since the entire Territory is part of the United States. The English language, with many bizarre inflections and additions, is spoken; United States money is used; United States stamps are stuck on letters. Old-timers are inclined to lift their eyebrows in bored tolerance when a newcomer or *malihini* shows his ignorance by referring to Hawaii as a "foreign" possession.

Neither should service in Hawaii be included with other tropical duty, chiefly because of its climate. It is a land of sunshine, and the climate is as nearly perfect as at any spot yet discovered by man. The ancient Hawaiian vocabulary includes no word for weather. It was so even, with no changes, in those days, that there was no need to mention it. Rain is spoken of as "liquid sunshine," and the double rainbows and lunar rainbows are a sight to delight the aesthetic soul of man. Rainbows are so common that the university football team is known as the "Roaring Rainbows." Mothers never think of calling in their children, who slide around on the lawns, frolicking in the refreshing drizzle that blows down from the cloud-wrapped peaks of Mt. Tantalus. The normal temperature in Honolulu is seventy-two degrees, with an all-time low of fifty-eight degrees. On the hottest day on record in Honolulu the mercury soared to eighty-seven degrees; but at a time like that, the best thing to do is to hie yourself over to the Rest Camp at Kilauea in the mountains and relax. It isn't the heat, but the humidity can be terrific if the trade winds stop blowing for a few hours.

Until recently, Oahu was the only fortified island of the Hawaiian group. It ranks third in size among the eight principal islands. Hawaii is the largest of the group and gives its name to the entire Territory. It is generally called "The Big Island" and is the favorite vacation island because of its cool climate and its superb scenery.

Honolulu, meaning "abundance of calm," on Oahu, is the largest city in the Territory. It is a melting pot for Oriental and native Polynesian peoples, with a heavy infusion of Europeans and Caucasians. The Army and Navy personnel make up a floating population, and in normal times thousands of tourists pour in from all parts of the world. There are few tourists today, but their places are filled by defense workers. In a week the place is landscaped, and in a few months these small communities take on an aspect of permanency.

It is a changed Honolulu to the old residents of the city. Everything is hustle and bustle, and the easy, leisurely, graceful way of living has been changed to a jittery, rushing existence like that of any other commercial center. In the old days pedestrians had the right of way; storekeepers had time to be polite to customers; taxi drivers twined a lei of fragrant flowers around their hat bands before starting their day's work; diving boys came up smiling if they were lucky enough to retrieve pennies and dimes. Today diving boys hold out for twenty-five-cent pieces! It is all a new and different Honolulu. A great deal of the charm is gone, but its natural beauty remains.

Regardless, though, of conditions, from the time one sights Diamond Head Honolulu seems to cast a spell, whether you be a newcomer or a "come-backer." The many-fingered harbor itself is a gem, surrounded by purple mountains that seem to rise directly out of the opal sea. At the right as you approach the harbor entrance the world-famous Waikiki Beach, in the shape of a crescent, gleams beneath its fringing coconut palms. Directly ahead rises the Aloha Tower, flanked on one side by the largest pineapple-shaped water tank in the world and on the other by the municipal electric plant. Beauty linked to commerce *was* the keynote of Honolulu; today, WAR linked to commerce has taken its place, with beauty relegated often to the out-of-the-way places and quiet corners which remain as Hawaiian as ever.

One of the most endearing things about the islands is the custom of presenting flower leis to incoming visitors or to departing friends. The florists on the mainland must have taken their slogan "Say it with flowers" from the Hawaiians, because flowers seem to be the language of these kindly people.

The visitor, smothered in leis of Hilo violets, fragrant *pikake*, spicy carnations, ginger, and even orchids, will experience an indescribable thrill as the Royal Hawaiian Band plays "The Song of the Islands," followed by "Aloha." This word has many meanings and is a world-famed greeting. Its most common interpretations are: love, welcome, and farewell.

Where to Live

Residential districts popular with naval officers are Kahala, Manoa, Waikiki, and Nuuanu. The Halekulani Hotel with adjacent bungalows on Waikiki Beach, eleven miles from Pearl Harbor, is the home of many Navy couples. It has the atmosphere of an exclusive home.

The Pleasanton Hotel at Punahou and Wilder Streets is also popular with Navy people, especially those having children who attend school at Punahou.

The Niumalu Hotel, next to Fort De Russy and right on

the beach, is more of a family hotel. There are numerous other hostelries, of all sorts and sizes, ranging from the private residence type to the expensive Royal Hawaiian, which is the last word in modern hotels. It is the haven of movie stars and other celebrities, and worth the price, if you have it. (Rates $12 per day, up.) The Moana is under the same management as the Royal and is famous for its beautiful Banyan Court. It is next door to the Royal Hawaiian on Waikiki Beach.

The largest hotel in the business district is the Alexander Young (European plan), and the second largest is the Blaisdell, located in the shopping area.

As to clothes, take your entire wardrobe. Honolulu women have a tendency to follow the seasons in dress, although there are strictly speaking no seasons to follow. There are times when lightweight woolens, a topcoat, and even a short fur jacket can be worn with comfort. You will see a few velvets and tweeds, but they are comfortable only when the kona winds blow. The shops are exceptionally good, particularly those at Waikiki, that specialize in sports clothes; so you will do well to wait until you arrive in Honolulu to add to your wardrobe. An interesting fact is that prices for clothing compare very favorably with mainland prices in comparable boom towns.

Schools

All schools are crowded, and it is advisable to register children as far in advance as possible, in private schools. The public schools are good, and the ones attended by Navy children are Kapalama, Stevenson, and Roosevelt.

The University of Hawaii is an accredited liberal arts institution specializing in agriculture and sugar technology. It is a land-grant university which is fully accredited by the Association of American Universities. It offers courses leading to the B.A. and M.A. degrees in all standard fields of study.

Some Things You May Like to Know

An automobile is a necessity, since Pearl Harbor is ten miles from Honolulu, and the city itself covers a vast area. The increasingly heavy traffic is one of its greatest problems. It seems as if everyone in Honolulu is on wheels of some kind, with the cars varying from the latest model Packard to ramshackle Fords of ancient vintage. Walter Winchell says, "Filipinos always buy a car together, instead of all owning the machine, each claims a part, one a horn, another a hub cap, still another a wheel." There are strict parking laws and efficient traffic officers always on the alert for minor violations, although speed demons seem often to go unnoticed. The motor trips are beautiful and the roads are excellent. Taxis are high.

Honolulu is proud of the fact that it has never had a case of rabies, so if you plan to take your favorite wire-haired or your beautiful Persian cat along, you should know beforehand that your pet will have to remain in the Territorial Government Quarantine Station for 120 days at a cost of 25 cents a day. There is no way of getting around the law, so you will only waste your time trying!

Food is necessarily higher in Honolulu than on the mainland, and prices continue to increase daily. The native markets are interesting with their tempting arrays of Hawaiian fruits and vegetables. June, July, and August are the months for the delicious sun-kissed pineapples. Mango, breadfruit, avocado—each has its season, though papaya seems to ripen the year round. Meat from the mainland is expensive, but native beef from the ranches of Hawaii and Maui is good.

"Hawaii Is the Land Where—"

According to Walter Winchell, visitors and newcomers in Honolulu are referred to as *malihinis*, while old-timers or people who have not necessarily been born in Honolulu but have lived there for a long time are known as *kamaainas*.

In Honolulu the following terms are used in speaking of directions: There is no north, south, east, or west; the directions are *mauka*, meaning toward the mountains; *makai*, toward the sea; *waikiki*, toward Koko Head, and *ewa*, toward west, or Schofield way.

Officially, the language of Hawaii is English, but it is an English interspersed with a large number of Hawaiian, Oriental, and Spanish words. You will be surprised how quickly some of these words and expressions will work themselves into your vocabulary. A *haole* is a person of the white race. A porch or veranda will always be a *lanai*; a woman will inevitably be a *wahine*; you will say *pau* as a utility word for "ended, finished, completed"; *kapu* means "keep out" and the signs are usually on the property around town and in the country. *Pilikia* means trouble, and everyone but yourself you'll soon agree is throwing a lot of *hoomalimali*—or bologna to you!

Swimming, surfing, golf, and tennis are the most popular sports. The Oahu Country Club in Nuuanu Valley has a beautiful golf course where many naval officers play. Waialae Golf Club is the championship course of all, and always has a long waiting list for members. Horseback riding at Fort Shafter and at Schofield Barracks is available for Navy personnel upon application.

The Kilauea Military Camp on the Island of Hawaii also welcomes Navy families. Applications for a two-weeks stay are made through the Recreational Department at Fort Shafter. No tour of duty in Hawaii is complete without a visit to the other islands, particularly the Big Island. There is place service twice daily, and the Inter-Island Steamship Company has sailings twice a week.

While you are on Hawaii, or on the way back to Honolulu, you should take a trip to the island of Maui, the "Valley Isle," to see Haleakela, the world's largest dormant volcano. If you fly back to Oahu you will pass over Molokai, the "Friendly Island," on one small isolated coastal plateau of which is located the famous leprosarium in which Father Damien did his heroic work for an afflicted people. There are other things besides lepers on Molokai, however, notably huge fields of pineapples, the only deer hunting in the islands, and one of the fanciest model cattle ranches stocked with thoroughbreds in the world. If you want to see Hawaii at its leisurely best perhaps you'd better take a trip to the "Garden Isle," Kauai. It has its scenery boosters too, and the natives think nothing of linking Waimea Canyon and Grand Canyon together in one breath—usually rather to the discredit of the Colorado River job.

What to Buy in Honolulu

Lauhala rugs
Lauhala mats
Lauhala purses
Lauhala hats
Lauhala knitting bags
Lauhala door stops
Tapa cloth from Samoa and Tahiti
Coral beads
Shells
Flower prints

Carved woods (koa and monkey pod)
Etched glass
Ming horses
Hand-blocked linens
Luncheon sets
Handkerchiefs
Dresses (beach apparel)
Oriental goods
Rattan furniture

What to See and Do in Hawaii

The Pali
Diamond Head
The Blow Hole
Cooper's Ranch
The Mormon Temple
Chinese Temples
Queen Emma Museum
Aquarium
Old Mission
Iolani Palace (the only throne room in the U.S.)
Iolani Barracks
Bishop Museum
Academy of Arts
Orchid gardens
Flower show (April)
Aala Market

Shack of Robert Louis Stevenson at Waioli Tea Room
A real luau
Hula lessons
University of Hawaii (see sausage tree)
Sugar plantation
Pineapple plantation
Pineapple cannery
Night-blooming cereus
The House Without a Key
Mochizuki Tea House
Lau Yee Chai (Chinese restaurant)
The Good Earth
Trader Vic's
South Seas

Visit the Big Island, and if possible fly one way.

See the volcanoes, Mauna Loa, Mauna Kea, Kilauea.

Inter-island trips to Maui, Kauai, Molokai, and Lanai are of interest.

See Santa Claus arrive in an outrigger canoe.

The Y.W.C.A. offers interesting courses in flower arrangement, short story and article writing, speech and personality classes, French and Spanish, Chinese cooking, water color, block printing, Lauhala weaving, plain cooking, and Hawaiian quilting.

DUTY IN ALASKA

(Navy wives are not allowed in Alaska now, either, but in the hope of eventual normal times let me tell you about life there as we have known it.)

The very mention of your husband's orders to the Naval Air Station, Sitka, Alaska, or to Dutch Harbor, at Kodiak, makes you shiver, doesn't it? Well, that is because you are not up on your Alaskan geography perhaps! Alaska covers a lot of territory. Most people are surprised to learn that it is somewhat larger than the combined states of Texas, California, and Montana. Also the climate varies greatly in different sections. For instance, in Sitka it is similar to that of Seattle, Washington, with temperatures ranging from about 20 degrees minimum to 80 degrees maximum, with very little freezing weather; in Fairbanks, 580 miles north, the thermometer sometimes drops to 70 degrees below.

A very helpful information bulletin is sent out by the Bureau of Navigation in regard to service in Alaska, but somehow, the most comprehensive and carefully prepared bulletin by a man never tells a Navy wife the hundred and one little things that are of especial interest to her. Such as: Is there a beauty parlor in Sitka? There is, my darling, but brace yourself for its prices; A manicure costs $1.25, while a shampoo and set cost from $2.50 to $3.50. The supply of cosmetics is limited and of a poor variety, as well as being expensive, so it is suggested that you include a goodly supply of your favorite kinds. Many Navy wives learn to do their own beauty work, or they work out a system of mutual aid.

Maybe you are the optimistic type who has visions of a retinue of Eskimo servants dog-sled driving you over the frozen roads. Well, you are doomed to disappointment, because the Indians, even the fairly intelligent mission-trained ones, apparently have no desire to better themselves financially. Training them has been tried by experts, but they have usually not gotten to first base on that score and have given up. The half-breeds, or "breeds," as they are called, are inclined to be rather independent and indolent after they have saved up a few dollars. The present Commanding Officer in the past year has not been able to get a servant. Maybe these Eskies are just smart. After all, why should one work puttering around a house if he has enough dried fish for the winter and a good suit of woolies?

The Naval Air Station is situated on Japonski Island which is about one mile long and a half mile wide, lying immediately adjacent to Sitka on Baranof Island. Stone causeways connect it to the group of small islands on which the Army base is situated. Boats are operated on a half-hour schedule between Japonski Island and Sitka. Needless to add, an automobile is not a necessity, but a private boat is a great convenience. There is bus service for all personnel on the island.

Sitka has three schools, two Indian and one white, the latter being a grade school combined with high school. The public school system on the whole is creditable. The teachers are imported from the States and employed by the Territorial government. The University of Alaska is located at Fairbanks in the Tanana Valley. It is a federal land-grant college and specializes in courses in agriculture. It is also well known for its School of Mines.

No, You Won't Live in an Igloo!

On the Naval Air Station there are five very complete and commodious sets of quarters which are assigned to the Commanding Officer, the Executive Officer, the Personnel Officer,

the Medical Officer, and the Marine Officer. The quarters
are of concrete and frame, covered with asbestos.

Ten additional sets in the form of duplex three-bedroom
houses are under construction, and the B.O.Q. at present
boasts four suites, along with 56 rooms and 38 baths. Also
in the process of construction is a low-cost housing project
consisting of 67 duplex houses or 125 sets of quarters for
married enlisted men and civilian employees. Oil furnaces
are used for heating and electric stoves are furnished for
cooking in all government quarters. Rents in Sitka are high,
and the houses and apartments are small and poorly furnished.
There are no real-estate agencies, so anyone desiring accommodations in Sitka should write in advance to the Personnel
Officer at the Naval Air Station.

The three best apartment houses are: Tower Apartments
(1 and 2 bedrooms, $60 to $80), Rands Apartments ($60 to
$80), Kettleson Apartments (newer but poorly furnished, $60
to $80). Houses are at a premium. The only first-class hotel
is the Sitka Hotel, consisting of 66 rooms with minimum rates
at $5.00 per day. There are four or five second-class hotels
with *very* poor accommodations and very high rates.

Prices are all out of reason. Just to give you an idea: A
hamburger costs $0.65; laundry is almost prohibitive, shirts
$0.35 each, sheets $0.20 each, one suit of underwear $0.50.
Food prices in town are very high, but the Commissary
prices are average. Milk can be obtained in limited quantities,
but the station has a "mechanical cow" and the commissary
sells good milk and cream therefrom.

The stores carry about the same type of merchandise found
in similar stores of small towns of the United States, but in
Alaska, because of the freight rates, prices are necessarily
higher. It is wise to lay in an extra supply of useful articles
from the dime store before you go north. Mail-order shopping
from catalogues will be the solution to some problems, and
will be a pleasant way to spend your leisure.

The most recent news about living conditions in Dutch
Harbor is not too encouraging. It doesn't look as if Navy

dependents will go there in the immediate future. There are no quarters available except the ten sets for the heads of departments which are now under construction. A B.O.Q. is included in the plans. The quarters will be of frame construction with electric stoves for cooking and a central steam plant for heating. The answer to the possibility of procuring suitable furnished houses or apartments and servants in the vicinity is NO.

The climate is wet and *windy*, with the heaviest rains in October. There will be gusts of wind, the velocity going to 100 miles per hour.

A grade school is promised. This is a new base that doesn't sound awfully attractive unless you have a yen to do some real pioneering.

Clothes

In the cities of Nome, Juneau, Fairbanks, Anchorage, and Haines one sees fashionably dressed women. No doubt Sitka will join this cosmopolitan group with the arrival of the feminine contingent of Navy wives. Take along your regular wardrobe, but be sure to include plenty of good rubber rain clothes. The rainfall, though seldom heavy, is consistent, averaging about eighty-three inches a year, if that means anything to you. If it doesn't now, it will before a year has passed.

Raincoats and umbrellas of yesterday were drab affairs, indeed, in somber colors such as funereal black, murky brown, and navy blue. Today one can look cheery in a downpour on the gloomiest day, what with cherry or lemon-yellow slickers, snazzy little capes of rubberized silk, and umbrellas that not only shed rain but look as though they were dreamed up as Christmas tree ornaments. You may have to wrap yourself in cellophane in Alaska during the rainy season, but you might as well make it pretty cellophane.

But these are your summer rain clothes; for winter a heavy gabardine trench coat with a hood will be a joy. And be sure to include plenty of overshoes and boots.

A good warm topcoat will be a necessity, or if you own a fur coat or a fur-lined coat, take it along. You may take a trip into the interior by dog-sled or go up to Fairbanks during the winter Ice Carnival, which is the social event of the season. Lightweight woolens and tweeds, along with the average wardrobe needed on the station for social affairs, should be included.

Diversions

Alaska is noted for its beautiful scenery. It is the Land of the Midnight Sun! In the more northern cities like Fairbanks street lights are not turned on in the summertime. There is no need. The Northern Lights, indescribable in their everchanging beauty, and the fjords of the Inside Passage remind one of Norway; while the dazzling white glaciers, mirror-like lakes, and valleys strewn with exquisite wild flowers bring back summers spent in Switzerland.

Snow-crowned Mount Edgecumbe, an extinct volcano, dominates the harbor entrance to Sitka. You will be fascinated by the totem poles which in the early days were small carved grave posts or tombstones. With the coming of the white man, tools became plentiful and the totem pole art flourished. From living trees the coastal tribes made "family trees" depicting grotesquely decorative figures of their mythological ancestors. Sitka's outstanding landmark is the old Russian cathedral of St. Michael, dedicated in 1848.

Fishing may be said to be the most popular sport, though shooting and hunting are available. No license is required for fishing, and deep-sea fishing for salmon and halibut is excellent, while trout fishing in the many and various streams makes this a fisherman's paradise.

Big-game hunting is such an expensive sport that few can indulge in it. First of all, one must procure a license for hunting which costs $50, then engage the services of a registered guide at $10 per day in addition to supplies and all the extras that are necessary to the success of this type of sport.

The Welfare Department maintains a 38-foot cabin cruiser

(sleeping nine) which may be obtained for trips by application to the proper authorities. There are also several excellent cabins which may be used by fishing and hunting parties.

On the station there is an Officers' Club with monthly dues of $1.00 per person. Dances are held frequently. Badminton courts are installed in the hangars, there is a skeet range and an archery range, and the Recreation Building is equipped with pool tables and bowling alleys.

SERVICE IN THE CANAL ZONE

The headquarters of the 15th Naval District are located on the *Pacific side* of the Isthmus. The naval activities at this terminal include the Radio Station, Balboa, the Radio Station Summit, and the Naval Ammunition Depot. Balboa is the normal base of the Special Service Squadron. Panama City, the capital of the Republic of Panama, with Balboa and Ancon, are the principal cities on the Pacific side.

On the Atlantic side are located the Naval Air Station and the submarine base at Coco Solo, the Gatun Radio Station, the Naval Magazine, and the Navy Radio direction finder station at Toro Point near Fort Sherman. Cristobal and Colón are the leading cities on the Atlantic end of the Canal.

Climate

Panama is always hot, though it has two seasons, the dry and the rainy. The former extends from about the middle of December to the first of May and is characterized by relatively low humidity, constant, monotonous trade winds, and practically no rain. During the rainy season, May to December, the humidity is very high and it rains every day. The rain isn't usually continuous, but instead comes in short, heavy showers. The water pours on the tall, regal palms, washes the façades of the stately old cathedrals and palaces, and likewise gives the naked little Panamanian urchins a much-needed ablution as they play in the streets. It is very damp and everything mildews, so a dry closet is a necessity.

Living Conditions at Coco Solo

Government quarters of concrete construction (a few of frame) are provided for officers on duty at the submarine base and at the air station. When any are not occupied, they are assigned on a temporary status to the Inshore Patrol, Naval Intelligence, and Section Base personnel. Most of these quarters are new and very comfortable with three bedrooms, two baths, large combination porch-living room, dining room, kitchen, and servants' quarters.

There are practically no suitable furnished or unfurnished houses for rent near by, and the inferior accommodations that are to be had are very high in price.

Panama isn't what it used to be when it comes to servants; in fact they are scarce and of a very indifferent type. The Panamanians and Negroes find working in restaurants preferable to domestic service, and many have government work.

The Washington Hotel, fronting the sea, in a parklike enclosure, is expensive, but it is always crowded with Navy people. It is government owned and is the only place on the Atlantic side to stay. Nowadays, when all nations are busy with their own knitting and problems of state at home, one does not see the cosmopolitan group of travelers that used to congregate at the Washington Hotel. Instead, it is filled with Service men and pretty young girls and Navy wives who are following the ship.

Living Conditions on the Pacific Side

In the 15th Naval District located in Balboa there are eighteen sets of quarters, including those of the Commandant. Those not occupied by heads of departments are assigned according to rank. The quarters are rather high concrete bungalows on stilts, excepting those of the Commandant, who resides in state in a large two-story house.

For the many officers who have to live in Panama City, finding a suitable house is quite a problem. Furnished houses for rent are almost unheard of; and the unfurnished ones have very high rentals. There are a few modern apartments, but all have long waiting lists. Before the construction of a new apartment house is even nearly completed, all the apartments are rented. The average rent for a two-bedroom apartment is $90, and $70 is asked for a one-bedroom apartment very indifferently furnished.

The Tivoli Hotel is always crowded with Navy people, though it is quite expensive. The food is good.

Schools

The public schools are under the management of the Panama Canal, and they are excellent. A good junior college (2 years) is located in Balboa. Tuition is $20 per month. The school year begins in September and ends in June.

Transportation

The Panama Railroad is the principal means of transportation across the Isthmus from Colón to Balboa, a distance of forty-seven miles. There is no motor road, although there is one being rushed to completion. There are three regular passenger trains each way every day, in addition to a "scooter," which has limited first-class accommodations. The shuttle trains ply back and forth on schedule, and the one-way trip requires one hour and twenty minutes. The fare to naval personnel and their families is $2.80 a round trip.

A private car is a necessity. It is advisable to ship down an old car rather than a new one. Weather conditions are hard on cars. A closed car is preferable for comfort, though an open car has more resale value.

Clothes

Take plenty of washable clothes; dry cleaners are practically nonexistent. Give emphasis to shoes. Store all your furs and your husband's blue uniforms in the States. You'll not need them.

Markets

On the Atlantic side food is obtained through the Army, Navy, and Panama Canal Commissaries. There is also a native market in Colón.

On the Pacific side there is no Navy Commissary, but necessary provisions may be obtained from the Panama Canal Commissary and the Army Commissary at Corozal. There is a native market in the city of Panama where fowl, fruits, vegetables, and fish can be bought reasonably. The fish is excellent. The milk from the Commissary is good, and cold-storage eggs are plentiful. The meats are reasonable, but vegetables, although of fair quality and variety, are expensive.

Recreation

Officers and their families enjoy a variety of sports in Panama, including golf, tennis, bowling, badminton, sailing, fishing, and swimming (if a place can be found where the water is clean and free of sharks). Despite the rain, golf is played all year! The following clubs are available: Panama Golf Club, an eighteen-hole course about six miles from Panama; Fort Amador Golf Club; and Pedro Miguel Golf Club at the Mira Flores Locks.

The Stranger's Club in Colón and the Union Club in Panama City give reciprocal privileges. The dues are nominal for Service personnel.

Cities and Shopping

On the Pacific side of the Isthmus is old Panama City; on the Atlantic side is modern Cristobal. They represent two different worlds, two civilizations, two religions, and two races. Panama sells crucifixes and Cristobal sells Frigidaires; Panama smokes black tobacco, Cristobal smokes yellow; Cristobal sleeps on Beauty Rest mattresses, Panama in feather beds. It is a country of anachronisms.

Colón's streets are lined with Hindu shops, shops that once held wonderful displays of Oriental goods, perfume,

Panama hats, and fascinating goods that were so tempting to the feminine shopper. Today their stocks are sadly depleted. The optimistic merchants carry on, however, always hoping and cheerfully promising a new shipment on the next boat. English china is said to be about the only real bargain today. It is less than half United States prices. Silver may also be ordered at a discount, but Chinese linens have advanced in price with each shipment, and French perfumes are a luxury of the past—even that "Christmas Night" that the bootleg perfumers used to mix up in washtubs and sell for $7.50 an ounce to pop-eyed tourists.

LIFE AT GUANTANAMO

Guantanamo, Cuba, is one of the principal marine bases. It operates in conjunction with and under the U.S. Naval Operating Base at Guantanamo Bay. Since an automobile is a necessity, perhaps it might be best to approach Guantanamo by automobile and train and ferry. Outside of airways, if you can find an easier and shorter approach than three days, be sure to let us know!

Trunks and all heavy baggage should arrive in Havana on the steamer with you, as everything is subject to inspection by customs; however, for Service personnel the authorities do not make a rigid inspection. They are mostly concerned that not more than two cartons of American cigarettes are carried.

When you arrive you will be welcomed on this more or less isolated base with open arms. The women will be avid for States news and the sight of the last word in clothes; therefore, look your best. The Officers' Club is the rendezvous for social activities, and because of lack of outside entertainment facilities, it is utilized to a great extent.

Climate

The climate is tropical, averaging during the day in summer months 87 degrees, but the nights are usually cool. During the winter months, light blankets are welcome at night. The atmosphere is dry, and medical officers state it is one of the most healthful of tropical stations.

Quarters

The married officers' quarters are limited in number (as usual) although it is expected that sufficient quarters will be available for all officers ordered to the station. Married officers should by all means find out if quarters will be available prior to the departure of the family from the United States.

The new quarters for officers are of tropical frame construction, consisting of a large living and dining room, entrance hall and porch, kitchen, three bedrooms, two baths. All the floors are tiled, and a garage and servants' quarters are in a building detached from the house. Electricity is used for cooking and heating.

All public quarters are furnished throughout except for mattresses, pillows, bed and table linen, hangings, china, silverware, glassware, and kitchen utensils. It is wise to bring table and silverware as it is expensive in Cuba.

Some Things to Take to Guantanamo

Curtain material—cretonne or otherwise
Floor lamps
Table lamps
Utility tables
Card tables

Flat silver
Visiting cards
Inexpensive crystal ware
Linens
Blankets

Drapery material for curtains should have body to it as the constant wind tends to make light materials stringy in appearance.

Clothes for Guantanamo

Women should bring an ample supply of clothing suitable for a warm climate, including slacks and shorts. Patterns and materials to be made up locally should also be brought.

Bathing suits
Hosiery (available in ship's service store)
A plentiful initial supply of shoes, sizes recorded at store in U.S.

Evening dresses of wash materials: organdy, gingham, cotton, lace, etc.
Ample supply of children's outer garments
Riding or jodhpur boots, riding breeches, coats (if you ride)
Summer hats (none are available locally)
One outfit of heavy clothing—sweaters and a light coat
An evening wrap

(THE NEAREST DIME STORE IS SANTIAGO.)

Servants

Yes, you can relax and enjoy life in Guantanamo! Cooks and nurses are plentiful, and the wages paid all servants are controlled by station order. All servants who are Jamaicans, Cubans, or Chinese are required to pass a rigid physical examination at the Station Dispensary before they may be hired. Except for a tendency to move rather slowly, they are quite efficient and good natured.

Schools

The Naval Operating Base is proud of its new school, which employs thirteen teachers. The grades cover primary, elementary, and high-school work. A small tuition fee is charged, and students purchase their own textbooks from the school authorities. There are no private schools on the station or in the vicinity.

Marketing

On the station a commissary store is in operation which carries a comprehensive stock of well-known brands of canned groceries, cold-storage meats, fruits, and vegetables. Once in a while it is impossible to get celery or lettuce, but on the whole the marketing situation is satisfactory.

Local meat, fowl, and vegetables are obtainable but are of an inferior quality. In season, local oranges, grapefruit, papaya, pineapples, bananas, and mangoes are available and of good quality. During dry seasons the milk supply is limited. A new milk plant has just been established on the station, which will produce a better grade of milk at slightly lower prices.

Recreational Facilities

Swimming, tennis, baseball and softball, sailing, motor boating, hiking, hunting, shooting, fishing, picnics, horseback riding, band concerts, club dances, nightly open-air movies, a good library and reading room comprise the recreational facilities.

Radios: Long-wave sets are suitable only after dark and during the winter months. Short-wave sets can be used any time. Radio sets can be purchased at the ship's service store at a greatly reduced price.

Riding: The mountain and beach trails are picturesque and beautiful. There are about 160 private mounts. The monthly feed bill for a horse is about $8.00.

Hunting and shooting: Game in Cuba consists of deer, ducks, large blue pigeons, doves, and wild guinea. Trap shooting and skeet are available.

Golf: It is hoped that a nine-hole course will be constructed in the near future to replace the course abandoned because of the expansion of the base.

Clubs: A well-appointed Officers' Club is in operation, also a Club for Chief Petty Officers which is available for married Petty Officers. There are no hotels, restaurants, or like accommodations available.

San Juan and Saint Thomas

Owing to the strategic importance of Puerto Rico and the Virgin Islands in the Caribbean, the activities of the 10th Naval District have been greatly expanded in the past year. A submarine base and an air patrol group have been established at Saint Thomas, and the Naval Air Station at San Juan has been greatly enlarged.

Puerto Rico means "Gate to Riches." We acquired this island from Spain in 1898 in a treaty after the Spanish-American War.

The three "Virgins," Saint Thomas, Saint John, and Saint

Croix, were bought from Denmark in 1917 to be used as a future naval base.

At first, after the first World War, it looked as if we had been overenthusiastic about extending our offshore domain, but the picture has changed. Today these islands are worth a good deal more to the United States than Uncle Sam paid for them. They serve as a covering air base for the Panama Canal. The Virgins have maintained their identities after a fashion; the Spanish influence is definitely felt in San Juan, while the Danish atmosphere is apparent in Saint Thomas. Withal, though, they are both intensely American and the Puerto Ricans refer to mainlanders as continentals. Another Caribbean paradox!

Lying in the path of the trade winds, both islands have a tropical climate. Likewise living conditions are similar except that so far Saint Thomas is totally unspoiled! By plane, San Juan and Saint Thomas are only forty minutes apart, but the boat trip requires eight hours.

Living Conditions in San Juan

At the Naval Air Station at San Juan there are thirty sets of quarters for officers, and under construction for the 10th Naval District are eleven additional sets and an apartment house for twenty-four families. All are of concrete construction. At the air station electric stoves for cooking are furnished, while gas is used in the district houses.

Houses and apartments are scarce. The best ones are Ocean Walk, Borinquen Park, the Valencia, and the Miami. Several more are under construction. Few of the houses or apartments are furnished, and all rentals are high. Prices range from $50 to $90 per month. You may be lucky and find a charming old Spanish casa with a patio that will be the delight of your life. It pays to shop around in San Juan.

The public schools are out of the question for American children, but there are twenty private schools in San Juan, including several good Catholic convents. The University of Puerto Rico is located at Rio Piedras and specializes in agriculture and engineering. Its liberal arts courses are not of particularly high standing, but it does have a splendid School of Tropical Medicine.

Native Puerto Rican servants were plentiful until recently. On the whole, though, they were never very efficient. Their scarcity today is a greater blow to the pride of people who used to employ them than to smooth household running.

Food is always a lively topic of conversation, probably because most of it is imported. Mondays and Thursdays are "boat days," and parties usually follow on Tuesdays and Fridays, when hostesses can be sure of fresh vegetables. On the whole, food is expensive, especially meats. There are good dairies on the island, and the milk is delicious and plentiful.

A small car with a short wheelbase is a necessity. The roads are good, but just try to turn a Cadillac on one of the narrow winding streets of San Juan! You'll wish you had brought Junior's motor scooter instead.

Whether or not to take furniture? If you do, be sure to take something inexpensive in wicker, because the termites devour everything except solid native mahogany. Antiques are just their dish, and you can practically see your favorite whatnot vanish before your eyes.

There are two important golf clubs: the Berwind Country Club, with Service dues $6.00 per month, and the El Moro, or Army Club, whose dues are $1.00 per month. The Condado Hotel is expensive but popular, and the Escambron is famous as a night club and for its bathing beach and elaborate cabañas.

San Juan, the largest city on the island, is a wide-awake capital, not the siesta-inclined, tropical town featured in the movies. Its White House or Casa Blanca is now occupied by the Commanding General of the Puerto Rican Department.

The official residence of Puerto Rico's Governor-General is La Fortaleza, and it is reputed to be the oldest building under the American flag. It is painted a rather sickening raspberry pink but otherwise is quite dignified. A tremendous old battle-scarred Spanish Fort, El Morro, stands guard at the entrance of the harbor.

"Puerto Rico reeks of romance and tragedy! Its charm and mystery are intangible, yet beauty and sadness are there." There is also, if one looks for it, plenty of sunshine and pleasant living.

Navy Life in Saint Thomas

The early history of Saint Thomas is like that of many other places in the Caribbean. The development of the islands was left to overseers of absentee landowners. As a consequence of the usual neglect, there are few monuments, imposing buildings, palaces or other manmade landmarks of the early days.

Lucky you, to be going to this outpost while it is in the making and before its charm is spoiled! Of course pioneering always has its inconveniences; yet Saint Thomas will offer you special compensations. To begin with, you may have a difficult time finding a place to live, but when you do, you may be sure your house will be on a hill. All the houses are built on ledges of sloping hills, thereby giving a terraced effect.

Though scarce, houses are cheap. They are made of island limestone cement, on account of being in the hurricane zone. Roofs are of corrugated iron, and the houses usually have two stories since that makes them cooler. All houses have upper "galleries"—not porches.

You will be enchanted with the native servants. They have musical voices and speak in parables; also, they are very polite and gentle. Crime is exceedingly rare, although precautions against it are common. For instance, if one owns a fine banana tree the idea is to encircle its base with a ring of flour. This circle constitutes a curse for the thief, so it and your fruit will not be disturbed. If any banana-eating boy is running around with flour on his feet, the authorities know what to do.

Laundry is no problem at all. It is done by a local washwoman who will do everything for a family for about $8.00

or $10.00 per month. There is no dry-cleaning service, and cleaners in San Juan are only fair.

Most of the food is imported from the States, so it is necessarily a bit higher. The Navy Commissary and Marine Commissary sell at average government prices. Local fruits, such as papaya and oranges, are plentiful, but the dairies are not too satisfactory.

An automobile is a necessity, and a small old car is recommended. Again one finds those narrow winding streets similar to the goat alleys of San Juan. Don't forget to stay on the left side of the road, just as you did in Manila. Gasoline sells for about $0.15 a gallon.

There is a private school for Service children at Bourne Field, and the high school in town is average, though no color line is drawn.

The town of Saint Thomas boasts three hotels, all on the American plan. The 1829 has rates at about $50 per week. (There is a color line here.) The Grand has the same rates. (No color line.) The Bluebeard has slightly higher prices. Rates may be a little less to Service personnel. None of these hotels takes children. There is one boardinghouse, which gives a monthly service rate of $150 per couple.

Dronningensgade (Danish enough for you?), which is the Main Street, is an eloquent relic of the past. Formerly warehouses, its stores and shops are thick-walled, narrow buildings whose owners are given to telling stories of the days when barks, schooners, brigantines, and full-rigged ships came to Saint Thomas laden with millions of dollars' worth of fancy merchandise. Brocades from China, cashmeres from India, laces from Ireland, perfumes from France were the cargoes of the ships that lay to in the harbor. Today the merchandise in these shops includes charcoal burners, laces, hats, paints, oils, corsets, and cigars.

The shopkeepers are often more interesting than their stores. One aged shopkeeper will not sell any of her jugs because her husband, when he was alive, was fond of them.

Another cannot part with certain pots because some day she may need them.

The St. Thomas Islands Co-operative is an interesting commercial enterprise. Not so long ago the United States found that practically all the natives were on relief and poorly fed. So a system was worked out whereby an organization would purchase all their handiwork and resell it at standard prices. Organized in 1931, the Co-operative has now become the hub of all island industry. The natives make beautiful embroidery, basketry, and furniture; and these are sold at standard prices. There is no bartering.

There is a daily plane service between Saint Thomas and San Juan, except on Sunday. The round trip costs $15. The Alcoa Steamship Line has ships direct from New York every two weeks. There is daily airmail out of San Juan.

The *Catherine* or *Katy*, an interisland boat, steams across to San Juan twice a week. For a number of years she was a drab Cinderella performing her round of duties; but with the influx of visitors she was redecorated, private baths and suites were installed, and her departure from San Juan, which takes place at night, is attended by all the fanfare of a transatlantic sailing of yesterday.

At present there are no government quarters for officers, but eight sets have been authorized. These will be constructed of local limestone.

There is very little furniture to be had on the island, so it is suggested that a complete outfit of inexpensive wicker be brought along; also linen, bedding, dishes, and kitchen utensils.

Wash clothes are the order of the day, and for the evenings too, so bring along a good supply. You should have enough shoes to last through your entire stay.

Golf, riding, and swimming are the popular sports. Tennis and handball courts are being laid out, and softball fields are planned. The Marines have a Beach House on Lindbergh Bay equipped with dressing rooms and a bar. This bay has the only bathing beach on the reservation. Swimming piers similar to those in Guantanamo Bay will be built on the east shore of Great Krumm Bay near the barracks.

The Marines also maintain a riding stable and play polo every Sunday. There are about thirty mounts for horseback riding.

Naval Missions in South America

Almost every country of South America has a United States Naval Mission stationed in its capital, in addition to its naval attachés. A detail in such a place can be wonderfully interesting, and the social round is quite formal and intense. Remember that the seasons are just reversed! July is the height of the winter season which gets under way with the celebration of the Ninth of July, their Independence Day.

Buenos Aires is as formal as Washington. There is great punctilio about leaving cards and returning calls. Argentine women dress in the French tradition of elegance, and spend most of their time at it. At Argentine parties the important thing is to see and be seen. Dinner is served at nine or later. Tea is an important meal every day at five. There is no café society, for the Embassy Club, the Charleston, the Africa, and one or two others are the only respectable night clubs. Dinners at home almost invariably demand black tie, though occasionally white ties are de rigueur. During the season there is opera in the old Teatro Colon, and on Sundays everyone goes to the polo games.

Rio is less formal than Buenos Aires. The winter season is the gayest time of the year. Santiago, Chile, is a popular detail. The Chileans are gentle and informal, and living in Santiago is very inexpensive. Viña del Mar on the Chilean coast, in addition to being a recreational resort, is noted for its flowers. The hydrangeas grow as big as a horse's head, soft cool cushions of cloudy pink and blue, and the roses are the size of butter plates. In the autumn, Santiago has its opera season, followed by concerts and lectures. Just before Christmas everyone goes to hear the Bach chorals, beautifully sung in the dark old church of Saint Augustine.

Lima is a city of the past, rich in colonial treasures and proud of its heritage. The aristocracy keeps its Spanish titles, and the atmosphere of Spanish royalty lingers on in Peru. It is still locked in the Spanish tradition. The wives of Peruvian naval officers lead quiet lives, have large families and small pay; so you will not expect to be entertained by them. It is not at all unusual for a husband to appear at a dinner party without his wife.

The atmosphere is extremely gay for diplomats, attachés, and naval representatives of the American missions. To speak Spanish is a very valuable asset and will prove an open sesame. The Peruvians are never critical of how poorly one speaks Spanish, but the lack of effort is deeply resented. They are a very gentle people and extremely careful of their manners and dress. It is said of them "They will follow you to Hell if you are courteous, but not to Heaven if you are rude."

What the future holds in the way of naval missions, legation duty, and when and where new Ambassadors will be sent remains to be seen! At present, Iceland, Trinidad, Bermuda, and others are claiming our attention as naval bases. The Navy wife welcomes new places and new experiences as she serves at the side of her husband. Hers is a life of high adventure, of service, and of courage.

Navy Wives

(By permission of Margaret Tayler Yates.)

We are the silent partners in a notable Company
We work with the Navy Department and the various ships at sea
Free and happy-go-lucky—a transient, motley mob—
Still, for the "good of the Service," we have to be on the job.
We pack at a moment's notice; strange places we explore
To make a home for our husbands whenever they come ashore;
We hop a transport at Frisco, at Norfolk or Puget Sound:
We brave typhoons in the China Sea to follow our men around.
We "doll up" a room in Manila, or shack in Samoa or Guam,
Or perhaps a flat in the U.S.A. so Harry or Dick or Tom
Can find a home when they come ashore, whatever the land or clime;

And we bear them children, whom they can love whenever they
  have time.
Allied with a fighting unit, a fighting unit we;
Ours to fight the lonely hours and blue uncertainty.
We've the butcher, the baker and "rank" to fight; we fight for a
  place in the sun
But the hardest fight is our "Navy pay"—a fight not always won.
But, oh, we love the life we lead, it never grows stale or slow;
Whenever we feel the itching foot we can pack our things and go
For whatever we are, whatever we're not, whatever we might have
  been
We have learned to greet Adventure, if it helps our COUNTRY
  win!

APPENDIX

HERE is some general information concerning the United States Navy of today, including military and naval terms that should be in every Navy wife's vocabulary. It is taken from *What The Citizen Should Know About the Navy*, by Hanson Baldwin, 1941, but several changes have been made since the declaration of war which we have included. Future changes may be in order. This skeleton outline is tentative.

The Commander-in-Chief of the United States Navy is the President of the United States.

The Secretary of the Navy is a civilian, who now has a civilian under-secretary, an assistant secretary and an assistant secretary for air. He represents the President in exercising his command function.

The Chief of Naval Operations is appointed by the President and holds the rank of full Admiral during his tour of duty, which is four years.

The Commander in Chief of the United States Fleet is no longer known as "Cincus," the traditional Navy abbreviation, but as "Cominch." He is the Commanding Officer of the fighting forces at sea.

The Navy Department in Washington is the center of administration of both shore and seagoing establishments.

The Navy Department is the head of a vast hierarchy of rank and comprises in addition to the offices of the Secretary and his assistants a number of bureaus and offices.

The principal divisions are:

1. Bureau of Navigation (charge of naval personnel, charts, hydrographic surveys, etc.)
2. Bureau of Ordnance
3. Bureau of Ships
4. Bureau of Yards and Docks
5. Bureau of Supplies and Accounts
6. Bureau of Medicine and Surgery
7. Bureau of Aeronautics

8. Bureau of Construction and Repair
9. Bureau of Engineering
10. Major General Commandant of the Marine Corps
11. Judge Advocate General of the Navy
12. General Board

The United States is divided into fifteen territorial districts, and in addition to these are districts of the overseas possessions of the United States.

Headquarters of these districts are shown below.

District	Headquarters
First	Boston, Mass.
Second	(Included in first and third)
Third	New York, N.Y.
Fourth	Philadelphia, Pa.
Fifth	Norfolk, Va.
Sixth	Charleston, S.C.
Seventh	Charleston, S.C.
Eighth	New Orleans, La.
Ninth	Great Lakes, Ill.
Tenth	San Juan, Puerto Rico
Eleventh	San Diego, Calif.
Twelfth	San Francisco, Calif.
Thirteenth	Seattle, Wash.
Fourteenth	Pearl Harbor, Hawaii
Fifteenth	Canal Zone, (Balboa)
Sixteenth	Cavite, Philippines

Each district has its Commandant, who has complete charge of the naval activities within the geographical limits of his district. The Commandant is in turn responsible to the Chief of Naval Operations.

GLOSSARY OF NAVY TERMS AND
NAUTICAL EXPRESSIONS

Abandon ship: To abandon ship is to cause all hands to leave the ship for their safety, when a ship is in danger of sinking, or threatened by destruction by fire. All personnel including passengers on every ship are assigned abandon-ship stations. For passengers on a liner or a Navy transport, the abandon-ship station designates the lifeboat in which the passenger is to leave the ship and the location on deck where the passengers for each boat are to assemble at the order, "Prepare to abandon ship." On the first day at sea there will be an abandon-ship drill, during which all passengers physically able to do so must assemble at their assigned stations, in order that there may be no misunderstanding in case of an emergency, and for instruction in adjusting life preservers.

Abeam: At right angles to the keel of the ship.

Aboard: On or within a boat or vessel. This word is seldom used by Navy personnel; the term *on board* is much preferred by seamen.

Above: This word is used in naval parlance to denote movement upward from the keel to the upper deck, or a relative position at a greater vertical distance from the keel. The term *upstairs* is never used; on board ship all means of ascending from one level to another are called *ladders*; and in place of saying *going upstairs*, one says *going above*; or *up on deck*. Altitudes higher than the upper deck, except the bridges, are *aloft* and not *above*.

Absentee: Any person in the Navy who fails to return to his ship or station by the hour of expiration of his leave or liberty is an absentee.

Accommodation ladder: A ladder suspended at the side of a ship to permit personnel in boats to ascend to the deck of a ship. In the Navy the term *gangway ladder*, or, informally, *gangway*, is the more common term. The treads of a gangway ladder are at right angles to the side of the ship, and the slope of the ladder is such as to resemble stairs. (Compare with Sea ladder.)

Action: In naval parlance this means hostile action; the use of the ship and its armament in battle. In the British Navy *battle stations* are called *action stations.*

Action, clear for: Clear for action means to make all final preparation, except going to battle stations; to prepare the ship for battle.

Aft: Toward or in the direction of the stern; opposite to forward.

Afternoon watch: The watch from noon to 4 P.M.

Aide: An officer assigned as a personal assistant to the President, the Secretary of the Navy, or an Assistant Secretary of the Navy, a Flag Officer, or in some cases an officer of lower rank in command of a naval unit comprising a number of ships. Not all officers assigned to staff duty are designated as aides. Those designated as such normally are Chiefs of Staff, Flag Secretaries, and Flag Lieutenants.

Aiguillettes: The insignia of an aide. Dress aiguillettes consist of a heavy braided loop of gilt cord, passing around the shoulder and attached to a button or pin in front; suspended from this loop at the point where it is attached in front are two gilt pendants. The origin of the aiguillettes is uncertain but is said to have been a coil of line carried by an aide to picket a General's horse. Undress aiguillettes consist merely of loops of cord surrounding the arm and attached at the shoulder. An aide to the President wears aiguillettes on the right shoulder; others wear them on the left shoulder.

All hands: The entire crew of a ship, officers and men, except those specifically excused by regulations covering the particular situation; i.e., "All hands up anchor"; or the call of the boatswain's mate at reveille, "Up all hands, rise and shine."

Aloft: Above the upper deck (except the bridges, which although above the upper-deck level are not considered aloft), usually applied to stations on or in the masts.

Alongside: By the side of, side by side; a boat comes alongside a ship's gangway; a ship goes alongside a dock, or alongside another ship at anchor or at a buoy. When two or more ships alongside each other are riding to one anchor, or to a mooring buoy, they are said to be *nested,* and collectively comprise a *nest.*

Anchor: A portable metal weight designed with flukes to bite into the ground, or bottom, which, secured to the ship by chains, is used for holding the ship in position when it is not underway or secured to a dock, buoy, etc.

Anchor's aweigh: The situation when the anchor is being hove in, at the instant the anchor is free of the ground. After the anchor clears the ground, the ship is free to use its engines to maintain its position or to proceed to sea.

Anchor watch: Men detailed to remain alert, during the night, when a ship is at anchor, to be immediately available to take any necessary action such as veering chain or letting go a second anchor in case the ship, due to current or wind, should drag or be in danger of dragging her anchor.

Armament: A general term comprising all weapons, guns, torpedoes, depth charges, etc.

Armor: The steel plate distributed principally on the sides and decks of a ship, to protect its hull, turrets, magazines, and engineering space from shells and bombs.

Astern: In a direction opposite to the course or heading of the ship; in the wake of the ship.

Attached to: This is the general form of expressing the assignment of naval personnel; i.e., attached to and serving on board the U.S.S. ——.

Avast: A nautical word meaning discontinue, cease; i.e., avast heaving.

Awash: On a level with the surface of the sea.

Awning: A sheet of canvas spread over certain sections of a ship's deck for protection from the sun.

Aye, aye, sir: The traditional Navy acknowledgment of the order of a senior, indicating that the order is understood and will be executed.

Barge: A boat carried by a flagship for the use of the Flag Officer; i.e., the Admiral's barge.

Battle cruiser: A large ship, approximately the tonnage of a battleship, carrying guns of more than 8″ in caliber.

Battleship: The most heavily armed and armored type of warship; the backbone of the Fleet.

Beach: A general term used frequently as a substitute for shore; i.e., *hit the beach* used for *going ashore* on leave or liberty, also said of a ship which goes aground.

Beach guard: A detail of Navy personnel to control the activities of a landing.

Beam: The extreme breadth of a ship, also one of the principal horizontal steel girders which support the decks.

Bearing: The direction of an object from the ship.

Bear a hand: Make haste, hurry.

Belay: To make fast, as a rope.

Below: In the direction of the ship's keel; the term *downstairs* is never used on board ship; the correct expression is *going below*.

Bell: Each ship has a large bell so situated that its sound when struck can be heard on the upper decks and in many portions of the lower decks; this bell is used in marking the passage of time, being struck each half-hour.

Bell buoy: A buoy located to mark a danger to navigation, or the entrance to a channel, fitted with a large bell which is rung by the movement of the buoy due to action of the waves.

Berth: The term is used principally in the Navy to designate the assigned anchorage, dock area, etc. to be used by a ship; figuratively, it is used in relation to an officer's assignment to duty; it is also used to designate a sleeping place in a stateroom, but the more common word in this sense is *bunk*.

Bilge: The bulging, lower section of a ship's hull. Water which may leak into a ship settles in the bilges. In wooden ships this leakage was such as to necessitate daily pumping, hence the word bilge has come to be used in the Navy as a verb meaning elimination due to failure, or failure to meet required standards.

Billet: On board ship, the assigned location for sleeping; hence, figuratively, in a broader sense, a good billet indicates a desirable assignment to duty.

Binnacle list: The binnacle is the stand containing the compass in the vicinity of which, at sea, the Officer of the Deck is stationed in order to watch the steering of the ship.

Bloomers: Canvas secured to the front plate of a turret and enclosing the barrel of each turret gun for a short distance from the turret face plate, for the purpose of keeping spray and other forms of dampness from entering the turret through the holes in the face plate through which the guns project.

Bluejacket: The most common term for Navy enlisted men. The word *gob* sometimes so used is not dignified, and is very distasteful to naval personnel.

Boat cradles, or skids: The supports on the deck or on overhead beams in which the boats rest when hoisted on board.

Boatswain: A Warrant Officer whose specialty is seamanship, including the handling of boats and anchor gear.

Boatswain's mate: A Petty Officer in a deck division of the ship's company whose duty is to supervise and direct the performance of the general duties of a portion of the division.

Boom: A long spar used in the handling of cargo boats, etc.

Boot: A term of comparatively recent origin used to signify a new recruit, or a recruit recently received on board a ship from a training station.

Bootlick: To flatter or cater to, with a view to one's own advancement, or other personal advantage.

Bow: The forward end of a vessel.

Boy: The general designation of an officer's mess attendant.

Bridge: The high structure in the forward part of the ship from which the ship is maneuvered and navigated. Some ships have more than one bridge, usually in the same location but at different levels.

Brig: The compartment of the ship in which prisoners are confined.

Broad command pennant: A swallow-tail pennant indicating that the ship carrying such pennant is the ship of the senior officer of an organized naval unit comprising several ships and when such officer is not of flag rank.

Brow: A large gangway provided for communication between a ship and dock.

Bulkhead: A vertical partition separating one compartment, or room, from another. There are no walls on board ship.

Bunkroom: The number of junior officers on many ships is such that from eight to twelve officers are assigned to a compartment fitted with bunks and lockers, chairs and tables. Compartments so fitted are called bunkrooms.

Buoy: A float usually moored to the bottom in such position as to mark a danger to navigation or the limits of a channel.

Buzzer: A signal for firing the guns in salvo. Guns may be fired while the buzzer is sounding.

Cabin: The quarters on board ship of a Captain or Flag Officer.

Camel: A float placed between a ship and a dock, or between two ships moored side by side, in order to prevent projections from the ship's side from fouling.

Camouflage: The use of various colors of paint in order to reduce the distance at which a ship or aircraft is visible.

Can, or tin can: A figurative term applied to destroyers, sometimes derisively but more often sentimentally by officers serving in, or who have done considerable service in, destroyers.

Captain: A rank next below Rear Admiral, but this term is used on board his own ship in addressing any officer who has been ordered to command, no matter what his actual naval rank.

Carrier: A common abbreviation for aircraft carrier.

Catapult: The mechanism installed on board battleships and cruisers for projecting seaplanes from the deck of the ship into the air.

Caulk: To drive oakum into the seams of a ship, or into the seams (spaces between planks) in the deck of a ship; hence, figuratively, to sleep on deck, and thus *caulking off* means taking a nap.

Censor: Because of the necessity for secrecy as to naval operations during war or national emergency, all communications from a ship must be examined to insure that no unauthorized information is divulged. Such examination is called censorship. Mail which has been so examined is stamped, "Passed by censor."

Charlie noble: The galley smokepipe. This name is said to come from a Captain Charlie Noble of the British Merchant Marine whose ship was noted for its highly polished brass galley smokepipe.

Charthouse: That compartment in the bridge structure of a ship designed for the workroom of the navigator and within which the charts are stored ready for use.

Chief Engineer: The senior officer attached to the engineer department of a ship.

Chief of Staff: The senior aide to a Flag Officer commanding a type, force, or fleet.

Chief Petty Officer: The highest rating of enlisted personnel.

Chit: A chit, when signed, is an acknowledgment of receipt of stores, or services, the value of which is to be charged against the signer's account.

Chow: An informal name for food, or a meal.

Chronometer: An instrument resembling a clock for measuring time with extreme accuracy, for use in navigation computations.

Civil Engineer: An officer of the Civil Engineer Corps of the Navy.

Clear: To free from obstructions, to leave a dock or port, etc.

Clear ship for action: The final preparation, other than going to battle stations, to prepare a ship for battle.

Coaming: The raised wood or metal border of a hatch, or the raised doorsill in the openings between compartments. Coamings are designed primarily to prevent the flow of water on the deck down a hatch or from one compartment to another.

Colors: The national ensign. In port Navy ships in commission hoist the colors at 8:00 A.M. and haul them down at sunset; at sea colors are hoisted when and so long as they can be distinguished, in the presence of foreign shipping, or in sight of land. In time of war colors must be hoisted before the firing of a gun.

Colors, strike the: To strike the colors means to haul them down as a token of surrender.

Commander: A navy rank next below Captain; in large ships when several of the heads of departments may have the actual rank of Commander, only the Executive Officer is referred to, or called, the *Commander*.

Commodore: A navy rank between Captain and Rear Admiral now obsolete except for a few officers on the retired list.

Commutation of rations: An allowance in money made to officers and to enlisted men under special circumstances in lieu of rations in kind. This allowance is usually less than the officer's mess bill.

Compass: An instrument to indicate the magnetic meridian, or in a gyroscopic compass the true meridian by means of which the ship may be steered upon a definitely determined course.

Complement: The complement of a ship is the authorized strength in officers and men.

Confidential: In these days of war all information concerning vessels of the Navy is confidential, and divulging such information may result in serious legal action.

Conning tower: The armored station in the vicinity of the bridge within which the Captain controls the operation of the ship during battle.

Convoy: A group of noncombatant ships sailing under naval control and usually under escort of combatant ships; this term is also used at times in a collective sense, to include both the combatant and noncombatant ships sailing under one command.

Court-martial: A court of justice composed of officers all of whom if practicable are senior to the accused, for the trial of disciplinary offenses.

Coxswain: The lowest Petty Officer rating in the deck force; also the enlisted man who steers and is in charge of a ship's boat and its crew.

Critique: A formal presentation to officers who have taken part in it, of a detailed history of the conduct of operations during a fleet exercise, including a critical examination of decisions reached, plans made, and the manner of execution of such plans.

Cruiser, battle: A vessel of large tonnage carrying guns of 12" caliber or larger.

Cruiser, heavy: A vessel of from 8000 to 10,000 tons standard displacement carrying a battery of guns in excess of 6" in caliber.

Cruiser, light: A cruiser not in excess of 10,000 standard tons and carrying no guns of greater caliber than 6".

Davit: One of a pair of F-shaped uprights projecting over the side of a vessel for suspending a boat.

Deck: All plank or metal floorings of ships are called decks.

Demobilize: The process of returning to peacetime conditions after having been mobilized for war.

Dependent: A legal dependent is a lawful wife, a child under 21 years of age, own or legally adopted, or a mother, provided she is in fact dependent and receives the major part of her support from her son in the Navy.

Depth charge: Explosive charge carried by antisubmarine vessels for the destruction of enemy submarines so designed as to explode at a predetermined depth below the surface.

Destroyer: A comparatively small high-speed naval vessel whose armament comprises torpedoes, depth charges, and guns of 5" caliber or less.

Disbursing Officer: The officer of the Supply Corps charged with making all cash disbursements, including the payment of officers and men.

Distress signal: The letters SOS, by radio, flashing light, or other means. Ships at sea keep guard at definite intervals on a designated distress frequency, which is used by any ship making a radio distress signal.

Division: The crew of a ship is organized in groups, each of which is called a division. Each division has a specific assignment of duties, and an assigned portion of the ship within which it bunks and messes and for the cleanliness, good order and preservation of which it is responsible.

Division of ships: Ships of each type are also organized in groups called divisions. A division of battleships usually comprises three ships; cruisers, three to five ships; destroyers, four to six ships; submarines, four to six ships. An officer commanding such a group is a Division Commander.

Dreadnought: A modern battleship; so called after the British battleship *Dreadnought*.

Dress, full (ship): To full-dress ship is to decorate a ship by flags in honor of a national holiday or a ruler of a country.

Dud: A shell or bomb which fails to explode.

Dungarees: Work clothes made of dark-blue denim, used on board ship by the engineer's force and by others when engaged in certain forms of work.

Duration: The period of the war.

Duty: The officers and crew of a ship are organized in two watches, and each watch in two sections. In port one section is required to remain on board. Such section is called the duty section.

Embark: To go on board a vessel.

Ensign: The national flag; also the junior commissioned rank in the Navy.

Epaulet: An ornamental gilt shoulder badge worn with dress and full-dress blue uniforms. The epaulet is said to have originated with metal shoulder pieces worn by officers to protect their shoulders from saber slashes.

Escort: To accompany merchant shipping by a warship for protection; also a ship of war so engaged.

Esprit de corps: A spirit of common devotion, honor, interest, binding together persons of the same professions, organizations, ships, etc.

Executive Officer: The second in command on board a ship.

Field day: A day for general cleaning of all parts of the ship; usually Friday.

First Lieutenant: The officer, head of department, responsible for the cleanliness, good order, efficiency, and neat and trim appearance of the ship as a whole, and of all parts thereof.

First watch: The four-hour watch from 8:00 P.M. to midnight.

Flag: The insignia of an officer above the rank of Captain carried by a ship in which such officer is officially embarked.

Flag Officer: An officer above the rank of Captain in the Navy.

Flag Lieutenant: The personal aide of a Flag Officer whose customary duties embrace supervision over all forms of visual signaling on board the flagship.

Flag Secretary: The personal aide of a Flag Officer charged with supervision of correspondence, filing, etc.

Fleet: An organized major subdivision of the Navy under command of a Commander-in-Chief.

Float: A raftlike platform used at boat landings to facilitate embarking or disembarking from boats.

Flotilla: In the United States Navy, an organized group of destroyers comprising two or more squadrons.

Flotilla leader: A ship, usually of the cruiser class, operating as flagship of a flotilla Commander.

Flourish: A series of notes on a bugle as a part of official honors.

Force: An organized major subdivision of a fleet, i.e., the battle force, the scouting force, etc.

Forecastle: That portion of the upper deck of a ship forward of the superstructure.

Forward: In the direction of the bow of a ship.

Foul: Entangled; i.e., a foul anchor is one entangled with its chain or cable.

Funnel: A smokestack of a ship.

Furlough: Leave of absence.

General quarters: The condition of a ship when all hands are at battle stations and ready for action.

Gig: A boat designated for the personal use of the Commanding Officer of a ship, or of a Chief of Staff, if below flag rank.

Guard duty: In each group of ships there is one detailed to be

responsible for certain activities requiring the presence on board
of certain definite personnel. At times a different ship may be
required to retain on board ready for service certain personnel
of the medical department; a ship so designated has the medical guard duty.

Gunnery Officer: The officer, head of department, specifically
charged with the preservation and efficient operation of the
ship's armament.

Hammock: A swinging bed made of canvas, suspended from
hooks.

Hangar: A building, or a compartment on board ship, for stowage
of aircraft.

Happy-hour: An entertainment on deck, usually by the ship's
personnel, for the entertainment of the crew.

Hash mark: The slang term for service stripes worn by enlisted
men on the left arm below the elbow on dress uniforms; each
such stripe represents one completed period of enlistment.

Hatch: A door or covering for a hatchway. Also applied to the
hatchway itself.

Hatchway: A rectangular opening in the deck of a vessel for
passage below.

Heave: To hoist or lift up.

Heave to: To stop a ship at sea.

High seas: Waters outside the territorial limits, i.e., more than
three miles from shore.

Hold: That part of the vessel where the cargo is stored.

Home port: The officially designated operating base of a ship,
to which dependents of personnel serving in such ship are
entitled to government transportation.

Home yard: The Navy yard designated as the place to which a
vessel will normally be sent for repairs or overhaul.

Hull: The body of a vessel.

Jack: A flag smaller than the national ensign and usually in
design comprising only a portion of such ensign; i.e., in the
U.S. only the blue field and stars. Hoisted on a staff at the
stern of a U.S. public vessel when such vessel is not underway.

Jacob's ladder: A rope ladder with wooden or metal treads.

Jalopy: A slang term for an outmoded or broken-down automobile or airplane.

Junior Officer of the Deck: A junior officer serving as assistant to the Officer of the Deck. This is the method by which young officers obtain sufficient experience to qualify for watch duty.

Keel: The chief and lowest timber, or girder, of a vessel extending from stem to stern and supporting the whole frame.

Knot: A nautical mile—2025 yards; a unit of speed per hour; i.e., 15 knots—15 nautical miles per hour; also, an interweaving or tying of thread, cord, or line.

Leeward: The lateral drift of a vessel to leeward of her course, caused by wind and sea.

Liberty: Permission to leave the limits of one's station for a period of 48 hours or less; this term is used only in relation to enlisted personnel; for officers such permission is called shore leave.

Lie to: To stop and drift at sea, i.e., awaiting a pilot or boarding officer.

Life lines: The lines at the edges of upper decks to prevent personnel from falling overboard.

Life raft: Warships are unable to carry many boats when cleared for action, and in action any boats carried may be put out of commission. Many rafts are carried in the hope that in case the ship is sunk, men can support themselves by holding on to the rafts until rescue vessels arrive.

Lights: The lights in various parts of the ship are required to be extinguished at definite times unless an extension of time is given by the Commanding Officer; some are eight o'clock lights, some nine o'clock, and some ten o'clock. Except when a ship is darkened for purposes of security certain definite lights are required by a ship underway, known as running lights, or by a ship at anchor, known as anchor lights.

Line: Line is the general term for what in civil life is called rope; large lines or wire lines are frequently called hawsers. The word line is also used to designate a formation of ships in which the relative bearing of the ships is 90 degrees from the course.

Lines of a ship: The form or contour of the hull of a ship.

Log: The official record of the ship's location, movement, operations, etc. in which are recorded all events which might have any bearing in relation to any officer or man of the crew.

Lucky bag: The locker or compartment in which the police Petty Officer places all personal belongings of members of the crew which are found lying about the decks or in unauthorized places. The name of the class book prepared and issued annually at the Naval Academy by the First (senior) Class.

Mail clerk: Each ship has a post office with a mail clerk in charge; the mail clerk is an enlisted man assigned to such duty at his own request.

Mess: An organization for the purpose of preparing and serving food. In flagships there are the Admiral's Mess, comprising the Admiral and such staff officers as he may select; the Captain's Mess, usually just the captain; the Wardroom Mess, comprising the Executive Officer as mess president and all other officers above the grade of Lieutenant (J.G.) and officers of such grade as assigned as watch and division officers; the Junior Officers' Mess; the Warrant Officers' Mess; the Chief Petty Officers' Mess; and the General Mess, which includes all other personnel.

Mess bill: Officers are allowed a certain sum for subsistence, but this sum is less than an officer's proportional share of the cost of running the mess, i.e., his mess bill, which must be paid in advance.

Mess, cigar: A cigar mess is an independent organization, organized to sell soft drinks, cigars, cigarettes, candy, etc.

Mess president: The Executive Officer is president of the Wardroom Mess; the senior line junior officer is president of the Junior Officers' Mess.

Mess share: The mess share is the prorata worth of the stores and such equipment belonging to the mess as has been purchased with mess funds. An officer joining a mess must make an initial payment of the current value of the mess share in addition to his mess bill.

Mess treasurer: The Wardroom, Junior Officers', Warrant Officers', and Chief Petty Officers' messes are supervised each by a mess treasurer elected monthly from among its own members. The officer so elected performs this duty without pay, in addition to his other duties.

Mine: A heavy explosive charge in a steel container designed to float, or rest on the bottom, or to be suspended below the surface by a float or held at a fixed depth by an anchor, exploded by contact with a ship's hull, by induced magnetism, or by sound waves from propellers, with a view to injuring a ship in its most vital area below the water line.

Mine layer: A vessel designed to lay mines.

Mine sweeper: A vessel designed to remove or explode mines by means which normally insure her own safety.

Motor launch: A type of large open boat provided for transportation of enlisted personnel, stores, etc.

Motorboat: A type of boat having a canopy which is provided for the use of officers and their guests.

M. T. boat: A motor torpedo boat—a special type of high-speed motorboat designed for operation near shore bases, and carrying one or more torpedoes.

Navigator: The officer, head of department, responsible under the Commanding Officer, for the safe navigation of the ship, and care, preservation, and operation of all instruments and mechanism in connection therewith.

Navy yard: A Navy shore establishment designed and operated for the construction, repair, outfitting, and supply of Navy vessels.

Old man: A term usually applied to the senior officer on board a ship, the Captain, or, in flagships, the Admiral.

Orderly: An enlisted man, usually a Marine, assigned to attend a Flag Officer or Commanding Officer, for the purpose of carrying messages or orders. A time orderly is assigned to inform the Officer of the Deck of the time to strike the ship's bells to indicate each half-hour period, and to remind the Officer of the Deck of any required action in accordance with the daily schedule. A mail orderly is a man detailed to carry mail between the ship's post office and a shore post office.

Passageway: Spaces which on shore are called corridors or halls on board ship are called passageways.

Patrol, shore: The shore patrol comprises officers and enlisted men detailed by competent authority to assist civil authorities in maintaining order and discipline among naval personnel on liberty.

Pay: The money received as salary. The actual amount received is greater than this salary by the amount of the allowances. The allowances are greater when an officer has dependents than when he has none. The word pay is also used to mean the act of sealing seams in a wooden deck with hot pitch (a solid black resinous substance obtained from boiled tar). The outer plank of a deck (next to the side of the ship), because of the difficulty in keeping this seam watertight with oakum and pitch, is called "the devil." Hence the expression, "the devil to pay and no pitch hot."

Peacoat: A short overcoat of a style sometimes called a reefer worn by enlisted personnel other than Chief Petty Officers.

Pennant: A long, narrow strip of bunting carried at the masthead of each Navy ship in commission, except when it is supplanted by the flag of a flag officer or the broad command pennant of an officer below flag rank in command of a division or squadron. A broad command pennant is triangular in shape with a swallow tail, white in color with edges outlined in blue for the Commander of a division of large ships or a squadron of destroyers, and outlined in red for a division Commander of destroyers or submarines. In destroyers and submarines the official number of the squadron or division is shown by numerals of the same color as the edging superimposed on the white field.

Pilot, sky: The ship's Chaplain is frequently referred to as the sky pilot.

Pipe: The boatswain's pipe is a special form of whistle capable of variation in tone by the position of the fingers in relation to the opening by which the air escapes.

Pipe down: A series of notes on the boatswain's pipe to indicate the completion of an all-hands evolution. The order to the Boatswain was "pipe down"; hence, figuratively, to stop what you are doing; generally used in the sense of "make less noise."

Pitch: The alternate rise and fall of the bow and stern of a vessel due to action of the sea.

Port, hole: The round openings in the side of a ship for light and ventilation.

Pulling boat: A boat propelled by means of oars.

Quarter: A sector limited by bearings 45 degrees abaft the beam and astern, on each side. Also means mercy when used in the sense "to cry for quarter."

Quarters: Living accommodations; also, the assembly of officers and crew for muster or inspection.

Quarter-deck: That portion of the deck in the vicinity of the gangway ladder used by officers. Originally the quarter-deck included such gangway and extended to the stern of the ship; in modern ships such gangway may be forward, or in the waist. The quarter-deck is the ceremonial portion of the deck and reserved for the use of the Captain (and the Admiral in flagships).

Quartermaster: A Petty Officer rate. The quartermaster is an enlisted man, assistant to the Officer of the Deck, whose duties include at sea the supervision of the steersman and the collection of data required to be entered in the log, and in port maintaining a lookout for approaching boats or other matters of interest taking place in the harbor.

Rudder: A frame of wood or metal by which a vessel is steered.

Sabotage: Destruction or damage to property by disloyal persons or enemy sympathizers.

Sail: To leave port; usually on an extended cruise.

Sailing orders: Ships are frequently placed on sailing orders at a definite time, from two to six hours before the expected hour of departure. At the hour the ship is placed on sailing orders all personnel must be on board unless ashore on duty.

Salute: Salutes are of two classes, hand salute and gun salute. The hand salute is a mark of military respect rendered by enlisted personnel to officer personnel, and by junior to senior officers. It is acknowledged by returning a similar salute. A gun salute comprises a number of discharges of a small type of gun called a saluting gun, in honor of Flag Officers of the Navy, General Officers of the Army and Marine Corps, and certain civil officials such as the President, Secretary of the Navy, etc.

Salvo: A simultaneous discharge of guns, torpedoes, bombs, etc.

Scuppers: The enclosed drains from the waterways of a ship's deck to a point of discharge near the water line.

Secure: An order implying: Discontinue the exercise and return all material to its normal stowage.

Selection: The process by which officers are chosen for promotion.

Sentry: A person, usually a Marine, stationed as a guard or watchman.

Sextant: An optical instrument for measuring the altitude of heavenly bodies for purposes of navigation.

Shore duty: Officers of the U.S. Navy alternate between duty attached to ships—called sea duty—and duty attached to shore stations. In the junior grades the periods of sea duty are much longer than the periods of shore duty.

Shoulder marks: The insignia of rank worn by officers on white uniforms and overcoats.

Skipper: A term frequently used as a nickname in referring to the Captain of a ship.

Smoke screen: A dense cloud of smoke from the funnels caused by incomplete combustion of fuel oil, or from specially designed chemical tanks, to shield ships from observation.

Smoker: A form of entertainment held on board ship for the pleasure and amusement of the crew, usually consisting of boxing and wrestling matches during which free smokes are provided.

Squilgee: A hoe-shaped instrument with a rubber edge used for drying wooden decks, similar in results obtained to a windshield wiper.

Stanchions: Vertical cylindrical posts extending between decks as supports for the deck above.

Stand by: A term used as a warning to be ready.

Station: An assignment to duty; on board ship each officer and man has a definite battle station, and a station for each general drill such as fire, collision, etc.

Station, naval: Naval stations are small, usually independent or semi-independent, naval activities of the nature of a base, i.e., Naval Station Guantanamo, Samoa, etc.

Station, naval air: Each location on shore fitted and organized by the Navy for the operation of aircraft is called a naval air station.

Steady as you go: An order to the steersman to hold the ship on the heading at the instant the order was given; hence, figuratively, continue in the present direction.

Steerage: Commercially that part of the ship allotted to passengers paying the lowest fares.

Steerage way: The lowest speed at which the vessel can be accurately steered.

Strike: To lower. Hence, to strike the colors means to lower or haul down the colors in token of surrender. To strike below means to lower any object to a lower deck level.

Striker: A man assigned as a helper and apprentice with a view to qualifying for a definite position or rating.

Strip ship: The removal from a warship of material not essential for war operations.

Stripes: The insignia of rank of naval officers worn on the sleeves near the cuffs on blue uniforms and on the shoulder marks with white uniforms.

Supply officer: An officer of the Supply Corps, charged with matters pertaining to pay, general stores, and the general mess.

Taps: A bugle call indicating lights out in living quarters and quiet to be maintained about the decks.

Tarpaulin: A piece of canvas used to cover anything for protection against the weather.

Tattoo: A roll of the drum or a bugle call sounded five minutes before taps as a warning to retire to quarters and turn in. This word is from the Dutch *tattoe* which indicated the time to close all taps or taverns in a garrison town.

Topside: Slang for upper decks.

Transom: A built-in long seat in a stateroom or other living quarters.

Truck: The topmost point of a mast.

Turn to: To begin work.

Turret: The oval-shaped armored structures, capable of rotation, in which the main battery guns of large ships are emplaced.

Underway: Not anchored or made fast to any other object.

Visa: An endorsement upon a passport by a consular agent of the country one desires to visit, authorizing such visit.

Wake: The track of disturbed water astern of a ship, caused by the action of the propellers and movement of the ship.

Wardroom: The space provided on board ship as a messroom and reception room for officers junior to the Captain and senior to the junior officers.

Waterways: The gutters around the edge of the deck.

Whaleboat: A type of small boat pointed at each end, so named because it is the type most frequently used in harpooning whales.

Yardarm: The framework extending from a mast from which signal flags are hoisted.

BIBLIOGRAPHY

Naval Customs, Traditions and Usage, Leland P. Lovette, U.S. Naval Institute, Annapolis, Md., 1934.

Annapolis Today, Kendall Banning, Funk & Wagnalls Company, New York, 1938.

The Fleet Today, Kendall Banning, Funk & Wagnalls Company, New York, 1940 (?).

The History of Our Navy, John R. Spears, Charles Scribner's Sons, 1899.

Navy Men, James B. Connoly, Van Rees Press, New York, 1939.

Story of the Submarine, D. Appleton-Century Company, New York, 1916.

What the Citizen Should Know About the Navy, Hanson W. Baldwin, W. W. Norton & Company, New York, 1941.

The Navy's Best Stories, Harry Hockey, Wetzel Publishing Co., Los Angeles, Cal., 1940.

Naval Leadership (Some Hints to Junior Officers and Others), A compilation for and by the Navy, Fourth Edition, 1939.

The Bluejackets' Manual, U.S. Naval Institute, Annapolis, Md., 1940.

Fighting Ships, Sampson Low, Marston and Co., London, 1940.

Taschenbuch der Kriegsflotten, J. F. Lehmans Verlag, Munich, Germany, 1940.

Ships' Data, U.S. Naval Vessels, Government Printing Office, Washington, D.C.

Your Navy, Claude Banks Mayo, U.S.N., Parker and Baird, Los Angeles, Cal., 1939.

Ships and Sailors, William H. Clarke, Page and Co., Boston, 1938.

Life at the U.S. Naval Academy, Ralph Earle, U.S.N., G. P. Putnam's Sons, New York, 1917.

Annapolis, William Oliver Stevens, Dodd, Mead & Company, New York, 1937.

Modern Submarine Versus Major Warship, D. S. Dillingham, U.S. Naval Institute Proceedings, Vol. 67, No. 458, April, 1941.

Naval R.O.T.C. Students, Frederick Nelson.

Submarines, Admirals and Navies, Colin Mayers, Associated Publications, Los Angeles, Cal., 1940.

American Naval Songs and Ballads, Yale University Press, New Haven, Conn., 1938.

On the Bottom, Edward Ellsberg, Dodd, Mead & Company, New York, 1929.

Mahan on Naval Warfare, Edited by Allan Westcott, Little, Brown & Company, Boston, 1941.

Sea Duty, Yates Stirling, G. P. Putnam's Sons, New York, 1939.

Blow All Ballast, Nat A. Barrows, Dodd, Mead & Company, New York, 1940.

Hell on Ice, Edward Ellsberg, Dodd, Mead & Company, New York, 1940.

Men Under the Sea, Edward Ellsberg, Dodd, Mead & Company, New York, 1939.

With the Help of God and a Few Marines, G. A. W. Catlin, Doubleday, Doran & Company, New York, 1919.

Military and Naval Recognition Book, J. Bunkley, D. Van Nostrand Company, New York, 1941.

Fix Bayonets, John W. Thomason, Blue Ribbon Books, New York, 1926.

A History of the Marine Corps, Clyde H. Metcalf, G. P. Putnam's Sons, New York, 1939.

Enemy Sighted, Alec Hudson, The Macmillan Company, New York, 1941.

Naval Ordnance, U.S. Naval Institute, Annapolis, Md., 1939.

Navy Directory, U.S. Navy Department, Bureau of Navigation, Washington, D.C.

Life and Letters of John Paul Jones, Mrs. Reginald de Koven, Charles Scribner's Sons, New York, 1913.

Bluejacket, Fred J. Buenzle, W. W. Norton & Company, New York, 1931.

Submarines, Frederick A. Talbot, J. B. Lippincott Company, London, 1915.

We Dive At Dawn, Kenneth Edwards, Reilly & Lee Company, Chicago, 1941.

Full Ahead, Felix Riesenberg, Jr., Dodd, Mead & Company, New York, 1941.

Sons of the Hurricane, James Hottell and Thomas Molloy, J. B. Lippincott Company, New York, 1938.

What the Citizen Should Know About the Coast Guard, Hickman Powell, W. W. Norton & Company, New York, 1941.

Guardsmen of the Coast, John J. Floherty, Doubleday, Doran & Company, New York, 1935.

The U.S. Coast Guard, Evor S. Kerr, Jr., Robert W. Kelly, New York, 1935.

"Hospitals on Wings," *Hygeia Magazine,* S. R. Winters, February, 1939.

"Heroes of the Deluge," *Popular Mechanics,* April, 1940.

"With the Air Patrol in the Southwest," *Travel Magazine,* July, 1939.

Entertaining Without a Maid, Elizabeth Lounsberry, Harper and Brothers, New York, 1941.

Toward a New Order of Sea Power, Harold and Margaret Sprout, Princeton University Press, Princeton, N.J., 1940.

Adventures in Good Eating, Duncan Hines, Bowling Green, Ky., 1939.

A Navy Second to None, George T. Davis, Harcourt, Brace and Company, New York, 1940.

Etiquette, Emily Post, Funk & Wagnalls Company, New York, 1938.

The Navy, Charles A. Beard, Harper and Brothers, New York, 1932.

U.S. Navy Regulations, Government Printing Office, Washington, D.C., 1920. Reprinted in 1932 with all changes up to and including No. 14.

Watch Officers' Guide, Russel Wilson, U.S.N., U.S. Naval Institute, Annapolis, Md., 1935.

How to Be a Naval Officer, Yates Stirling, Robert M. McBride and Co., New York, 1940.

Navy Life in Peace Time, Margaret J. Codd, A. Flanagan Co., Chicago, 1924.

Our Navy, Charles J. Finger, Houghton Mifflin Company, Boston, 1936.

Navy Wings, Harold Blaine Miller, Dodd, Mead & Company, New York, 1937.

Room to Swing a Cat, Frederick J. Bell, Longmans, Green and Company, New York, 1938.

Etiquette, Margery Wilson, Pocket-book Guide, New York.

School of the Sea, Leland P. Lovette, Frederick A. Stokes Company, New York, 1942.

Fighting Ships of the U.S.A., Victor Fl. Blakeslee, Artists and Writers Guild, Random House, New York, 1941.

New River, N. C., 54; life in, 60-62; expenses in, 60-61
Nursery schools, 212-215
Nurses, Navy, 240-241

Oahu, 279
O.A.O., the One and Only Girl, 6, 12, 13, 14, 20, 78; of the aviation cadet, 31-32
Opal Locker Naval Air Station, 35

Paca House, 23
Pallbearers, 243, 245
Panama, expenses in, 291, 292
Panama City, 290, 293; life in, 291-292
Pantry, stocking of, 165; emergency shelf, 166-167
Paul Jones, the Founder of the American Navy, a History, 106
Pay, Ensign's, 21, 143-145; aviation cadet's, 32; base, 132
Pearl Harbor, 24, 41, 105, 110, 269, 282
Pensacola, 25-26, 233; life in, 27-29; clothes for, 27-28; expenses at, 28
Pensions, 140, 155, 249-250
Petty Officers, 259
Pickens, Fort, 27
Piping the side, 118-119
Pontchartrain, Coast Guard cutter, 70
Powell, Hickman, quoted, 65n., 68, 70
Precedence, 182, 226-227
Preparatory schools, 215
Presents, wedding, 100-104; acknowledging, 101; displaying, 102; general information, 102-104
Puerto Rico, 297-300

Quantico, life at, 57-59

Randall House, 23
Randolph Field, 25

Ranks, equivalent, of Navy, Army, and Marine officers, 228; how to distinguish, 228-229
Ratings, distinguishing, 257-260
Receiving calls, 168-169
Receptions, 162; wedding, 99-100; in Washington, 223; President's, 224-225
Records, social, 138; financial, 138-140; legal, 140; automobile, 140-141; of dates, 141
Red Cross, 73, 191, 241
Red Pants, 55
Reef Points, 18
Regular Veterans Association, 250
Reimbursement for transportation, 137, 202-203
Rescue chamber, 47
Rescues, beach, 72-73
Returning calls, 169-170
Ridout, Mrs. Hester, 22
Ring Dance at Annapolis, 12-13
Ring Dance at Coast Guard Academy, 66
Rio de Janeiro, 1, 66, 274, 303
Roberts, General Charles D., 247

Safety deposit box, 152
Saint Croix, 297-298
Saint Thomas, 66, 297, 298; life in, 300-303; expenses in, 300-301
St. Thomas Islands Cooperative, 302
Saluting, 265; the quarter-deck, 115; guns, 116-118; hand, 119
Samoa, 155; life in, 274-278
San Diego, 233; life in, 59-60
San Juan, 297; life in, 298-300, 302; expenses in, 298
Santiago, Chile, 303
Savings and investments, 147
Scholarships, 215-218
School of the Sea, The, 220
Seating, of wedding guests, 91; according to rank, 227-228
"Semper Paratus," in *National Magazine,* 64n.